LOOKING for GOODWILL

LOOKING for GOODWILL

Pat Price and Scott Price

May your Life be filled with Goodwill!

Pat and Scott

Providence House Publishers

PROVIDENCE PUBLISHING CORPORATION

FRANKLIN, TENNESSEE

Printed in the United States of America

10   09   08   07   06   1   2   3   4   5

Library of Congress Control Number: 2006930956

ISBN-13: 978-1-57736-374-3
ISBN-10: 1-57736-374-4

Cover and page design by Joey McNair

PROVIDENCE HOUSE PUBLISHERS
an imprint of
Providence Publishing Corporation
238 Seaboard Lane • Franklin, Tennessee 37067
www.providence-publishing.com
800-321-5692

To all the men and women, past and present,
who have served in the United States Army, Navy,
Air Force, Marine Corps, and Coast Guard

CONTENTS

ACKNOWLEDGMENTS

We wish to express our thanks to the professionals at Providence Publishing Corporation for their creativity and expertise, especially Melissa Istre, Holly Jones, Andrew B. Miller, Joey McNair, Tammy Spurlock, and our dedicated editor, Nancy Wise, for her many helpful suggestions and thoughtful advice. Scott's business partner, Jay Siegrist, deserves a special word of gratitude for his brotherly support of this project and his unfailing patience.

How can we ever adequately express the genuine delight we found in every single person we interviewed? They are the treasured substance of this book. For their trust, their extraordinary insights, and their overflowing goodwill, we are forever grateful.

We also give honor and undying love to our dear mother and wife, Dr. Ann H. Price, and to our sister and daughter, Rachel Kathryn Price, whose good hearts always inspire our hearts.

"Has there ever been good news?"

PROLOGUE

"One who diligently seeks good, finds goodwill."

This ancient proverb sums up eleven exhilarating months of seeking and discovery. It all began when, not long ago, we saw a small cartoon in *Barron's* financial news magazine.

A father and his young son are watching the evening news on television, and the boy says to his dad, "Has there ever been good news?"

To us, it seemed more sad than funny that, with a steady diet of modern TV news, many young people might well have a pretty grim view of life, and yet, we knew there were good people all around us doing good things every day.

An idea was born. We decided to take a single year and travel the entire country, visiting every state in search of goodwill. We determined to interview randomly selected people from all walks of life and ask them about the good things in their lives. We would give people an extraordinary opportunity to ponder the positive, then we would compile their words into a book called *Looking For Goodwill.*

Our journey began with little prior planning, but with abundant enthusiasm and an unwavering conviction that goodwill was out there in abundance. We were not disappointed. In fact, the breadth and depth of goodwill we discovered during our quest far exceeded our expectations.

Across thousands of beautiful miles, we sought and found wonderful people full of goodwill. In retrospect, we now marvel at how readily people trusted us and opened up to us so completely. When describing this great adventure to friends and family back home, we frequently were asked, "How do you get people to talk to you?" or "Aren't people suspicious?" It gave us genuine delight to always be able to respond positively about the splendid reception we were receiving across America.

Everyone was so gracious to us. Our standard approach went like this: I, Scott, would smile and introduce myself: "I am Scott Price from Nashville, Tennessee." We'd shake hands. Gesturing towards Pat, I would say, "This is my son, Pat. He just graduated in May ['03] from Lipscomb University in Nashville." Often the person would warmly congratulate Pat. Invariably, Pat put out his hand and gave a friendly handshake accompanied by a friendly smile. Although Pat was born with spina bifida, his outgoing personality always seemed to put people at ease and allowed them to see past his wheelchair.

"We are writing a book together." This almost always increased the intensity with which they were listening. "It's called *Looking For Goodwill*. We are visiting every state in the Union and asking people about the good things in their lives and in their communities." Often, we would tell them about the cartoon and confidently re-state our view about good people doing good things all around us. When we asked, "Could we interview you for our book?" no one turned us down. People seemed intrigued by the idea, and everyone responded positively when we asked for permission to record the interview. Not only were they gracious, they also gave us vigorous encouragement to continue.

One pattern we developed—as you'll see from the book—was that Pat would do the interviewing and Scott would act as scribe. In the book, to make it clear who was speaking, we've stuck with referring to ourselves in the third person. It may seem a little strange, but you'll understand our thinking. Please forgive us in advance for any confusion this may cause.

Our quest led us to all kinds of people. We intentionally did not set quotas or even keep track of young or old, male or female, race or ethnicity, or foreign visitors or American citizens. Although we kept a detailed journal about our new friends, their words, and the places we found them, we purposefully decided against keeping track of such distinctions. We were looking for goodwill. Guess what? It isn't age, gender, or ethnically specific, but it is definitely out there! We looked diligently all across this great land and absorbed the goodwill whenever, wherever, and in whomever we found it.

As you'll find as you read our account, we learned a lot as we went along. Our procedures evolved, as sometimes did the questions we asked. For example, when we first started, we hadn't decided to get photos of all our new friends. We've regretted that, especially since we don't have a picture of Jim Pankiewicz, our very first participant. We had actually purchased a new video camera in Nashville the night before we started our quest with the thought that we would film each interview. However, we were concerned that being on camera might make some folks a little uneasy or less forthcoming, so we never used it. We apologize if the accompanying snapshots fail to fully capture the joyous goodwill we found so abundantly in our interviews.

These people made us feel so good! We also found that occasionally some of our questions needed to be explained. Eventually, we honed our list of questions to:

1. Is there a place in your state which you especially enjoy? What is your favorite place, and why?

2. What is the best thing about your town?

3. Of all the people you know, is there one who "stands out" for consistently doing good things? Who is it?

4. Which person, living or dead, would you most like to meet, or meet again?

5. What is the best decision you have made? (These questions about "best decision" and "best thing" often precipitated the longest pauses, the most contemplation, and the deepest reflection. Pat explained that "best thing" differs from "best decision" because the best thing that has happened in your life may be something over which you had absolutely no control.)

6. What is the best thing that has happened in your life?

7. Do you have a goal which you still hope to achieve?

8. If you had an opportunity to begin a new career, what would you choose to do? (This question sometimes struck folks as meaning, "What would you do now if you were beginning a new career?" To others it meant, "What would you do if you could go back in time and begin a new career?" Neither interpretation really concerned us because our hope was that the question would simply prompt some positive reflection.)

9. Do you have a message of encouragement or words of advice for our readers all across the land?

Our notes from our process reflect that beginning with Inna Kourdeltchouk in Versailles, Kentucky, we concluded all of our interviews by presenting the person interviewed with a ten-dollar bill and asking each one to help spread a little goodwill. We requested that each interviewee use the money to do something good and we asked each to write and let us know how they decided to use it. We thought it would be interesting to see how a wide variety of people would choose to use such an unexpected gift.

(Occasionally, an interviewee would ask us if we had seen the movie *Pay it Forward*; we still have not. We were told that its story involves a somewhat similar effort to encourage others to spread goodwill.)

We loved the random process of selecting interviewees, and we have had our joy multiplied many times over by their thoughtful responses, and also by the varied ways in which the money was put to good use.

We want to share the story of our journey with everyone we meet. Not because of us, but because of the people we met everywhere we went. We want you to get to know them and perceive the vast reservoir of goodwill in their hearts. One hundred six interviews comprise a relatively small sample in a nation of 295 million souls. However, the one hundred and six good-hearted individuals in this book are illustrative of the goodwill all around you. You don't have to look far to find it.

Our fond hope is that you will be inspired to seek goodwill yourself—and spread it—right where you are.

There is good news every day—if you are looking for it!

TRIP ONE
KENTUCKY & OHIO

Kentucky

July 11, 2003, Friday
Jim Pankiewicz (PAN-kuh-witz)
Hodgenville, Kentucky—birthplace of Abraham Lincoln

A temple-like shrine houses the crude log cabin in which one of America's greatest presidents was born. Inside, we meet Jim Pankiewicz, the young U.S. Park Service employee on duty. This is our first interview, and we are feeling our way along.

Jim is youthful, clean-scrubbed, and courteous; we especially regret having been so excited (and unprepared) for beginning our search that we forgot to make a photograph of him. We began so spontaneously, so excitedly, so unscientifically, and we are admittedly disorganized.

A recent graduate of Northwest Missouri State, Jim plans to go to graduate school at Western Illinois in the fall of 2003. Jim was born in St. Joe, Missouri, and his favorite places include St. Louis, the Ozarks, and Kansas City.

When asked about the best things in his home state, Jim says, "The farmers, the corn fields, and the cattle in the northwest corner of Missouri. There are good people in those small towns, and I especially like the countryside—the beautiful, peaceful farmland."

Although brief, our visit with Jim is all positive. The goodwill we find in him is most pronounced in his wistful sincerity as he expresses his obvious and genuine affection for the land—the countryside he roamed as a boy.

We interview Jim inside the Lincoln temple and our conversation is prematurely concluded by the arrival of a blonde, fiftyish, female tourist who enters, looks at the log cabin, and proclaims, "I went to Grenada . . . and they have got people living in smaller places than this!" She then begins to pepper Jim with questions. We step outside.

This was all new. We went to a bench and talked about how we could improve.

Engraved in stone above the monument's doorway are Lincoln's inspiring words: "With malice toward none—with charity for all."

We resolved to take that spirit with us throughout our quest.

This great president, inspiring poet, and orator began his life in the most humble of abodes—a one-room log cabin in what is still a relatively remote corner of Kentucky's hills and woods.

As we drove away, we talked about what a fascinating experience it would have been to interview Abraham Lincoln for this book. "We are looking for goodwill. Who is the best person you know? What is the best decision you have made?" Out of this conversation an idea began to germinate: why not add a question about which person, living or dead, you would most like to meet? We added this to our inquiries.

Lesson 1: Try to seek out people of goodwill in settings where we can talk without being interrupted.

Lesson 2: Have a set, deliberate pattern for interview. Later, we add getting a photograph and giving a gift.

Abraham Lincoln's birthplace, Hodgenville, Kentucky

July 11, 2003, Friday
Holly Bischoff
Bardstown, Kentucky—where Southern composer Stephen Foster
wrote "My Old Kentucky Home"

In our earliest conversations about the interview process, we contemplated seeking out four citizens and one public official in every state. We soon realized four people would create so much information that we would be forced to cull certain interviews, something we did not want to do; and that a public official might not always be available. We decided we would gladly take note of goodwill found in anyone, anywhere we found it. This was fortunate, as on a Friday afternoon at a quarter to five, the county courthouse had closed.

We casually cruised around Bardstown looking for a person in a place where we might find goodwill. We saw a lone suburban cowboy standing on the sidewalk along Main Street with his amplifier plugged in somewhere so he could play his guitar and sing cowboy country tunes. We passed an antique shop, then Hurst's Drug Store, which featured a soda fountain and counter service. Two older ladies were enjoying an early dinner (or a very late lunch) at the counter.

Another loop of the courthouse square led us to the local information center where we were met by the very friendly and direct Holly Bischoff. We explained that we were looking for goodwill; we wanted to know about the good things in her life and in her community. She agreed to be interviewed.

Pat asks about the best place in Kentucky and Holly enthusiastically says, "I can't figure out why God put me in the most wonderful country in the world, in the most beautiful state, and the nicest town! I was born in Lincoln County [Kentucky] . . . guess I'll be buried there . . . but this [Bardstown] is my favorite place. I came to Bardstown from Lincoln County at age fourteen; my mother was a schoolteacher."

Booming doesn't precisely describe Holly's voice so much as it bespeaks her joyful spirit. When asked about the best decision she has ever made, she smiles and says, "Marrying my husband, Kent, and having our three children. We have three really nice children."

Holly immediately responds when we ask about the best thing that has ever happened in her life. "Kent coming home safely from Vietnam. Bardstown lost more boys in Vietnam, per capita, than any other town our size. My husband lost so many friends. I had a baby while he was over there, and I would worry, and worry, and worry. So, it was glorious to have Kent make it home."

Pat asks Holly about her desire with respect to a new career, and she says, "Well, I'm basically an optimistic person and I don't mind growing older . . . you have your birthdays and you just be glad you're still here! I am content right where God put me."

Holly Bischoff's words of advice to our readers: "To those to whom much is given, much is expected. I couldn't ever begin to repay it all."

Holly Bischoff

This lovely woman was so friendly, open, matter-of-fact, and direct in her responses, so cheerful and good-natured that we felt an immediate bond. Her goodwill emerged in her "Honey, here it is" speech patterns and revealed her inner joy.

We headed back to the car, loaded our gear, then realized we had forgotten (again) to make a photograph of our new friend. Scott dashed back in and quickly snapped Holly's picture.

July 11, 2003, Friday
Inna (EE-nuh) Kourdeltchouk (Koor-DOLL-chuck)
Versailles, Kentucky

"You can't get lost if you don't know where you are going." We used this light-hearted refrain over and over with each other and with many of the good people we met on our trips.

We purposely avoided planning a specific route or a specific itinerary. We launched out on July 11 because a cousin in Ohio invited us for a family get-together, which she dubbed "Pickle-Fest." Thus, we left Nashville with the aim of reaching Wheelersburg, Ohio on Saturday, July 12, but without any preconceived notion of where we might travel while getting there. Hodgenville and Bardstown had just looked and felt like good places to stop along the way.

This provided us with the most delightful, enchanting sense of freedom! How grateful we felt, from that very first day to the very last, to be able to do such a thing. To actually, really and truly, go wherever we wanted. To be physically, financially, and politically able to do so.

So, as we left Bardstown, we talked about heading toward Frankfort, Kentucky's state capital.

Driving out on the highway, Scott called home and dutifully reported our progress. When he ended the call, Pat said, "Dad, you missed the turn to Frankfort."

"No problem," Scott replied. "We'll just take the next exit we come to and go wherever it leads."

That is how we came to visit Versailles—not the palace in France and not pronounced like that either. It's "vuhr-SALES" in Kentucky, and it was the absolute perfect place for us to be on that warm Friday evening in July.

It was a special community night, and many people gathered in the few blocks around the county courthouse. Everyone was casually walking in the streets, and the steps of the Baptist church were filled with black and white children eating hot dogs and/or pizza. Local groups set up barbeque grills on the sidewalks and cooked steaks or ribs or chicken. There was music, crafts, flowers, six or seven antique cars and hot rods proudly on display, a sea of friendly faces and ready smiles. The chief of police was being repeatedly and unceremoniously dunked in a dunking machine set up right in front of the storefront police station.

It was as though we had been magically transported to an idyllic, modern Mayberry. The comfortable, happy sense

Kentucky & Ohio

of contentment was palpable, and it was a great delight to be here.

After dinner, we made our way around the courthouse square looking at things, but really looking for goodwill.

Inna caught our eyes. We can't tell you with any sort of precision exactly why she seemed to be the one to approach out of the hundred or so people on the square.

She sat at a small card table set up behind her car's trunk. On the table were jars of all sizes, filled with honey. The labels bear the name Kourdeltchouk, and Scott asked her, "Is this your honey?"

Revealing an un-Kentuckian accent, she said, "Is my father's hobby and my grandfather's bees." She had a winning smile. We explained our quest and she consented to be interviewed.

"I am originally from Lutsk, Ukraine. We came to Versailles thirteen years ago when I was eight years old and I love it! It is so quiet and so very peaceful." Her emphasis on the word "peaceful" is pronounced. She says, "There are many kind people here and everyone knows each other. My three siblings and I knew no English when we came here, but everyone treated us so kindly, no one made fun of us—they taught us."

Pat with Inna Kourdeltchouk

When Pat asks her opinion of the best place in the state of Kentucky, Inna says, "Berea College. It is even smaller than Versailles! The campus is so beautiful—like in early colonial days. It's one hour away from here, it's little, and it's so peaceful." She positively glows when speaking of peaceful-ness, a treasure we often overlook or take for granted. [Exactly ten months later, we would see precisely the same look in the eyes of Zineta Imamovic, a refugee from war-torn Bosnia whom we would find and interview in Fargo, North Dakota.]

A happy sophomore in pre-dentistry at Berea, Inna tells us, "I go at no cost; my family's circumstances allowed my admission."

When Pat asks, "Who is the best person you know?" Inna smiles self-consciously and says, "My fiancé. He is an all around great guy. He is so nice and so romantic. He is originally from Ukraine too, and he just graduated from the University of Kentucky."

Her best decision, Inna says, was deciding to go to Berea College. "There are no cars for students; we have great professors and wonderful people. I am so happy there!"

This young woman is a bright ray of sunshine; the sweetness of her spirit shines through. In her we find a refreshing desire to speak of how much she treasures the peace we have been blessed with in the USA.

Our notes, made contemporaneously with the interview, included the following notation: "gave $10 and address." This leads us to believe that we probably did not do the same with Jim Pankiewicz or Holly Bischoff. The idea of asking each person to help spread some goodwill just came to us.

For the rest of our journey, we gave each person we interviewed a ten-dollar bill with the following instruction: "We want you to help spread some goodwill. Use this ten dollars to do something good. Anything you choose. It can be something good for you, your family, or your community. Just do something good with it and send us a note telling us how you decided to use it. We'd like to include that in the book, too." We thought it would be worthwhile to see what people might choose to do with an unexpected and totally unrestricted gift. The responses were inspiring and uplifting.

We enjoyed a beautiful summer twilight drive through Kentucky horse country on U.S. 60 to Lexington, then I-64 to Morehead, Kentucky, where we rested for the night.

Kentucky & Ohio

Ohio

July 12, 2003, Saturday
Judge Dick Schisler
Wheelersburg, Ohio

The morning provided an interesting example regarding back roads. We got off I-64 at Olive Hill, Kentucky, and decided to generally aim north on Highway 2 and Highway 7. That especially scenic stretch of road runs through Carter, Load, and South Shore up to the Ohio River. We saw deep woods, few houses, more roadside signs relating to church worship times than all other types of signs combined, and only two political posters, both of which extolled the virtues of a candidate for the office of coroner.

Judge Dick Schisler

The dapper Judge Dick Schisler presides over a municipal court with county-wide jurisdiction in Portsmouth, Ohio. First appointed by the governor and subsequently reelected, he has been a judge for nine years. We talk on the front porch of our cousin Kate's house in the countryside near Wheelersburg. A delicious breeze keeps us cool and gives just the right amount of "flutter" to the crisp new American flag flying from a pole attached to the front porch.

"The best thing about Portsmouth is the way people pull together in times of difficulty," Judge Dick tells interviewer Pat. "For example, we had an ice storm not long ago that left us without power for about a week. People were so unselfish, and many invited others to come stay in their homes. Folks not only took us in, there was another family staying for three days down in the basement. Everyone was willing to pitch in and help each other. I like that. It's a large-scale example of how people here are willing to help one another out."

When asked about his favorite place in Ohio, Dick says, "Right here! I was born in Portsmouth, and if anyone had told me when I graduated from high school that I would end up living here, I'd have said, 'You're out of your mind!' But, after college, law school, and some time working in Cincinnati and

Washington, D.C., I came to have a greater appreciation of my hometown's beauty and character."

"The best person I know," Dick says, "is my wife, Sally. She is my best friend and altogether the best person I know. She's always helping others and she is so friendly." He laughs out loud and tells a great story—at his own expense—that illustrates Sally's friendliness in every circumstance. "On our honeymoon, we went out to dinner and I was wearing a light-colored khaki suit. After we were seated, I excused myself to the men's room. After using the bathroom, I began to wash my hands and to my horror, the water came out of the faucet so forcefully that it splashed all over the front of my pants—in the worst possible location. There were no paper towels and the blower/dryer on the wall was at too great a height to do me any good. Frantically, trying to think of what to do and realizing time was slipping away, I resorted to using the box of souvenir matches in my coat pocket. I carefully lit each one and oh-so-carefully waved it back and forth in front of the offending spot. I know I must have looked like I was deranged. When I finally felt presentable enough to go back to our table, I worried that Sally would be upset with me for having been gone so long. Instead, I found her happily talking to the people at the table next to ours—she had learned everyone's name and graciously introduced me."

> A couple of weeks after our visit, it was announced that our local homeless shelter was running low on funds. I gladly took the $10 you had given me, added $70 of my own, and sent $80 to the shelter.
>
> Peace,
> Dick

The mental picture of Dick Schisler scrambling to light matches and dry his trousers has stayed fresh in our minds all along our way, and we have enjoyed sharing much laughter with others as we have re-told his "best person" story many times.

The judge says the best decision he ever made was "to marry Sally. As I told you, she is my best friend. We have lots of parallel interests, and as a result of our decision to marry, we have two fine sons. Also as a result of that decision, I joined the church she was a member of, the Episcopal church, and that decision has produced invaluable results—for me personally, for our family, and for others, I believe."

What a tribute to his wife! We feel so grateful to hear someone we have just met, outside our normal orbit of friends and family, who speaks so positively and lovingly about his wife. Pat and almost all young Americans hear a steady drumbeat of news about failed marriages, divorce, and infidelity. The goodwill expressed by Dick Schisler in describing his genuine love for Sally is the first (but not the last) dose of "goodwill marriage medicine" we would find down the road and across America.

Pat's final question of, "Do you have any words of encouragement or advice for our readers?" resulted in Dick's reply of, "Anytime you meet somebody, assume you'll meet them again, and treat them well." We like that idea.

July 13, 2003, Sunday
James "Jim" Poole
Aberdeen, Ohio

Leaving Wheelersburg, we drove west from Portsmouth along old U.S. Highway 52, which parallels the beautiful Ohio River all the way to Cincinnati. The rich farmland, deep green woods, and the sprawling river cast an enchanting spell on a quiet Sunday morning. No other cars overtook us, and we met fewer than ten heading in the opposite direction. Not only were we as free as the clouds, it seemed as though we had the country almost to ourselves!

Aberdeen is a very small town beside the river; we turned off the highway, cruised a single block, and saw a small riverfront park completely empty except for one man sitting on a bench facing the wide river. Nestled beside him was a cute little girl.

We unloaded Pat's chair, approached the two, and introduced ourselves: "We are looking for goodwill" and gained an interview.

Jim Poole is soft-spoken and genial, and he is obviously devoted to the little girl. We are interrupting their shoreside time together, but the child doesn't fuss or fidget. She is obviously quite comfortable in Jim's arms.

When Pat asks about the best place in Ohio, Jim says, "Right in this area. I have been all over this state and I'm always glad to get back here. I was born in Ripley, about six or seven miles down the road, and I have worked at the power plant [we had passed it on the river a few miles out of town] for thirty years. Lived here in Aberdeen for fifteen years."

People living in the country and living in small towns generally seem to love being right where they are. Jim makes no mention of, nor offers any criticism of, Columbus, Cincinnati, Cleveland, Toledo, or Dayton. Their considerable array of sights and attractions do not compare to a simple park bench beside the river in Aberdeen.

To Jim, the best thing about Aberdeen is the climate. "You know, the seasons. The changes in the seasons are real pretty. We get a little bit of each and it just makes this a real good place to live, really."

To this point, Jim has been polite, but a little restrained. But when Pat asks him, "What is the best

Jim Poole and granddaughter Ashleigh

thing that has ever happened in your life?" Jim lights up, hugs the child by his side on the bench, and says, "This little girl. This is my step-granddaughter, Ashleigh. She's twenty-three months old. I never had any children of my own, and then she came along. She's just been the best! Not ever having any children, I didn't know what I had missed." He gazes at Ashleigh with loving eyes.

Jim thinks a few moments about who might be the best person he knows, then replies, "It's hard to pick just one. I've met lots of good folks. I don't think I could single out just one." We tell him how fortunate he is.

Similarly, when queried about his best decision, Jim ponders the question, looks down the river, and says, "I don't

Kentucky & Ohio

know. I've made good ones and I've made bad ones. I hope more good ones than bad ones."

Pat closes out the interview by asking Jim for words of advice or encouragement. Jim says, "Well, I'd say—not ever having any children—have children, and enjoy them and enjoy your grand-children. I never realized how much a child could mean until she [Ashleigh] came into my life. I'm old . . . I'm almost fifty-five, and I missed a lot."

This was one of those times when we wished that we had a camera filming the interview. We wish that at some disap-pointing or unhappy moment in her teenage years Ashleigh could watch a video of this beautiful morning and see the expression of pure joy on her grandfather's face as he spoke so lovingly about her to two complete strangers alongside the Ohio River. This was exactly what we are looking for!

Oh, the power of love! In just twenty-three months, Ashleigh's little life transformed Jim's!

As we loaded up the car, Jim and Ashleigh went to play on the swings nearby.

July 13, 2003, Sunday
Joan Mineer (MUH-neer)
Maysville, Kentucky

Just west of Aberdeen, Ohio, in an open field next to a Dairy Queen ice cream stand, we saw three cars parked in the grass and a few folks setting up tables for a flea market. As we would many times in the future along the way, we slowed down, turned around, and drove back to a place, believing someone was waiting to meet us and be interviewed.

Sweet Joan Mineer actually lives just across the Ohio River from Aberdeen in lovely Maysville, Kentucky. The river shim-mers quietly in the Sunday morning sunshine, as if posing for a portrait by some aspiring young artist. We explain our search for goodwill; Joan is so immediately friendly and so enthusiastically cooperative that we feel as though she has been our friend for a long time. Starting the interview, Pat asks her about the best thing that has happened in her life. There is a long, quiet, contemplative pause. Joan's eyes moisten and she says, "I may cry." Her deep sense of gratitude is so outwardly obvious. She says, "My heritage. My being raised by Christian people in a Christian community. My ancestors."

Joan's opinion of the best place to live may stem from her previous reply. "Well, I think the land around Lexington, Kentucky is the prettiest. But, I just love the hills of eastern Kentucky. The hills hug you!"

When Pat asks, "Of all the people you know, is there one who stands out for consistently doing good things? Who is the best person you know?"

Joan says, without hesitation, "Oh, number one would be my maternal grandmother, Myrtle. So many were influenced for good by her strong values."

Pat stumps her a bit with his next question: "What is the best decision you have made?"

"Um, give me a clue."

Pat obliges by explaining that "best thing" differs from "best decision" because the best thing that has happened in your life may be something over which you had absolutely no control.

After some thought, Joan says, "I took my children to church and I taught them good values. It seems like I'm repeating myself, but what I received, I passed on."

When Pat asks her to talk about the best thing in her town, Joan replies brightly, "It is so historical. The area has a lot of history and you can really dig into it."

Joan Mineer and Pat

Joan has some heartfelt words of advice: "Take the time to be with your children, and take the time to teach your children."

Kentucky & Ohio

When we ask to take her picture for this book, Joan smiles sweetly, says, "Of course," and sits right down on Pat's lap for the photo. Such remarkable personal warmth and such a sunny disposition! This positive interaction with Joan early on inspired us to keep searching for more people of goodwill. Her kind spirit encouraged us.

July 13, 2003, Sunday
Keyshawn Sanders
Cincinnati, Ohio

Keyshawn Sanders and a young lady enjoy a shady spot on the lovely plaza in the center of downtown Cincinnati, Ohio, when we introduce ourselves and tell them about our nationwide search for goodwill.

Amiable and open, Keyshawn, who was born June 6, 1964 in Fort Myers, Florida, tells us that his best decision had been to attend college at Florida State University, where he had played free safety for Coach Bobby Bowden's football team. "I decided to stay in college and get my degree instead of trying to go pro. That was right for me."

Pat asks, "What is the best thing about Cincinnati?"

Keyshawn responds, "That's a hard one." After a few moments of reflection, he says, "The best thing is that we have lots of programs for kids. And we help the homeless too. There's a good community spirit."

Keyshawn enthuses that the best thing that happened in his life was joining the fire department in Cincinnati. "I've been here about twenty-two years."

The best person he knew, he says, was his grandfather, William Sanders. "He instilled a lot of moral values, and he basically taught me how to be a man."

Pat asks Keyshawn about the best place in Ohio and Keyshawn replies, "I would say Cedar Point up in Sandusky, Ohio. It's a great amusement park." Looking at Pat with a big smile he says, "Oh yeah, you will love it. You will love it!"

"My message of encouragement would be, keep the faith, continue to pray, and always believe," Keyshawn says.

We give the ten-dollar bill to Keyshawn and give him the "go and do good" instructions—part of which is take your time and think about it. He replies, "I don't need to think about it, I'm going to give it to my mamma. It'll help her."

On this first weekend of interviews, Scott just carried a few tens in the left front pocket of his slacks. When he pulls the bills out of his pocket and peels one off for Keyshawn's use, two casual visitors nearby on the plaza quickly make their way over to our small gathering and ask if Scott is doing magic. We explain that it is magical but not magic, and make our departure.

Pat and Keyshawn Sanders

Thinking back on that day, we have often laughed and surmised that the two latecomers just saw the money and were looking for some goodwill of their own.

Funny how things work out. The first person we had approached on the plaza seeking an interview was a young woman finishing a sandwich. She graciously explained that her lunch break from her job at a nearby drug store would be over in just under ten minutes. She didn't turn us down; the lack of time would not allow her to be interviewed. Leaving her, we spotted Keyshawn and he proved to be exactly what we were looking for—a man of considerable goodwill.

And a man his grandfather taught well. Look at that picture of Keyshawn with Pat. We had met Keyshawn no more than ten minutes before, yet he made us feel completely welcome in his city. He is an excellent goodwill ambassador for Cincinnati.

These earliest interviews with Keyshawn, Joan, Jim, Dick, Inna, Holly, and Jim were all such delightful experiences. They opened up to us. They responded joyfully to the idea of what we were doing. They encouraged us. In spite of (or because of?) our spontaneous beginning, our adventure was off to a great start.

Kentucky & Ohio

Kentucky

July 13, 2003, Sunday
Sonny Hart
Elizabethtown, Kentucky

On our way back to Nashville, we passed through Elizabethtown, Kentucky, which everyone in Kentucky and Tennessee calls "E-town."

There we met Sonny Hart, a commercial construction project manager who was born in his grandmother's house in Louisiana, in August of 1950. Sonny was eager to participate.

Sonny has a clear idea of the best place in Kentucky. "Even though we moved here in May of 1990, we haven't traveled that much," he admits. "But we were real impressed with Lake Cumberland in south central Kentucky. We take a camper down there and hike around that lake. It's beautiful and very peaceful."

"The best thing about E-town is the size of it. It's livable, it's friendly, and it's still small enough. The city government is 'open-door.' Everything you need is here, plus you are only forty miles from Louisville."

Sonny says his mother is the best person he knows. "She's a really strong, faithful Christian. She has always worked hard to help others, and she cares for people so much, and she's had the most influence on me. She has gone to Ukraine twice with me on mission trips, and the folks over there think of her about as much as I do."

In response to Pat's question about the best thing that has happened in his life, Sonny thinks for a few moments before saying, "Number one was meeting K. K. [his wife] when I was sixteen years old. Number two was being asked to go to

Pat with K. K. and Sonny Hart

Ukraine in 1993. That ten-day mission trip changed my life in a lot of ways, for the better."

When Pat asks what was the best decision he had made, without hesitation, Sonny replies, "To hang on to K. K. and marry her on June 12, 1970. We were both nineteen."

Sonny's message of encouragement is: "'Do good unto all men, especially to those of the household of faith.' I love that verse of Scripture."

It's refreshing to meet a man who still relishes meeting, holding onto, and marrying his sweetheart, whom he's known since the age of sixteen. It's encouraging to meet someone who really enjoys living and working in his town and who has found added vitality in working to help others in a faraway land.

As we head for home, the glowing sunset matches the glow we feel in our hearts at having found so much good-will. This has been a good beginning.

I have succeeded in using the $10 for a person in need, as you requested. Every Wednesday evening we pick up . . . an elderly sister for Bible class. She is living on a fixed income and has only our Christian family to depend upon. One day when we took her home she said that she was saving up for some new stone in her driveway since it was getting soft and she didn't think it would hold up through the winter.

I arranged for our company truck driver to go to the quarry, get some stone, and meet me at [her] home. We deposited the stone she needed . . . Boy was she surprised when she came home!

In Christ,

Sonny Hart

Kentucky & Ohio

.

TRIP TWO

NORTH CAROLINA

July 20, 2003, Sunday
Carolyn Weissenrieder (VEE-sen-REE-der)
State Capitol Steps
Raleigh, North Carolina

This leg of our journey began with a trip from Nashville to Chapel Hill, North Carolina, where, along with Scott's wife (and Pat and Rachel's mom) Ann, we watched Pat's younger sister, Rachel, compete in a tennis tournament at the University of North Carolina. She played very well, and we all enjoyed exploring the Chapel Hill campus and town together.

After the tournament ended, we drove to Raleigh and arrived at the old capitol grounds in downtown just before midday. A couple of downtown churches were just completing their services and groups of worshippers stood and chatted along the sidewalks or went to their cars and headed for Sunday lunch. The park-like grounds surrounding the North Carolina capitol building seemed like a good spot to find a goodwill interview.

Rachel and Ann declared that they would wait in the car. They couldn't imagine that we actually intended to approach complete strangers and begin talking. Off we went.

Strolling along a shaded path, we see a young woman up ahead walking alone. This is different because we are approaching her from behind and she is all by herself. Up to this point, we had always approached each prospect head-on, able to look directly into their eyes and perhaps begin with a friendly smile. We don't want to scare her and we also don't want to be rejected. Well, all we can do is ask.

Carolyn Weissenrieder

"Excuse me, Miss," the introduction begins, "we are looking for goodwill." We sit down on the steps of the old capitol building and discover that Carolyn Weissenrieder is visiting North Carolina from her home in Tettnang (pronounced "TET-nahn"), Germany.

Pat asks Carolyn about the best thing in her life and she replies, "My family. My parents have always been there for me so I know that I am not alone."

When asked what she likes best about North Carolina, Carolyn laughs and says, "I just arrived on Friday. For a big city, it [Raleigh] is actually very small. I am staying in Sanford, North Carolina, while I do an internship in a private company that makes shredders."

Pat asks about her favorite place back home and Carolyn says, "I love swimming in the sea at the lake of Constance near the German, Austrian, and Swiss borders."

"Of all the people you know, is there one who stands out for consistently doing good things?" Pat asks.

Carolyn replies, "My mom. I admire everything about her."

Carolyn says that the best decision that she ever made was going to Australia. "For one year, I worked and lived and traveled there . . . all on my own. I was nineteen." We are dumbfounded! Carolyn seems so young to be in America all alone, and the thought of her having ventured off to Australia, alone, at an even younger age, seems so incredibly bold. What an adventurous spirit! She volunteers that the best place she visited while in Australia was Ayers Rock, in the Outback Northern Territory.

When Pat asks this unpretentious world traveler to give a message of encouragement for our readers, Carolyn cheerfully obliges with, "You can do everything you want to. If you have the will to do it, just do it!" Carolyn has brought goodwill with her all the way from Germany.

We feel elated to have met and talked with Carolyn so easily. She was neither the first nor the last person we would interview who was not a native of the place where we met.

We were headed back to our car when we realized that Scott forgot to take a picture of Carolyn. He ran back in time to see her entering the North Carolina State Museum and made the accompanying shot of her standing beneath a replica of the Wright Brothers' famous first flying machine.

July 20, 2003, Sunday
Russell C. Rybka (Rib-KUH)
Holly Ridge, North Carolina

Driving south and east from Raleigh, we enjoyed a delicious barbeque lunch and vast pine forest countryside. In an intentional departure from our random quest, we aimed for Holly Ridge, North Carolina, because it is the home of thirty-one-year-old Russell C. Rybka, a captain in the United States Marine Corps. A Cobra helicopter pilot, Russell is stationed nearby at the Marine Corps Air Station in New River—close to the Second Marine Division at Camp Lejeune. Russell is Pat's cousin, the son of Scott's sister, Elizabeth, and he has just returned home from his first tour of combat duty in Iraq. He would later take a second tour of duty in Iraq from July '04 to February '05. We wanted Russell in this book.

Already in our driving across Tennessee, Kentucky, Ohio, and North Carolina, we had seen hundreds of mail boxes adorned with small American flags, as well as a multitude of yard signs, billboards, and restaurant marquees proclaiming, "We support our troops" or "God Bless

North Carolina

America." The spontaneous outpouring of goodwill and patriotic affection for our country, and for the young people who are in harm's way on behalf of the rest of us, was wonderful to see. Not organized by state or local governments, and not promoted by local civic clubs, these personal manifestations of love for country and love for our defenders are a powerful force for good.

[That generalized love is made all the more acute when your own kin, a child you have watched proudly since his birth, is pressed into combat.] The joy at his safe return is unrivaled in its sweetness. And so, the joy was palpable as Pat was able to interview his cousin. Russell's small home is immaculate, spare, and peaceful. Iraq is very far away.

Scott with Russell Rybka

Pat asks his cousin, "What is the best thing about Holly Ridge?"

"The low cost of living makes us [the Marines] able to live comfortably. It's close to the beach and close to work. That's a nice combination," Russell replies.

Pat inquires, "What is the best thing that has happened in your life?"

Russell repeats the question out loud, then says, "Being in this family; meeting Paula [who would become his wife in 2004]; taking a chance in ROTC; becoming an aviator; having a great job, great family, and great friends."

According to Russell, the best places in North Carolina are the beautiful Blue Ridge Mountains and historic Wilmington.

When Pat asks, "Who is the best person you know?" Russell thinks a bit and says, "My whole family—parents, my sister, aunts, uncles, and cousins. The time and effort, the moral and financial support they have all given me. This goodness—you and this book."

Russell says the best decision he made was switching from Naval ROTC to the Marine Corps. "In college at Auburn I was in the Naval ROTC. In my senior year, I decided to change over to the Marine Corps. In Naval ROTC, I had a guaranteed aviation slot, which I would not have in the Marines' program. I made the decision to go into the Marine program [anyway], and I got an aviation contract. I love being a Marine and getting to fly!"

Pat asks Russell for words of advice and he says, "Keep your family and friends close. Treat your family as friends and your friends as family."

As these words were written, Russell was redeployed at the end of June 2004, to serve with the Twenty-fourth Marine Expeditionary Unit in Iraq. As you read these words, may your heart be connected to the hearts of all those brave men and women who have served and are honorably serving in our Army, Navy, Air Force, Marine Corps, and Coast Guard.

September 2, 2003, Tuesday

We never actually sat down and mapped out a grand strategy for covering every single state in one year's time. Instead, we decided to approach the travel portion just like the interview portion—as a huge adventure. On a few evenings we did sit in our library and gaze at a good atlas, pondering the most efficient way to cluster several states at a time. Inexpensive airfares allowed us to implement a fly- and-drive method which served us quite well.

TRIP THREE
VIRGINIA
& WEST VIRGINIA

Virginia

September 3, 2003, Wednesday
Marcia (MAR-sah) Short
J. W. Adams School
Pound, Virginia

We tried to weave our book travel into family activities. Thus, we set out in the general direction of Princeton, New Jersey, on the afternoon of Tuesday, September 2, 2003, with the SUV loaded full of Rachel's necessities for college dorm living. We drove eastward through Monterey, Clarkrange, Big South Fork, to Pine Knot, Kentucky, and spent the night in Corbin, Kentucky.

While this is unquestionably the story of the people in whom we found great stories of goodwill, it is also important to note the physical backdrop against which their lives unfold.

On this particular day, our drive took us from Corbin, Kentucky, to Flat Lick, to Pineville and along a road marked "Kingdom Come Parkway." We saw all types of church buildings. The area was rocky, rough, and ultra-remote. It struck us as funny to see so many "No Trespassing" signs in an area where there seemed to be no one around except the two of us!

On twisting, darkly shaded roads that dropped steeply down into vine-covered ravines, we felt completely alone. We crossed into the state of Virginia on the quietest of back country roads. Soon, our road dead-ended into Highway 23, a four-lane highway that seemed positively modern compared to the back roads we had just traveled.

Turn right or left? We turned right and headed south. In moments, we reconsidered. Given that we aimed to end up north in Princeton, New Jersey, we quickly turned around and headed north on Highway 23. In less than one mile, we spied the J. W. Adams School and decided to stop.

The entry hall is bright, clean, and colorful. We introduce ourselves in the bustling office. Within moments, we are interviewing Marcia Short, the principal. We will spell her name "Marsah" throughout, as this unique pronunciation is indicative of her unique personality and background. Her office is spacious, immaculate, and graced with attractive feminine touches.

Pat begins by asking Marsah to talk about her hometown.

"Pound is very, very special," Marsah says. "I grew up here. I graduated from Pound High School in 1982, finished college in three years, and was back here in 1985. This is a very special place in my heart. My husband has had many job offers to go elsewhere with the state police and I always tell him, 'I wish you the best—I'm stayin' home.'"

Marsah has a warm smile on her face as she talks. "Pound is such a close-knit community. Out of 643 children enrolled in this school, there are not ten families that I don't know. And I will know them before school's out. We are like a family here."

Marcia "Marsah" Short

When Pat poses the question about the best person in her life, Marsah says, "Well, there are three. My mom, my dad, and my husband. They are all absolutely wonderful people. My mom is a monitor in the fiber optics class at Pound High School, and she always cooks special dishes for others. My dad knows and helps everybody in the community. Neighbors call, and Dad helps. He grows a big garden and gives all the food away!" Her loving admiration for her parents is wonderful to witness.

Marsah is so happy and so proud telling us about the good-will in her family and in her community. She continues, "Dad still lives where he was raised, in the Bold Camp community, and he still takes care of his parents, and my husband has been so supportive. He helps me."

Pat adds a new question: "Which person, living or dead, would you most like to meet?" We would discover it prompts an interesting variety of responses.

Marsah says, "My mom's father. I have done some family research and I would like to get to know him. I have enjoyed knowing Dad's folks so much."

Marsah says, with a soft chuckle, that the best decision she has made was her choice of career. "Though there are some times I regret it, I think my decision to go into education was the best. I have been able to help a lot of children. I think I have been able to help them grow up and do the right things."

Pat asks another new question: "Do you have a goal you still hope to achieve?"

Marsah says, "Well, I think about going on to get a doctorate, which might present new job opportunities. But I might miss the closeness with the children, which I love so much."

Pat asks about the best thing in her life and Marsah beams as she says, "Having the family that I have. They have given me such unfailing support. My mom and dad pushed education. My dad pushed me to excel and my husband has given me fifteen wonderful years of help and support and love."

Seeking to give still more opportunities for positive introspection, Pat has added yet another question: "If you had an opportunity to begin a new career, what would you choose to do?"

Not surprisingly, Marsah says, "I'd still go into education! It's really rough at times, but we are dealing with children's lives. Someone has got to care about them."

Marsah's words of encouragement are: "Even on a bad day, remember: good things happen to good people if you are honest."

Our interview is complete, and Marsah asks us questions about our book. "How did the idea originate? How do you pick the people?" She is genuinely enthused for us and for the idea. Getting such immediate, positive reinforcement makes our spirits soar. Doing this feels good.

Scott has an idea. "Could we interview one of your students?"

Marsah says, "Well, I would need to get the parent's permission." We think this may be too difficult to coordinate and maybe we should ease on up the road. Marsah's countenance brightens as she announces the solution. "We have a student whose mother teaches here. I'll ask her." Marsah makes things happen, and in a few minutes we meet Bryan Keith and his mother, Kelly.

September 3, 2003, Wednesday
Bryan Keith
J. W. Adams School
Pound, Virginia

A brand-new seventh grader, Bryan is a model of politeness and good manners. Such traits are not intuitive for seventh-grade boys, so it is obvious that Bryan has been well taught by his parents and teachers. He appears to clearly grasp our quest for goodwill and he gives succinct answers to our questions.

When Pat asks, "What is your favorite place in all of Virginia?" Bryan replies, "The Shenandoah River, fishing with my dad."

As you read those words, we hope a beautiful, idyllic scene of a father and son fishing together in a quiet bend of a beautiful river flashes across your mind's eye—as it did ours as we heard Bryan quietly speak the words. That is goodwill.

Trip Three

Pat continues with: "What do you like best about Pound?"

Bryan says, "It's peaceful. Everybody's real nice to everybody. There's lots of nice people."

Pat asks, "Is there one person who stands out for consistently doing good things?" Bryan ponders this one, then says, "Probably my pastor at church, Jerry Lusk. He is always going to other people's houses to visit or take care of them. He helped a lot of people after the flood here."

Bryan said he would most like to meet Michael Jordan. "I like basketball. He's a good player and a good person. He's not been arrested."

Bryan Keith and Pat

Children are paying attention. Everywhere. They are watching you, too.

When Pat asks the "best decision" question, Bryan thinks a while in silence, then says, "I haven't had to make a really big decision yet." One might think no concrete goal had yet solidified in Bryan's seventh-grade heart, but when asked, he responded immediately, "I want to be a professional basketball player in the NBA." (Watch for him.)

Pat asks Bryan what the best thing is that has happened in his life. Bryan's simple, honest response is, "My best friend's mom had cancer. We all prayed and prayed, and she was healed." How absolutely remarkable to hear a young boy sum up friendship, faith, community, and love in only fifteen words!

Here are his words of encouragement for our readers: (They truly are for you. Pat did not say, "Do you have a message/advice for us." He always asked ". . . for our readers") "Never give up! Lots of people quit. Keep on trying."

Virginia & West Virginia

Another great interview. We say our goodbyes to Bryan and his mom. Marsah is happy that we are happy. Then she says, "You know, you all really ought to interview my dad." She is beaming and it is clear that she understands what we are seeking. She sincerely wants to help two strangers passing through her community.

We ask, "Where can we find him?"

September 3, 2003, Wednesday
Roger Lee Mullins
Mullins Creek, Virginia

The directions to Marsah's dad's house began with the words, "Go right on the four lane," an unconscious acknowledgement that there is only one such roadway in the area, and also included the evocative words "Bold Camp Road." We wonder about the origin of the name, as we would about many fascinating place names we'd see all across the United States . . . Marked Tree, Arkansas; Point Blank, Texas; Mexican Hat, Utah; Walnut Shade, Missouri; Shoshoni, Wyoming. Recalling that Marsah had told us her dad had been "raised in the Bold Camp Community" we wondered whether particularly bold people had originally dwelled there in a mining camp?

We found ourselves well out of Pound and back up in the remote "hollows" of deep southwestern Virginia coal mining country.

What would this visit be like? We didn't really know what to expect, but we were not apprehensive, because Marsah, such a genuinely good-natured woman, had phoned ahead while we were still in her office to say, "Daddy, two men are here writing a book and they want to interview you, okay? You be looking for them. I love you." With such an introduction, we felt confident and enthused as we turned into the driveway of the neat "tan brick house on the right" Marsah had directed us to.

Roger Lee Mullins moved easily down the sloping hill behind his house and gave us a friendly wave; his big black dog galloped ahead to check us out. We could not have been more cordially greeted even if we had been morning coat-clad diplomats representing the Queen of England. At this writing, many months have passed since that meeting, and the warmth of Roger Lee's personality still burns brightly in our memory. He had been working outdoors in the morning sun and his light blue coveralls were damp with honest perspiration. As we made ourselves comfortable in the cool shade of his carport, he thanked us profusely for coming to see him and said, "You know, so many folks don't take the time to just stop and visit. I'm so glad you all came by." He radiated a big, genuine smile.

It is a struggle to put into suitable words the pure joy we feel at meeting such a man of goodwill. There is no exaggeration in saying that we immediately like him and he equally likes us. Utterly without pretense, Roger Lee pulls off his boots as we talk, and lets his sockless feet cool in the gentle breeze. Roger Lee Mullins is an original, one of those rare souls who is totally comfortable simply being himself and who feels no need to put on any airs. He is genuinely enthused about our desire to seek goodwill.

Pat asks, "Is this Bold Camp?"

Roger Lee replies emphatically, "This is Mullins Creek." We wonder, but do not ask, whether that is a longstanding name. No matter, we are glad to be with Roger Lee Mullins of Mullins Creek, Virginia.

When Pat asks about the best place in the beautiful, historic state of Virginia, the response could well have been Colonial Williamsburg, the Skyline Drive in the Shenandoah Mountains, Virginia Beach, or graceful Old Town Alexandria. Yet, not surprisingly, Roger Lee says, "I am well satisfied to be right here." The conviction with which the words are uttered reveals both an admirable intensity of affection for that place and a joyous sense of contentment.

With a liveliness one might expect from a teenager, Roger Lee says, "We are a small community, so everybody knows everybody. We have a low crime rate, and people are more down home here. It's easy to know everyone and get along. Nobody

Virginia & West Virginia

bothers me." He speaks not as a disagreeable hermit but as a man rejoicing in his many friendships and his independence.

Pat asks, "Who is the best person you know?"

Roger Lee Mullins replies with not one, but several persons. "Why, my immediate family. My wonderful wife, my daughter, and my mother and daddy. That's made me a better person all the way 'round."

When asked which person, living or dead, he would most like to meet, Roger Lee says, "It's hard to name just one, but I would like to meet my great-grandmaw."

Roger Lee says the best decision he made was a personal one. "When I met my wife, June Baker Mullins, and married her. We were from Right Fork [of the creek], she was from Middle Fork. I was driving a coal truck and saw her get off a school bus. The second best was having our daughter, Marsah, but I wouldn't have had her without deciding to marry my wife first."

Roger Lee Mullins and Pat

Pat asks, "Do you have a goal you still hope to achieve?"

"Well, I'd say seeing that my daughter has what she wants. I helped her go to college and I helped her get a master's degree, and if she wants to get a doctor's degree, I'll help her do that. As for me, I am well content," Roger Lee says.

In response to Pat's question about the best thing in his life, Roger Lee replies, "Well, as I've said, having my family. I was in the coal business for twenty-five years. I got in at the right time and got out at the right time. The good Lord has been good to me. I was able to retire at a young age and I like being on my own. I don't have to ask nobody for nothing! I worked coal sixteen to eighteen hours a day. My daughter and wife went with me. My daughter could do anything; she even drove a front-end loader!"

A single car passes by on the road; the driver honks the horn and gives Roger Lee a wave. Quite naturally, the driver gets a friendly wave in return.

Concerning a new career, Roger Lee tells us, "I suppose I could've done stuff with a lot less work, but I'm proud of the work I did. I'd do it the same!" It is a joy to hear a man speak so fondly of his work and to discern his sincere feeling of gratification at having pulled his own weight. Roger Lee strikes us as a man possessed of that unique American "can-do" spirit personified in President Theodore Roosevelt. We feel confident that if he had been given the opportunity, Roger Lee Mullins would have ridden with Teddy and the Rough Riders.

Roger Lee's advice to you is, "The biggest thing is—grow up and be a good citizen. And be a hard worker in anything you get into."

With the interview complete, we make a photograph and give Roger Lee an envelope with ten dollars for spreading some goodwill. This is another occasion we wish we had on film. Roger Lee, with the utmost sincerity, offers the money back. We explain that it is an unencumbered gift, not payment for the interview. He finally relents and says, "I'll double it—and more. I should be giving this back to you for what you are doing."

It lightens our hearts to see how much the very idea of our quest appeals to Roger Lee. At the outset of our journey, we had not anticipated how enthusiastic people would be, nor how the very idea of our quest would lift their spirits. So many people gave us so much encouragement along the way.

Roger Lee inquires, "Where are you headed next?" We explain that we have no specific itinerary, we just need to head generally north toward Princeton. Incredulous, he says, "Do you mean to tell me that when you got up this morning you didn't know where you were going?"

"Yes sir, that's right," we reply happily.

"And this evenin' . . . you're just gonna stop whenever you get tired?"

"Yes sir, that's right."

With a huge smile and a friendly clap of his hand on Pat's shoulder, Roger Lee says, "That's exactly how I'd do it if I was going with you!"

Though we certainly would have been delighted to have him join us in person, the fond memory of our brief visit with

Roger Lee Mullins stayed with us, across the many miles still to come.

What a good day! From Mullins Creek, we enjoyed a scenic drive to Clintwood, Haysi, and Grundy, to Princeton, West Virginia, where we got on the modern-as-space-travel Interstate 77 to Beckley, West Virginia, and rested for the night.

West Virginia

September 4, 2003, Thursday
Jillian Huber
Davis & Elkins College
Elkins, West Virginia

We departed Beckley in a torrential downpour and hoped that our Rachel was not facing such inclement weather on Princeton's freshman class outdoor adventure. We later learned that her group was in the rain every single day. They bonded. We were fortunate to generally have good weather throughout our travels—as rain makes it considerably more challenging to load and unload and also tougher to actually find a prospective interviewee.

We wandered a bit north and a bit east, and in the small town of Elkins, West Virginia, we stopped for fuel and a snack. Scott spied a statue of a distinguished-looking fellow on horseback and wondered aloud, "Who was Henry G. Davis?"

Pat, the former history major, said, "He was a U.S. senator from West Virginia, and was the Democratic vice presidential candidate in 1904 with Alton Parker. They lost to Theodore Roosevelt and Charles Fairbanks." Not many people know that.

For Scott, these trips were meaningful in multiple ways. Obviously, meeting more than one hundred new friends and being exposed to so much goodwill from coast to coast was exciting and memorable. Yet another unplanned benefit of the journey was simply riding through the country with Pat. Sharing the sights and the people was wonderful, and on top of that, Pat sharing his encyclopedic knowledge was educational, uplifting, and fun. Those memories are pure treasure.

From the gas station, we could see turrets atop a grand-looking old home perched on a hill above town. Curious, we headed in that direction and found the home, known as Graceland Inn, on the campus of Davis & Elkins College. The mansion was built early in the 1890s as a summer home for Senator Davis. Acquired by the college in 1941, Graceland was originally used as a residence hall. After a complete restoration in the early 1990s, the inn received its first guests in 1996.

We were greeted warmly at the front door by Jillian Huber, a student at the college whose studies include gaining practical experience in lodging and dining management by working part-time at the Graceland Inn. She cheerfully agreed to be interviewed and led us to a quiet conference room.

Pat begins by asking, "What is your favorite place in West Virginia?" Jillian responds, "The Canaan (Kuh-NANE) Valley and Blackwater Falls. It is amazing in the winter!" It is wonderful to see her open up and speak with us so enthusiastically. "I love to ski there. The area has not really been touched and it's very natural. You see deer and bears. I always feel kinda at home there."

Jillian Huber

"The best thing about Elkins is the people. It's a town of about 10,000 or so and everyone is very comfortable with each other. People are friendly and nice." High praise from a college student!

Jillian says, "Coming to school here is the best decision I have made. I could have skied elsewhere, but I was given a nice scholarship here, and it's just a half hour away from home. I get to see my parents all the time, and I landed a great job here at the Inn. That has helped me decide on a path in life."

Wholesome and earnest, Jillian continues, "I would like to be a ski-lodge owner, here or anywhere." Not just a ski bum or even a ski instructor—we love it that Jillian wants to own her own ski lodge.

When Pat asks, "Who is the best person you know?" Jillian pauses a while and says, "I can't narrow it down to just one." What a splendid predicament in which to find oneself! She says, "The entire college community does so much. There are many organizations at the college, like Upward Bound, for example, which do so many good volunteer activities."

Without delay, Jillian replies to Pat's living-or-dead-person question with, "Princess Grace. I went to Europe a couple of years ago and in Monaco I saw her garden. She was a powerful woman who reached out to a lot of people. She was beautiful and she also did a lot of good for others."

Pat asks: "What is the best thing that has happened in your life?" We are again privileged to see an expression of sincere gratitude on the face of someone we have just met in such a random fashion. Jillian tells us, "I have always been very fortunate. I have close friends and a loving family. I have been to Europe two times and to Canada. I've had opportunities to see the world. It has helped me live a better life seeing how others live."

Pat asks Jillian if she has a message of encouragement for our readers.

Her response for you: "Even through everything that's happened since 9/11, as long as you have family, friends and loved ones, and if you will stay strong, have hope and faith, everyone will be fine."

We are tempted by Jillian's gracious invitation to stay for lunch, but we feel we should press on up the road.

Dear Pat & Scott,

I wanted to let you all know what I did with the $10 that you had given me. There is a girl . . . that is about to have her first baby. She is a single mother who does not have support, but has been working like crazy to make money. I felt that she could've used a little extra money more than something else.

Sincerely,

Jillian Huber

September 4, 2003, Thursday
Willa "Sue" Grafton
Seneca Rocks, West Virginia

From Elkins we headed eastward into the Monongahela National Forest, an especially beautiful area of West Virginia we had never before visited. Verdant mountain forests, lovely rivers, and tumbling mountain brooks all combined to delight our senses and our minds.

Suddenly, we rounded a curve and saw rock cliffs that looked as though they belonged in a classic Oriental painting. They seemed mysterious, and we felt compelled to stop.

Willa "Sue" Grafton

We introduce ourselves to genial Willa "Everyone calls me Sue" Grafton, who we meet at the attractive visitors' center. A West Virginia native, Sue has worked at Seneca Rocks for the past six years. In response to Pat's question about her favorite place in the state, Sue says, "Spruce Knob. It's the highest point in all of West Virginia, and it's such a neat place. There's an observation tower and the area isn't so developed."

Pat asks, "What is the best thing about Seneca Rocks?"

"Besides the beauty of the rocks, the people here and the culture of the area are so special. You'll come back . . . there's something mysterious about this place," Sue says. How interesting that she used the exact word, "mysterious," that had prompted us to stop in the first place. Go see for yourself.

"Of all the people you know, is there one person who stands out for consistently doing good things?" Pat asks.

Sue says, "Fred Sites. He was nice to everyone. I have never met a nicer person." What a compliment! Wouldn't we all love to have someone think and say such good things about us? Comments like Sue's inspire us to strive more diligently to be nice to everyone.

When Pat asks about which person Sue would most like to meet, she says, "My grandparents. All of them were deceased at the time of my birth. I'd like to know them."

Scott & Pat Price,

It was a pleasure meeting the two of you. . . . After a great deal of thought, I donated the $10 to [a] single father who has custody of his three children. I told him that I looked at the $10 as very special seed money, which I hoped would grow into greater funds to help educate his children. I also contributed $20 to the children, assuring that the seed money had a good start in growing. Your "goodwill" has had a great start here in Pendleton Co., West Virginia.

Best wishes,

Willa "Sue" Grafton

She says she has a goal she still hopes to achieve. "I'm working on opening a business here. I'm always into a dozen different things, and I'm working on an arts and crafts gift shop to market works by local people in West Virginia and Virginia."

Sue chose to combine both the best-decision and the best-thing-in-life questions into one answer. With genuine pride, she says, "Having my daughter—she's terrific."

Asked about her choice given the opportunity to begin a new career, Sue laughs and says with confidence, "I like what I'm doing! Although I'm a registered forester, I really do more public relations now. I arrange arts and music events here, so I deal with people a lot—and I never thought of myself as a people person!"

Again we feel as though we have been granted a special opportunity to meet and hear from people who enjoy what they do. They are not claiming perfection, but they are forthrightly expressing a sense of joy at having work they like.

Here are Willa "Sue" Grafton's words of encouragement: "Laugh in the face of adversity and you will surmount all obstacles. When things get really bad, I just laugh and go on."

This friendly woman of goodwill has obviously confronted adversity before, and she has chosen to move beyond it with the help of good humor. We are happy to meet her.

September 4, 2003, Thursday
Diane Hypes
Moorefield, West Virginia

As we left Seneca Rocks, we took Highway 55, dropping in altitude alongside the Potomac River. While slowly passing through the little four- or five-block-long town of Moorefield, we saw *Moorefield Examiner* painted on a storefront window. We hadn't interviewed anyone at a newspaper yet, and there was plenty of free parking on the street. We went in and introduced ourselves to petite Diane Hypes, an Iowa native who is now a true West Virginia mountaineer. An electric fan softly stirred the air in her simple office as the interesting shorts-clad news editor calmly submitted to being interviewed by two total strangers who just walked in off the street.

A little unsure of us at first, Diane lights up when answering Pat's query about her favorite place in West Virginia. "Dolly Sods is my very favorite place. It's about a one-hour drive from here. It's one of the highest spots in West Virginia, probably 4,800 feet. It has climate and terrain that is similar to Canada. It has been preserved and put into the Monongahela National Forest. The trees are very different from here. This is a very hot valley, and when it is ninety-five degrees here, it will be seventy degrees there. It is absolutely my favorite place."

This is so interesting and exhilarating. Not only do we learn of a new, special place, but in the backs of our minds we are thrilled at how immediately she has trusted us enough to speak so openly and enthusiastically.

She continues to explain her fondness for West Virginia. "I had been all over the world twice, doing

Diane Hypes

an educational satellite project for the U.S. State Department out in the boonies of underdeveloped countries. I lived near Washington, D.C., but I loved visiting these mountains. I told someone someday I wanted to have my ashes dropped over the mountains of West Virginia. I realized instead I should go live there, and so I do. I live on top of a mountain in a house with no electricity, and I just got a phone two years ago." She has a nice laugh at herself. She exudes an air of determination and pioneer grit.

Pat wants to know the best thing about Moorefield.

Diane says, "The people. This is a small town, and the people here are very giving and very friendly. I grew up in a small town in Iowa; I like the setting. The people here are really very helpful, very friendly, and very accepting of your personality."

Pat queries, "Of all the people you know, is there one who stands out for consistently doing good things?"

There is no delay, no pause. Diane replies, "Brown Hott. He's one of the first two people I met in West Virginia. He died in 1994. He was positively the best! He was in the contracting business, did roads and heavy construction. He had no formal education, but he was one of the smartest people I've known. He learned his entire life. He just had an innate sense of the right thing to do at the right time. When we first met, I was a little impatient because I thought he was late coming out to work on the septic tank at my house. He told me I was on 'city time' and he was on 'country time.' Then he gave me the best advice: 'Don't come out here and tell us how we're living our life wrong and how we should change it. As a matter of fact, if I was you, I wouldn't say anything for about ten years!' He was absolutely correct."

What a story of goodwill is wrapped up in that advice, the way it was given and the way it was received. It is a fitting tribute to friendship and to Brown Hott.

Diane says that she would most like to meet Henry David Thoreau. "I enjoy his writing and I'd like to have a better understanding of his thinking."

Pat asks, "What is the best decision you have made?"

Diane smiles easily and says, "To move out here. I grew up on a farm in a rural area of Iowa. I went to the University of Iowa and studied journalism. As I mentioned, I did lots of traveling for the State Department, but as I visited out here I found the place where I am most happy. I told my mother I

Hi,

I just wanted to let you know that the $10 I received from you went, along with $15 of my own, as a $25 donation to the National Humane Education Society.

Diane Hypes

was sure I had been misplaced in life—these mountains just spoke to my soul. When I asked for a leave of absence from my work at the State Department, they said no. So, I quit and moved out here. This was twenty-five years ago. I had no job, no one knew me, and some thought I was a witch!" With a good-natured laugh, the *Moorefield Examiner's* news editor says she still enjoys keeping a broom collection. What a courageous and adventurous young woman she was to leave her job and move, alone, to the mountains of West Virginia!

In response to Pat's question about a goal yet to be achieved, Diane says, "Long term, I would like to have good health to be able to keep living the way I live. Independence. I don't have a lot of stuff. I would just like to keep at it." With a small wave of her hand, Diane indicates her work and this place. She continues, "I also enjoy endurance riding on mules." We are not surprised in the least. "I would love to get on my mule with my pack and just go. There are several hundred-mile trails I plan to do on my mule." This is one of the most original responses we got to this query.

Pat's next question brings a comprehensive reply.

"I think my whole life is the best thing that has happened to me!" Diane says. "I would do it almost exactly the same if I had it to do over. I am able to live where I want and how I want. I have a great job, and even though I don't have much money, I am fortunate to be able to travel and live the life I want to live." What a joy for us to hear another new friend express such profound gratitude.

We loved Diane's thoughtful answers, and we were especially touched at this point when she said, "I get to meet really interesting people every day. Unfortunately, much of the media concentrates on the bizarre and the absolute worst side of humanity. Every day I get to do stories about normal human beings living very valuable lives." Perceptively, she adds, "Just like what you are doing."

Pat asks Diane what she would do if given the opportunity to begin a new career. She says, "I love my career as a photographer and writer—but I could think of a bunch of new ones. The top two would be archeologist and psychologist. Somebody said, 'If you want to be happy for a year, win the lottery. If you want to be happy for your entire life, get a job you love.'"

Virginia & West Virginia

Pat asks Diane if she has words of advice. She says, "Live your life so that when death comes like a thief in the night, there is nothing left to lose or to be stolen!"

Wow! Jillian Huber, Willa "Sue" Grafton, and Diane Hypes. We have found a gold mine of goodwill in the mountains of West Virginia.

We met Ann's flight Friday morning in Baltimore, drove to Princeton, unloaded all of Rachel's gear from our car, and spent Friday and Saturday helping Rachel settle into her new dorm. On Sunday we said farewell to our new college girl, delivered Ann back to the airport, and turned for home.

TRIP FOUR
ALABAMA

September 11, 2003, Thursday
William A. "Billy" Noles Jr.
Birmingham, Alabama

On the way to Pensacola, Florida, to celebrate the eightieth birthday of Scott's fantastic mother, Katy (Does she have goodwill?—she would be an entire book!), we decided to also do our Alabama interviews. This time, we departed from our totally random search for goodwill. Scott is a native of Alabama, and there are three special people of such goodwill there that he wants to be sure you get to know them too.

Scott says, "I have two biological brothers, and Billy Noles is my third brother. Together we traversed the high school years . . . we were football teammates, classmates, and we always went on double dates. We each might be with different dates, but we were always with each other. Billy's mother, Pola, was one of the sweetest people I have ever known. She had a soft laugh that took hold of her and grew and grew. She always seemed easily amused by Billy and me. There are no friends like old friends, and Billy is one of my oldest and dearest. I just called him from the car as we left Nashville, and he said he would meet us anywhere for an interview."

Pat inquires about the best place in Alabama, and Billy says, "Gulf Shores, Orange Beach, Mobile Bay. If I could, I would retire down there in that area right now. It's beautiful."

"The best thing about Birmingham is its size. It's not a small town, but it's also not a great big metropolis. The rolling hills and greenery also make it attractive," Billy says.

Billy Noles

When Pat asks, "Of all the people you know, is there one who stands out for consistently doing good things?" Billy points at Scott and says to Pat, "Your dad is that man. He's my best friend from way back. I can still count on him." It's an embarrassing but heartwarming moment for Scott.

Billy talks about wishing he could meet his mother's father, who died in 1937 before Billy was born. "He fought in World War I and was decorated—awarded the Purple Heart. I'd like to know him."

Pat asks, "What is the best decision you have made?" Billy responds, "I have stayed in contact with some of my best friends. You know, you never forget people you have had good times with, and it's great to stay in touch through the years because you have so many things in common; not just old memories but new things like your children and their activities. We count our blessings together."

Billy's goals are simple. "Well, I haven't hit the lottery yet. So, I'm still working towards my retirement," he says. "I'd like to be a doctor, but I'm not smart enough. A good doctor can really help people and really make a difference for someone. If I was smart enough, that's what I'd like to do."

Billy says, "Meeting my wife, Janice, and marrying her was the best thing to happen in my life. We have been blessed with two wonderful children, and they have both done well so far—in college, in sports, in life. You know, all of that starts at home and I give Janice the credit." It's a loving tribute to his bride.

Billy Noles concludes the interview with this message of encouragement: "In life, if you work hard enough and long enough, and if you are honest and sincere, good things will happen to you."

We love Billy.

Trip Four

September 11, 2003, Thursday
Raymond T. Williams
Ozark, Alabama

Still aiming for Pensacola, we drove south from Birmingham and southeast from Montgomery into Alabama's "Wiregrass" region. Beautiful farms and small towns roll past our windows as we make our way to Ozark and one of Scott's college roommates, "The Electric" Ray Williams, so named because of his good-humored verbal zingers, his electric personality, and his excellent singing voice when leading his band, "The Burgundy Seven," during his high school and college years.

As one drives deeper into the South, the pace of life slows down and the hospitality quotient goes way up. When we arrived at Ray's home, he and his wife, Carolyn, had a huge dinner cooking for us. His warm, generous spirit inspired us, and his delicious dinner filled us up completely.

After dinner, Pat begins our interview by asking about the best place in Alabama. Ray says "My home, Ozark. I really love it. It has always been good to me. It's safe and secure, and you really know people. Let me give you an example. My daughter, Abigail, went to renew her driver's license when she was home from Auburn recently. She didn't have enough money with her to pay the renewal fee. So, the lady working in there paid it for her! She knew that I would pay her back, which I did. There is a level of trust here that you might not find in some places where people don't know each other as well."

When asked about the best person he knows, Ray says, "Well, let me tell you about three. One would be my father, B. F. Williams. He was such a good person because he helped so many people. He grew up poor, living with an aunt and uncle. He was very successful in the construction business and he always did good things for other people. Not hundreds— thousands. If he did well, he said 'Share it!' Another would be my wife, Carolyn. Her special goodness is a reflection of her dedication to Christianity. She is a person who truly believes in the goodness to be found in everyone she meets."

Ray then tells Pat, "And then there is your dad. I've never known Scotty to be mad at anyone. He has always been positive,

Alabama

no matter what the circumstances. That kind of goodness affects people."

Pat asks, "Who would you most like to meet?" Ray considers the question for a few moments and says, "Jesus is certainly the most significant person in history. I'd like to meet Him. A little more recently in history, I'd like to meet Robert E. Lee."

Ray Williams and Pat

Ray tells us the best decision he ever made was to marry his wife, Carolyn. "Her love has made me a better man and is probably the thing that has made me as stable as I am," he says. "Having our children with Carolyn is the best thing in my life. Seeing them grow up and be happy, well-educated, and independent people. All you have that really matters is your family and your friends."

When Pat asks Ray if he has a goal he still hopes to achieve, Ray explains, "I saw Shania Twain singing in Chicago, and I would also like to perform at a concert like hers, with 100,000 fans cheering me on. I enjoy the music business with my band 'Flambeaux.'"

Pat asks, "If you could begin a new career what would you do?" Ray replies, "That's hard to say. I have enjoyed my work in construction, I raise cattle, I'm in a rock and roll band." It is so good to see someone, especially a dear friend, who has felt joy in doing what is called work.

"I suppose I would have a restaurant on the Greek island of Spetses. I like Greek dishes and I love the Greek isles. I would name it 'Betsy's on Spetses' in honor of my sister, Betsy," Ray continues. We would confirm Ray's culinary expertise and his genuine charm as a host. He could even provide his own floor show as a singer!

Ray's advice for you: "As I reflect on my life and the things that have made a difference, I would say, 'enjoy your life, don't let it slip by. All the material things mean nothing.' My mother had such a great perspective about material things. She said that the only thing she didn't want to lose was her mind. Cherish your memories of people and places. And, you can be as warm and friendly as you want to be, and as fulfilled as you want to be."

Ray and Carolyn try very hard to persuade us to spend the night, even though they had very little advance warning of our visit. Their good hearts stir ours, and we are grateful for having had the opportunity to visit in their hospitable home. We smile as we drive into the summer night.

September 12, 2003, Friday
Charles S. "Charley" Willoughby
Mobile, Alabama

A true southern gentleman, Charley Willoughby was a law school classmate of Scott's, and they served together in the U.S. Marine Corps at Quantico, Virginia, and at Parris Island, South Carolina. On the road, Scott explained to Pat that even as a young man, Charley displayed an impressive level of character, integrity, and affability. His personal goodwill was notable even in difficult circumstances.

Settled in the handsomely restored historic home which now houses Charley's law firm in downtown Mobile, Pat begins our interview by asking Charley about his favorite place in Alabama. Charley says, "I have fond memories of Birmingham from the years I spent there in college and law school. I also enjoy Mobile. I've lived here for twenty-five years now, and I especially enjoy being on the water and sailing. I suppose my favorite place would still be my boyhood home in southeast Alabama, about twenty-five miles out in the country outside of Dothan. I still love going there and taking long walks in the woods. The peacefulness and the solitude provide a real sense of renewal."

Pat then asks, "What is the best thing about Mobile?" Charley responds, "Well, there are several things. I mentioned the water, Mobile Bay and the Gulf. We also enjoy a varied climate; the summers can be stiflingly hot, our winters are short and mild, and

Alabama

Charley Willoughby and Scott (bottom row, from left) with classmates on graduation day from Naval Justice School, 1975

spring is early and beautiful. We have quite a melting pot of people here which gives a nice flair to the city. Also, the Catholic Church is active in community life here. Catholic Social Services helped relocate a family here—one spouse is Catholic, one is Muslim, and they now own a popular restaurant here. They have resisted raising their prices because they say they want to pay back the people of Mobile for being so good to them." That is goodwill, received and passed on.

When asked about the best person he knows, Charley ponders a while and says, "It's hard to narrow it down to just one." (We often received this reply, and we would always interject, "Isn't that wonderful that you know so many good people!") He continued, "There are two especially self-sacrificing people who stand out. One, Edmond Jones, is a retired federal probation officer here in Mobile who has probably volunteered his time to help others more than anyone else I know. The second is a retired Catholic priest from Ireland, Monsignor Francis Murphy, who has really helped me come to appreciate the sacrifices made by members of the clergy in service to God and the Church."

Charley thinks for a while about who he would most like to meet. Finally, he says, "Thomas More. He was Lord Chancellor of England during the reign of King Henry VIII. And even though he was a dear friend of the king, Thomas More resisted the king's attempt to compel him to change a matter of conscience. He didn't acquiesce. He could not follow the king if it meant compromising his conscience. I wish I could live up to that example."

Pat asks, "What is the best decision you have made?"

Charley answers, "There are probably two. One is marrying my wife, Maureen, and the other is my decision to become a

Catholic after being raised a Baptist and wandering around for twenty-five years."

Charley says the best thing to happen to him was being raised by his parents with a high degree of integrity and faith which they imparted to him.

Asked about his goals, Charley replies, "This may not be typical, but I want to continue trying to resist temptation, and be able to live in a way that my family and I would be proud of. My goal is not to acquire great wealth, but to use my training as a lawyer to help others. My desire is to really help others and not just myself."

It's good to hear such positive thoughts being expressed so openly (by a lawyer!) in a modern world that is often focused on the negative.

Asked about choosing a new career, Charley says, "It might very well involve the study of forestry. I love being in the woods. If I could be outdoors more in a forestry job—not just an academic pursuit but something practical—I'd love giving that a try."

Here are Charley Willoughby's words of advice: "If we live our lives keeping foremost in our thoughts the happiness of others, we wind up a lot happier. If we follow the Golden Rule, ['Do unto others as you would have them do unto you'] we will wind up a lot happier. If we all did those, the world would have peace. I would also encourage your readers to read the ancient philosophers and learn from them."

It was a joy to see Charley, Ray, and Billy—three fine men of goodwill. Their dear friendship helped mold Scott and, by extension, influenced Pat and Rachel for good. We hope you enjoyed meeting them.

Alabama

RHODE ISLAND, MASSACHUSETTS, MAINE, NEW HAMPSHIRE, VERMONT & CONNECTICUT

Rhode Island

September 28, 2003, Sunday
Gordon Wilkins
Saunderstown, Rhode Island

We flew into Providence, Rhode Island, and rented a car to begin our search for goodwill in the New England states. We sat in the car at the airport deciding whether to go north or south—what freedom we possessed! Throughout our travels, we constantly reminded ourselves of how fortunate we were to simply travel our beautiful land so easily, so freely. No passes required. No border checkpoints. No one controlled nor even knew the routes we chose. We joyfully became a part of the great American romance with the road. Americans love the anticipation and excitement of a road trip and are captivated by the mystery and adventure of what and who may be waiting around the next bend in the road. Perhaps this helps to explain, at least in part, why so many people were so wonderfully enthusiastic about the very idea of our quest and the manner in which we pursued it.

We turned south, down Interstate 95 to Route 1, and chose an exit that said Wickford. It is a classic eighteenth-century New England waterfront village full of pretty shops, white picket fences, and leafy lanes. We looked carefully for a convenient spot and a likely interviewee in this lovely movie set of a village. Finding none, we drove out of town along a quiet country road until we saw a sign for the Gilbert Stuart Museum.

At five minutes after three, we arrived at a quaint, quiet, and remote spot where the great American portrait artist was born. There were no other visitors, just the two of us and four guides. We were given an excellent tour by seventh-grader Gordon Wilkins, who lives nearby in East Greenwich, and readily agreed to be interviewed.

Gordon Wilkins

Gordon is obviously bright and remarkably poised for his age. "This is the best place in Rhode Island. This area has beautiful scenery and it is relatively untouched. There are no big convenience stores, and the area is safe and peaceful," he says. "We live in a historic house and I really enjoy the richness of this area's history."

Quite naturally, when Pat asks who he would most like to meet, Gordon says, "Gilbert Stuart. I've learned so much about him working here, it would be interesting to meet him in person."

Gordon says his best decision up to this point in his life was to become a vegetarian and his continuing goal is to help people. What a good and noble goal for anyone of any age, and how unique for a seventh-grader.

When Pat asks Gordon about the best thing that has happened in his life, Gordon thinks hard about it but says, "I can't pinpoint a best point in my life yet." We tell him we hope the best is yet to come.

By way of advice, Gordon says, "I first visited here [Gilbert Stuart's Home] three years ago, and working here as a volunteer has taught me so much. It has made me appreciate the way we all live today. There were so many hard things in Stuart's day that we don't have to deal with." What an interesting expression of gratitude!

We make a photo and present Gordon with a spread-some-goodwill ten-dollar bill, then return to the road.

September 28, 2003, Sunday
Glen "Punky" Arthur
Newport, Rhode Island

Summer season had ended, but weekend tourists still filled the waterfront streets of old Newport as we drove into town. At Fort Adams, we met retired U.S. Navy Captain Glen Arthur, who is visiting his daughter Macie and her husband, U.S. Navy Captain Jim Pillsbury. Captains Arthur and Pillsbury have both been skippers aboard U.S. nuclear submarines, and Glen now lives in Gales Ferry, Connecticut (near Groton).

We were glad to meet this good man. He was relaxed and friendly, and he seemed happy to be interviewed by two strangers on a Sunday afternoon. Our quest seemed to really resonate with Glen. Born on a farm near Washington, Pennsylvania, Glen's father worked in the coal fields, and his mother died during his junior year of high school. A standout in football, he entered the U.S. Naval Academy at Annapolis, Maryland, and married his high school sweetheart on graduation day in 1955. In 1957, he began his work under the sea in the submarine service, initially in diesel, then in nuclear subs. Without being melodramatic, he explained to Pat how important the surveillance work was and how tense those Cold War days were, and something of what it was like to be at sea for one hundred days, then home for ninety days.

After twenty-two years of service, Glen retired from the Navy. Subsequently, he served five terms as a state representative in the Connecticut General Assembly. For good measure, he then served two four-year terms as commissioner on a state public utilities board.

We are fascinated by Glen's telling of this active life of service. Glen says the best place in Connecticut is, "Probably my home in Gales Ferry. It's a pretty place. I lost my wife in 1996; she had a brain tumor. She was my anchor and she made our house a home." He pauses. "I also enjoy the submarine museum in New London, Connecticut. I recommend you see that."

Glen says, "Gales Ferry is a little community, one of those where people come and go easily. We are part of a nice church. People are friendly. We get to see all four seasons of the year and enjoy lots of rocky, scenic shore. We are close to New York

Rhode Island, Massachusetts, Maine, New Hampshire, Vermont & Connecticut

City and close to Boston and all they have to offer. I'm an elder in our church. Anywhere I go in our little community, I see somebody I know. I like that."

When Pat asks, "Who is the best person you know?" Glen replies, "I'd say Admiral Hyman Rickover. When I first went to be interviewed about serving on nuclear submarines, Admiral Rickover said 'Don't sit. You won't be here that long.' But we talked at length and I was glad to serve under him. He was a guy that set big goals and really pushed for them. Admiral Rickover made our country better and safer. Not just in nuclear power, he pushed for better education, too. He was eccentric, but he would help you when you needed help. He really stood for things."

Glen Arthur

Glen says, "There are a lot of people I'd like to meet or see again, but I expect I would choose Rickover. He could be pleasant, and he could be fiery, but he was always interesting. I'd enjoy seeing him again."

Pat asks Glen about the best decision he has made. The Annapolis graduate-submarine Cold Warrior-State Legislator-Public Utility Commissioner lovingly says, "Marrying my wife, Dorothy, on June 3, 1955. She was my high school sweetheart."

We hope it thrills your heart, as it did ours, to hear a man whose life has been filled with distinguished achievement acknowledge that his best decision was marrying his wife! It is a joy to witness such a fond expression of genuine love and how good it is to hear about a strong, happy marriage.

Pat asks, "Do you have a goal you still hope to achieve?" Glen laughs. "I just finished my fourth retirement! Now, I would really like to spend some more time with my kids and grandkids," he says. "I feel good about the forty-one years I spent in public service. I have worked for good."

He continues, "My wife and I were blessed with six children and eleven grandchildren. They have been wonderful. Our oldest son had an aneurysm and died. I have four wonderful daughters. I have three sons-in-law; all 0-6's [Navy captains]; all commanding officers of nuclear subs! Who could ask for more? I have enjoyed a good life, and I have always tried to do my best in whatever I do. I seem to get much more back than I ever put in. Every time you give away—whether it's a dollar or a smile—it comes back to you twice over. It's not hard!" We agree wholeheartedly.

In response to Pat's question about choosing a new career, this happy, accomplished man quickly replies, "I'd do the same thing."

Captain Glen "Punky" Arthur gives a simple message of encouragement: "Anything you dream, you can do."

The interview is completed, and Glen's daughter Macie is cooking spaghetti in her kitchen. She extends a warm invitation for us to stay for dinner. We know we would be welcome, but we feel that we must press on up the road into Massachusetts before we stop for the night.

This has been a very good day. We knew we would always remember Gordon Wilkins and Glen Arthur.

Often, in conversations with others about our journeys, people have remarked about the explicit detail with which we recollect our visits and our subjects. People seem a bit surprised when we tell them in considerable detail about some specific person we met many months ago during our great quest. "You remember all their names!" we are often told. Perhaps our recall is so strong because we wanted to soak up all that we could about these good people to be able to accurately share it with others. Or, it may be because we were able to focus so intently on just one person at a time, almost always without distractions. Or it could be the mechanics: Pat has a fabulous memory, we taped each interview, and Scott took notes as well. Whatever the reason, these wonderful people and the goodwill they showered on us remain firmly etched in our memories.

It's hard to describe the elation we experienced during these months. The anticipation of going to a new place and meeting new friends, combined with the sheer joy of actually conducting an interview and finding so much goodwill, gave us a wonderfully memorable experience for which we continue to feel profoundly grateful.

Rhode Island, Massachusetts, Maine, New Hampshire, Vermont & Connecticut

Massachusetts

September 29, 2003, Monday
Abel "Abe" Correia (Korea)
JFK Memorial, Hyannis, Massachusetts

From Fall River, we reached Hyannis by mid-morning, thinking we might take the ferry out to Nantucket Island. At the ferry landing we perused the schedule, discovered the length of time involved in taking the ferry, and decided to look around Hyannis some more. We came upon the John F. Kennedy (JFK) Memorial, unloaded the car, and took in the lovely waterfront setting. Alongside the memorial, sitting in a folding lawn chair in front of a small booth was a smallish gentleman selling baseball caps bearing the JFK Memorial logo. He greeted us warmly; he had a big smile and an easy laugh. He was friendly and exuded goodwill. "My name is Abel—A-B-E-L—but everybody calls me 'Abe.'" He spelled out his last name too, and said, "You pronounce it like the war." This was certainly not planned. We thought we'd find someone on the ferry to Nantucket, but we happily took Abe where we found him and, after explaining our quest for goodwill, another interview was underway. Abe was already predisposed to spreading goodwill, and our explanation of our book's positive purpose just lit him up.

Pat begins by asking Abe about his favorite place in Massachusetts. With a smile, Abe says, "All of Cape Cod. This is a special place. When I was a youngster, I used to work on the ferryboats around here. I'm originally from New Bedford."

When Pat inquires about Hyannis, Abe says, "The weather here is nice. In the wintertime, when they get snow in Boston, we don't. We have a milder winter here." We tell Abe he should come see how mild winter can be in Nashville.

In response to Pat's question about one person who stands out for doing good things, Abe responds, "Ted Kennedy. He does a lot for folks and he's well known on Cape Cod. Hyannis Port is still home for him and he still comes down here most weekends."

Abe says, "I'd most like to meet General Douglas MacArthur. In World War II, I joined the Navy and served four years in the

South Pacific on a destroyer escort and landing troops. General MacArthur was a great general, and I'd like to meet him."

Pat asks, "What is the best decision you have made?" With a big smile, Abe says, "Getting married to my wife, Shirley. She's a wonderful wife. After the war, I went to Australia and did an amazing acrobatic act on the trapeze. I met Shirley in the same theater where we worked."

Abe tells us, "In everything I have ever done, I've tried to 'go by the book.' My goal has been to try to live a clean life." That's a worthy goal for all of us.

Pat asks, "What is the best thing that has happened to you?"

"Serving in World War II and surviving World War II," Abe answers. What a phrase. What a thought. What an accomplishment. We feel like we are somehow in a movie, watching this remarkable man speak so casually about his wonderful life.

Pat asks, "If you could begin a new career, what would it be?" This good man, part of our "Greatest Generation" says simply, "I like what I've done. I feel good about it. Tomorrow will be my eighty-third birthday!"

We are thunderstruck. Abe is not in a rocking chair on a porch somewhere. He is not taking it easy. On the eve of his eighty-third birthday, Abe Correia is out at the JFK Memorial, selling commemorative hats, working as a volunteer to raise tuition money for local needy kids to go to college. We are grateful to have met him. What an inspiration he is to us.

Pat with Abe Correia

As we complete the interview, Abe Correia leaves us with a message of encouragement: "My grandchildren are four-year-old twins, a boy and a girl. I tell your readers what I tell them. I try to explain what life is about: always be polite and courteous, and try to help others."

Such goodwill. Such wisdom. The inspiring memory of our few minutes with Abe will remain fixed in our hearts.

Rhode Island, Massachusetts, Maine, New Hampshire, Vermont & Connecticut

Indeed, we left Hyannis with hearts full of joy at having found so much more goodwill.

Excited about who might next cross our path, we wandered out on Cape Cod, staying as close to the shore as possible. Given the variety and quantity of lodging choices all along the way, it was obvious to us that in season, the Cape must regularly host vast crowds of vacationers. This day, it seemed as though we had it almost to ourselves. We were alone at Fort Hill, where we savored the exquisite natural beauty of broad green marsh which extended perhaps three-fourths of a mile out to the crashing waves pounding the shore. In the distance stood the lovely Nauset Beach Lighthouse, a warning for sailors and an enticement for artists.

At Truro, we decided we must turn back and begin making our way to Maine.

Pat and Scott at the *Mayflower*

September 29, 2003, Monday
Norman "Norm" Satterthwaite (SADDER weight)
Plymouth, Massachusetts

After lunch outdoors in perfect September sunshine on Cape Cod, we drove west by north-west and decided to stop at Plymouth Rock. With about a hundred other visitors, we gazed raptly at the now-enshrined spot where our brave forefathers stepped ashore in 1620. Scott started to snap a photo of Pat with a replica of the *Mayflower* in the water nearby. A pleasant voice behind us said, "Would you like for me to take a picture of both of you?"

The voice belonged to a spry eighty-eight-year-old gentleman with a head of pure white hair and what turned out to be a Scottish accent. Norman Satterthwaite, native of Dundee, Scotland, and longtime resident of Plymouth, took our picture and was ready to talk. Norm was delighted by our idea, and the interview began on a nearby park bench.

Pat asks Norm, "What is the best thing about Plymouth?"

He responds. "The ocean. The water. The tourists. I get to meet new people every day from all over the world."

In response to Pat's query about the best person he knows, Norm says, "I've met a lot." This is always good news.

"I'd say Rosalee Sinn of Plymouth, who I have known for many years. She has devoted her life to helping people throughout the world to have a better life. Through the Heifer Project, she helps send animals to Third World countries like Haiti. When the animal has its first offspring, the first recipient passes the newborn animal on to someone else who needs help. Isn't that a great idea?" We agree.

Norman Satterthwaite and Pat

When Pat asks, "Which person, living or dead, would you most like to meet?" Norm regretfully replies, "My son. He took his own life about a year ago—hanged himself on his fiftieth birthday." Norm accepts our expressions of sympathy with dignity. Despite such loss, Norm hasn't become bitter or withdrawn. On the contrary, his cheerfulness and his outgoing nature are what we remember most fondly about our visit to Plymouth Rock.

"What is the best decision you have made?" Pat asks.

Norm brightens perceptibly and says, "Getting married more than fifty years ago. Her name is Santina; she's from Sicily. A friend introduced us in Quincy. You know I'm a Scotsman, and Abe Cohen, who is Jewish, was my best man." He flashes a big smile. Norm is happy recalling the memory of this international wedding.

Asked about beginning a new career, Norm says, "I would like to have been a social worker."

That interest is reflected in Norm's words of encouragement: "We're only gonna go this way once; try to be helpful. If you can, do a little good along the line."

Rhode Island, Massachusetts, Maine, New Hampshire, Vermont & Connecticut

We thank Norm for the interview. We tell him we were hoping to reach Maine by bedtime in order to begin a new day of interviews the next morning.

Ever the cordial host, Norm says, "You guys are trying to do too much in one day! You should come by my house and have a cup of tea." This wasn't an I'm-being-polite-but-I-don't-really-mean-it invitation; Norm was sincerely seeking our company. While we hated to decline such a spontaneous, good-hearted gesture of goodwill, we still had to get through Boston, then northward into Maine. Our one-state-per-day schedule was a function of having to be back in Providence, Rhode Island, by Friday to catch our flight home.

We bid Norm a fond farewell, and as we turn back toward our rental car, we hear the friendly Scotsman saying to someone else, "Would you like for me to take a picture of both of you?"

How fabulous to randomly meet such a dynamic eighty-eight-year-old ambassador of goodwill.

I enjoyed meeting both of you at the waterfront in Plymouth and hope that you both enjoyed your trip around New England.

The $10 you have given me I am sending to "Project Hope to Abolish the Death Penalty," which is in Lanett, Alabama, as I am very much opposed to executing people . . .

May you both have a long and comfortable life.
Norman Satterthwaite

Through Quincy, through Boston, to quaint Newburyport for dinner, and through the night to York Beach, Maine, where we heard the ocean waves crashing against that rocky shore as we drifted off to sleep at the end of a very good day.

Maine
September 30, 2003, Tuesday
Priscilla "Pat" Metcalf
Bucksport, Maine (roadside stand)

We were up early and out in the fresh sea air, driving slowly along Maine's beautiful rocky coast. There were few cars there, but we saw more than a few solitary artists along the shore, striving to capture the special beauty of the place. The morning sunlight added a perfect touch to the pine- and sea-scented air. Already happy to simply be making our journey, we found a morning like this one multiplied our joy. The small villages of Ogunquit and Kennebunk were picture postcard examples of New England—trim, fastidious, and quietly prosperous.

At Belfast, we stopped at the local fire department with the expectation that we would be able to interview a good-hearted, colorful local firefighter. We unloaded, looked around and found four new fire trucks, two ambulances, and a museum full of well-preserved antique fire trucks and equipment. All were standing wide open, with not a single person to be found anywhere. Still, we enjoyed our free tour, and we were also encouraged by the obvious level of trust and community spirit manifested by the "open-for-business-whenever-the-need-arises" air at the Belfast fire station.

After driving through the town of Bucksport, we passed a tented roadside produce stand with one person seated inside and no customers. We found a place to turn around and went back. We met Mrs. Priscilla "Pat" Metcalf, who was comfortably ensconced amidst a bountiful harvest of fresh fruit and vegetables and a nice supply of jams, jellies, and homemade pies. Pat Metcalf gave us a friendly smile and said, "I saw you drive by. Thanks for coming back." We introduced ourselves, explained our goodwill quest, and began a delightful new friendship.

The lady tells us she was "born in Melrose, Massachusetts and moved up here two hundred years ago." She is a genuinely funny lady.

Pat asks her what she likes best about Bucksport, and she says, "There are not too many people, and the ones that are here are very friendly."

We've often heard people name their spouses as the best people they know, but Pat Metcalf has a twist: "My second husband, Stanley. I met him at a bar. I was playing the piano and he came in wearing a good-looking Coast Guard uniform. He's from Eastport." She continues, "Marrying Stanley was the best thing that's happened to me. He straightened me right out." She

Rhode Island, Massachusetts, Maine, New Hampshire, Vermont & Connecticut

pauses and adds, "Not totally. He didn't want me to come here today—but I did."

At this point, the older gentleman who had been working steadily in the yard around the house and in the garden from the time we pulled into the driveway, now strolled under the tent and busied himself straightening some of the produce on display.

His wife tells him, "These boys are writing a book." Stanley's only response—said with a classic Maine accent—is, "Don't give Martha (pronounced "MAHH-THAH") all the credit." As Stanley strolls out of the tent, Pat Metcalf explains that Stanley's remark made reference to the well-known television gardener, cook, and homemaker, Martha Stewart. We all have a good laugh.

She names her mother as the person she'd most like to see. "I was adopted, and she was very, very good to all of us," she says.

Pat Metcalf says that her goal is to keep on being happy.

She has such a cheery laugh and a twinkle in her eyes as she speaks to us. We are glad we turned around and came back. While we listen to her speak, we realize what a rare privilege we have been given. To be seated in lawn chairs on either side of the merry Pat on a sunny autumn day in Maine feels extraordinary!

When asked what she would choose to do if she could begin a new career, Pat proudly and confidently says, "I'd do the same thing over again. I was successful." Pointing across the highway at a building back down the road, she says, "I designed it and built it myself in the sixties. It's got log beams, and I still own it and rent it out. I used to serve breakfast and supper there, long enough to educate two daughters through college." This spirited, independent woman goes on to explain, "My first husband left me [as an aside, she adds 'black and blue'] and I had no help with the girls. I never served drinks until my girls got old enough for college. Then, the town women were angry at me because their husbands came out to my place for drinks. My first husband's cousin's husband was a big shot—well, he was one of three big shots who came to my place, and I'd have to drive him home when he drank too much. After doing that the third time, I worried about what his wife would think, so I went to the door and spoke to her. Well, she brought him and their thirteen-year-old son to my place for Sunday dinner, and they came every Sunday after that! And the big shot wouldn't have a drink on Sunday."

This saga of self-reliance, determination, and neighborly compassion just flows out of our new friend spontaneously and with such good humor. She is a joy to listen to, and to watch. She has a unique way of tossing her head ever so slightly to give emphasis to one observation or another.

At this point, a silver SUV pulls into the driveway next to the tent.

She says, "He's gonna buy something."

Indeed, the new visitor buys two magnificent fresh red tomatoes, each of which weighs one pound.

As Pat weighs the luscious red beauties, the visitor asks, "What'd you put to 'em?"

With comic timing that would rival Bob Hope's, Pat cheerily says, "My lovin' care!" How pleasant to observe a commercial transaction full of happy laughter and completely devoid of friction.

As the visitor turns to leave, the roadside merchant says with utmost sincerity and smiling eyes, "If you come back and want something and I'm not out here, come up to the house." It's fun to watch a fine business-woman in action.

Pat's advice: "If something comes to your mind to do, go do it. Don't listen to others who try to discourage you. And, don't be upset if you don't make it right away, keep at it. Keep trying."

Priscilla "Pat" Metcalf

This was such a memorable visit with such a remarkable woman, we hated to see it end. To this day, we still contemplate with amazement how easily we might have continued driving on past Pat Metcalf's roadside tent and thus have been forever deprived of the rich happiness and goodwill we found in her company.

Rhode Island, Massachusetts, Maine, New Hampshire, Vermont & Connecticut

September 30, 2003
Holly Manheim
Northeast Harbor, Maine

From Pat Metcalf's produce stand outside Bucksport, we drove to Mount Desert Island, home of Acadia National Park, Bar Harbor, Seal Harbor, and Northeast Harbor. The magnificent rocky Maine shore meets the deep blue Atlantic Ocean and the visitor is met with the rare combination of brisk ocean air mixed with fresh mountain air. In bright afternoon sunlight, the high temperature reaches sixty-two degrees.

We pulled into an open parking space in tiny, quiet Northeast Harbor. The shop directly in front of us had steps, so we opted for a gallery next door with a level entryway.

Holly Manheim, the gallery's director, was so immediately friendly it seemed as though we must have known her long ago. Although we had never met before, we were drawn to her kindhearted spirit. In earlier days, Holly was the mother of five children between the ages of five and ten, living in Camden, New Jersey.

A twenty-five-year resident of Northeast Harbor, Holly proudly says that she stays here all winter.

Note her response to Pat's question about the best place in Maine. "Somewhere [pause] about forty miles north of here. [pause] In the woods. [pause] In a canoe, on a river with white water." The pauses are for effect and emphasis, rather than to compose her thoughts. She seems to want to orally paint a scene for us to enjoy with her. She succeeds. "Out there in the williwags," she titles it. She speaks lovingly of Maine's "many wild rivers."

Pat asks, "What is the best thing about Northeast Harbor?"

Holly responds thoughtfully, "It is not just the people, that's easy to say. I think it is the way the people have taken care of these fine, old historical homes. They have preserved a part of American history we don't think of often. Many of the people here are well-to-do, but they are not rude or arrogant. They are very civilized and good-hearted, charitable people."

Responding to Pat's "Best Person" question, Holly says, "There is a little old lady who lives in my housing complex, and she seems to just radiate goodness. She was raised right near here on Cranberry Island. She's in her mid-seventies, and there is just something special about her; she has an extremely generous spirit. Her five children are the same way; they have the sunniest faces."

How nice for Holly—and now us—to know someone like that. Wouldn't it be so nice to be immediately thought of in the same way when a "best person" question is asked? Each of us possesses the capacity to be such a person.

Pat asks who she would most like to meet.

With a sunny smile of her own, Holly says, "I've met Margaret Mead, a few Rockefellers, and some very interesting clamdiggers. And, I expect, there are more still to come."

Pat and Holly Manheim

"Coming to Maine was the best decision I've made," Holly says. "I needed a good spot to raise my children, and all five grew up well. The past twenty-five years have proved it was a good decision."

When Pat asks about her goals, Holly says, "I would still like to have my own shop; perhaps sell antiques or clothing. It might also be fun to have a bed and breakfast inn on the Appalachian Trail in Pennsylvania!"

When asked about the best thing that has happened in her life, Holly replies proudly, "My five children and my eighteen grandchildren."

Here is Holly's advice: "Too often we get bogged down by what's happening to us. See the good part of it—look for the upside. Try to help others see something good each day. Everybody needs somebody to encourage. Rearrange your thinking!"

This was our twenty-fifth interview. While other interviewees may have thought about it, Holly was apparently the very first to understand, and was certainly the first to say something about the fact that we were actually spreading some goodwill while we were looking for it. Holly was also the first interviewee to speak directly to Pat about being in a wheelchair.

Holly asked if people treated Pat differently because he is in a chair.

When Pat said "Not really," she then told him that his visit had inspired her, and that his strength and his positive, outgoing spirit had brightened her day.

This bright, cheerful, encouraging woman was another special delight for us to meet. A beautiful person in a beautiful setting, neither of which was under our control.

We turned westward across Maine. After an excellent dinner at Scotty's restaurant (Pat's pick) in Newport, we drove on into the night along empty country roads under the magnificent beauty of a huge crescent moon. Near Farmington we stopped for the night at a quiet, old-time motor court.

New Hampshire
October 1, 2003, Wednesday
Tim Sullivan
Wolfeboro, New Hampshire

We awakened in Farmington, Maine, and looked out our small bathroom window to see that our motel adjoined an actual farm with cultivated fields, a big barn, and neatly parked pieces of farm equipment. Streams of lovely sunlight beamed through a light morning fog, accentuating the first flashes of red leaves beginning to adorn the trees on nearby hillsides. The tranquil, transcendent New England autumn beauty refreshed the soul. As we drove across totally rural western Maine into colorful New Hampshire, we felt as though we were swimming into a richly woven tapestry of reds, browns, purples, greens, golds, and occasional splashes of white birch or aspen. We headed through Pinkham Notch to tiny Jackson, where we stopped for a bite of lunch, and were most memorably fed by the sight of happy little sweater-clad schoolchildren at play and by the smell of astonishingly fresh and fragrant clean mountain air.

On we went, marvelously free, through Conway and West Ossipee. At the southern end of huge (and empty at this time of year) Lake Winnipesaukee, we cruised into the town of Wolfeboro, and looked around. On the back side of a small shopping center, we saw a law office sign and decided to go in.

We introduced ourselves to big, friendly Tim Sullivan who, despite the fact that we were strangers without an appointment and were interrupting his busy afternoon of lawyering, welcomed us cordially. He agreed to be interviewed, with the understanding that important incoming phone calls might temporarily interfere. They did so, but with hardly any impact.

With lawyerly precision, Tim tells Pat that his favorite place in New Hampshire is his home near Tuftonboro. "The woods are beautiful and quiet. That's where I like to be."

Tim says he enjoys Wolfeboro because of its friendly people. "I grew up in Manchester and I have really enjoyed the small town atmosphere here," he explains.

Tim tells Pat about two of the best people he knows. "Number one is my wife. She volunteers with Meals on Wheels, she visits the nursing homes, she gives a great deal of care and attention to the elderly. Number two is Dr. John Foley, of Dover, New Hampshire. He always goes above and beyond the call of duty in caring for patients."

Tim thinks a bit about who he'd most like to meet. "That covers a lot! The easy answer, of course, would be Jesus." He pauses, then says, "Abraham Lincoln. He was very interesting and intelligent." We think back to the humble log cabin in Hodgenville, Kentucky, where Lincoln's life—and our journey—began. It is endlessly inspiring to contemplate his rise from such a modest beginning to such historic heights.

Pat next asks, "What is the best decision you have made?"

Tim replies, "Other than marrying my wife, I'd say it was the decision to come up to this area to live in 1974."

Tim's goal is to maintain good health.

When Pat asks about the best thing that has happened in his life, Tim answers without delay, "I had heart surgery at the

Tim Sullivan

Rhode Island, Massachusetts, Maine, New Hampshire, Vermont & Connecticut

age of forty-nine, and I was so fortunate to have doctors who discovered and cured my problem."

Tim says, after a long pause to seriously contemplate the idea of a new career, "If I were beginning new today, I'd become a writer or a journalist. I'd like to do something where I could control my schedule." Spoken with the conviction of one who has long had his schedule if not controlled, then at least dominated, by others—lawyers, litigants, and judges. Interestingly, Tim doesn't seem at all bothered by our imposition on his busy schedule, and he appears to enjoy our visit, the idea of our goodwill quest, and especially our freedom of movement.

Tim encourages all of us to, "Always have a natural sense of wonder."

This is to let you know that **Mr. Timothy Sullivan** forwarded your $10 to us here at the Lakes Region Humane Society. Thank you so much.

This donation helps our animals here at the shelter in so many ways. As a private nonprofit organization, we rely solely on the kindness of others to continue our mission; dedicated to the loving care of abused, unwanted, and lost pets.

In 2002, donations like yours were used to provide medical care and a safe and warm environment, along with a caring staff for nearly 300 animals. We also provide community outreach to local nursing homes as well as provide services to schools teaching the pet owners of tomorrow about humane education.

Jane Harris
Lakes Region Humane Society

We wondered, as we drove through dark clouds and occasional rain along the deserted western shore of Lake Winnipesaukee, how we could have been so fortunate to randomly stop in Wolfeboro, randomly wander into Tim Sullivan's law office, and still be met with such goodwill and good cheer.

Though diligent, our search did not always seem easy or bear such fruit. Via Danbury and Lebanon, we reached Hanover, New Hampshire, in late afternoon and scouted around the beautiful green campus of Dartmouth University. Everyone seemed busy and was intently moving about in this quintessentially Ivy League setting. We searched the quaint main street shops and the local bookstore but found no interview prospect. We looked around all through dinner at the Hanover Inn but still found no one to interview.

This was such an unscientific enterprise. Looking back now, we wonder that we so easily met and interviewed so many people of goodwill. Well, we looked long and hard. However, the other important element of the equation is that there is a vast and remarkable reservoir of goodwill out there in our land. It's all around us, as you'll see if you take a look for yourself.

On that particular night, darkness closed in and pushed us northward to begin the new day in Vermont.

Vermont

October 2, 2003, Thursday
Norman Blodgett
State Capitol Building, Montpelier, Vermont

The morning air was brisk in Montpelier and we moved quickly across the street, even though there was almost no foot or auto traffic. Perhaps we'd get to see the governor before his official schedule began for the day in the nation's smallest state capital.

We signed in and introduced ourselves to quiet and courteous security officer Norman Blodgett, who told us that the governor had not yet arrived. No problem. We explained our quest and asked Norman if we might interview him. He pleasantly agreed.

We quickly learn that Norman is a man of few words. He responds to Pat's question about his favorite place by saying, "Worcester, Vermont. The change of scenery is beautiful, especially at this time of year. Sometimes we get snow here but not there, and other times there may be none in Montpelier, and a blizzard there!"

"Montpelier is quiet. People don't bother each other. You can leave your car unlocked at night." What mayor wouldn't love to have those same compliments given to his or her city or town?

When Pat asks, "Who is the best person you know?" Norman says, "The governor. Governor Douglas. He's outgoing and very friendly."

Norman says he would most like to meet his parents. "They've been gone for years and I miss them a lot," he says.

New Hampshire, Vermont & Connecticut

Rhode Island, Massachusetts, Maine,

We find it interesting that love of family transcends the culture's fascination with celebrity.

Next, Pat asks, "What is the best decision you have made?"

Norman says, "Getting married." By offering "just the facts, ma'am," Norman reminds us of Sergeant Joe Friday on the old *Dragnet* series.

Asked if he has a goal he still hopes to achieve, Norman says, "No, not really. I've done all I could really do."

Norman tells us that being saved was the best thing to happen to him, and that he doesn't think there's anything different he'd want to do as a career.

Norman leaves us with a simple message of encouragement: "Keep your chin up."

Norman Blodgett

Norman's answers were not abrupt, nor was there any hint of impatience in his tone or facial expression. He was straight out of Central Casting—the taciturn Vermonter. He wished us well and sent us on up to see the governor's office.

October 2, 2003, Thursday
Judy Moody
Governor's Office, Montpelier, Vermont

The governor's receptionist, Judy Moody, is ideally suited for her work. Her bright, open smile and her polite, friendly manner make us feel especially welcome. We have just come to see the office and we hope that the governor might arrive while we are there. Judy radiates goodwill, and so we seize the quiet early morning calm as an opportune time to gain another interview.

Pat's first query of, "What is your favorite place in Vermont?" prompts the reply, "The Northeast Kingdom, fifty miles north of here. That's where I'm from originally and that's where I live, in Irasburg. The lakes are gorgeous and clear. You should go up north and see Willoughby Lake. The people are great, and we have a great small school. We get lots of one-on-one with the children, and I like that."

Judy smiles as she talks about the best person she knows. "One would have to be my sister, Nancy Roberts. She is always doing good and she doesn't get the recognition she deserves. Also, I'd say the governor; he really helps a lot of people."

When asked who she would most like to meet, Judy's answer reveals her friendly spirit. "Oh, I don't know. I like everybody! How about the president?"

Judy says, "Having my children was the best decision I ever made. I have thirteen-year-old twin boys and a four-year-old daughter. They are just great."

Pat asks, "Do you have a goal which you still hope to achieve?"

Still smiling, Judy says she has several goals: "I want to do the best I can every day; to set forth good values for my children; to push them to do well in school and go to college. That's something I didn't have." She has such a positive spirit.

"What is the best thing that has happened in your life?" Pat asks.

Without a pause, Judy smiles and says, "Getting this job! Not everybody can work for a governor!" It seems obvious, but it is actually an insightful observation. She also points out that she worked for the governor back when he served as state treasurer. "You know, jobs are not as plentiful up around Irasburg. So, I'm very grateful to have this job—even though it means driving fifty miles, one way, to work."

Judy Moody

Pat asks, "If you could begin a new career, what would you choose to do?"

Judy says, "I hadn't thought about that." She pauses and ponders, then says, "I'd like it to be something with a degree and a way to earn a large income."

How could we not admire this hard-working, long-distance-commuting mother of three who wants to be and do better for her children's sake?

Here are Judy's words of advice: "Be the best you can be. I'm a positive person. Always look for the positive in every situation."

Another interview yields an unexpectedly positive goodwill quotient. Our early visit to Vermont's capital left us feeling elated, and as we departed Montpelier, we were especially grateful to have made friends with Norman Blodgett and Judy Moody.

From Barre to Bradford, we meandered alongside a beautiful, broad river and through classic New England woods. It was especially scenic backcountry driving—refreshing and uplifting.

October 2, 2003, Thursday
Larry Frazer
Windsor, Vermont

At Bradford, we headed south on one of America's most beautiful sections of interstate highway. I-91 parallels the lovely Connecticut River through magnificent farmland and gently rolling countryside. Oh, the majesty of our land!

We inexplicably felt the urge to get off the interstate and drive into the town of Windsor. We knew nothing about it and we knew no one living there. In brilliant mid-morning sunlight, we feasted our eyes on a classic Vermont village. Every building looked not only historic, but freshly painted. There were pretty flowers instead of trash, and lots of pumpkins, sweaters, and cornstalks. In a crisp, good way, we felt like we were on a movie set.

We parallel parked on the street for free and entered a building, which housed a bank on the left and an insurance firm on the right. We chose to go right, and there we met independent insurance agent Larry Frazer. After listening attentively to our description of this coast-to-coast quest, he seemed to embrace our pursuit and he spoke to us as friends.

Somewhat wiry and soft-spoken, Larry responds to Pat's question about his favorite place in Vermont by telling us, "My home in Hartland, just a few miles north of here, is such a nice little community. The interstate is right there, Boston is two hours, Montpelier is two and one-half, Dartmouth is just fourteen miles. Hartland is a wonderful place; about three thousand people. I've lived there fifty-three years and many people there still don't lock the back door."

Larry Frazer

"What is the best thing about Hartland?" Pat continues.

Larry immediately says, "The community spirit. Everyone helps each other out—in a quiet way if need be."

Pat then inquires, "Of all the people you know, is there one who stands out for consistently doing good things?"

"He just passed away," Larry says. "Henry Merritt was born in Hartland too. If anybody needed something done, he did it. Need to get snow off a roof? Henry would just do it and disappear. If somebody needed food, it would just appear. He always did good things and did it quietly. He gave three lots for Habitat for Humanity to build houses." Henry Merritt has left a wonderful memorial in the hearts of his neighbors and friends.

When asked about his own best decision, Larry says, "Going into the insurance business and staying in the Hartland area. I've been at it for thirty-one years, and I feel like I'm able to help folks."

Larry continues, "I want to see my two girls—one is twenty-six, one is twenty-eight—mature into their careers, and I'd like to see the growth of my agency to the ten-million-dollar level."

Rhode Island, Massachusetts, Maine, New Hampshire, Vermont & Connecticut

Pat then asks, "What is the best thing that has happened in your life?" Larry quietly responds, "About ten years ago, we owned a piece of property that we discovered had been contaminated by gasoline. It was dead weight, we couldn't sell it, and it was going to cost a fortune to clean up. Then the bank that had the loan went bankrupt and it looked like the same [would happen to] us, too. Three or four people came to us and quietly offered to help, with no strings attached." The emotion in Larry's voice amplifies the impact of hearing this wonderful account of genuine neighborly goodwill.

Pat asks Larry what he would choose for a new career.

"I'd like to own a restaurant—family-style—here in Windsor," Larry answers. "I might actually do it someday."

When Pat asks for a message of encouragement or words of advice, Larry is reluctant. "I'm not too philosophical," he says. Yet, after thinking a moment, he says, "No matter how dark the cloud, there is always a silver lining." Perhaps not the words of a philosopher, but certainly the voice of experience. Larry then adds, "Give yourself credit for trying."

We left, grateful to have happened upon Windsor, Vermont, Larry Frazer, and the good people in his life.

October 2, 2003, Thursday
Seeking

From Windsor, we decided to veer back into New Hampshire and try again to find one more person of good-will in just the right setting for an interview. We passed through Claremont and looked hard in North Walpole, a one-street town with no one visible at the library, fire station, or police headquarters. The few folks who live there must work elsewhere.

Now we needed to make some time, as we would fly out of Providence the next afternoon. Back into Vermont, we drove south on I-91 into and across Massachusetts, and down through central Connecticut past Hartford. Off the interstate, we wandered southeast, and somewhere near Haddam we found ourselves driving along eerily empty roads. Scott reminded Pat, "We can't get lost 'cause we don't know exactly where we're going." This was as much to reassure himself as Pat, because this particular "backwoods" seemed so unfamiliar. There was a rare twinge of unease about the possibility of getting into some tight spot and putting Pat at risk.

Not to worry. We came upon beautiful Chester, Connecticut, which, like Wickford, Rhode Island, and Windsor, Vermont, is chock-full of tranquil charm, tasteful and trim in every respect, its homes all well cared for and freshly painted in subtle hues. It is a living magazine layout with lots of strolling older couples, and a kayak or a canoe on top of at least 25 percent of the vehicles in town. We crossed the lovely Connecticut River on a tiny ferry, the only car on board. From mid-river, we saw a hilltop castle on the far shore. We wanted to learn more about it. Gillette Castle was built by an actor who portrayed Sherlock Holmes in early motion pictures, and although the house itself was closed, we were rewarded with a spectacularly beautiful view of the lower Connecticut River Valley from the castle's rocky porch.

Although people are the real story of this book, there were also places like this which inspired a strong sense of goodwill.

We followed our compass south, knowing that Long Island Sound was down that way.

Connecticut
October 2, 2003, Thursday
Leo Scillia (Suh-LEE-uh)
Niantic, Connecticut

We passed through Old Lyme and Lyme, trying to hug the coastline. Could we find another dose of goodwill before darkness fell?

We turned down a residential street and saw what looked like a nursing home. It was a senior citizens' center but had already closed for the day. We were heading out of the driveway when Pat said, "Hey, what's that old house next door?" We saw activity, a campfire, and tents. We unloaded and went exploring.

Setting up camp were three middle-aged men in Civil War uniforms; they were Civil War reenactors preparing for an event for local schoolchildren on the following day. They welcomed us with great gusto. This was amazing! How did we just happen to stumble into this scene, out of all the other places we might have discovered along the Connecticut shore, and at just that opportune moment?

The most voluble of the three is Leo Scillia, a native of Palermo, Sicily, and a longtime resident of West Haven, Connecticut. He teases us good naturedly about our southern accents, and explains that all three of these "Connecticut Yankees" are members of the First Maryland Brigade in the Confederate Army.

Leo is naturally funny and full of wisecracks; his two "Confederates" are obviously accustomed to listening to Leo, and they enjoy laughing with him around a campfire.

We are graciously invited to share their battlefield dinner of stew, bread, and wine. What spontaneous goodwill we have been shown all day long! We politely decline their kind generosity, and focus on interviewing Leo while they eat.

Leo Scillia

Pat asks, "What is the best place in Connecticut?" Leo gives a short laugh and says, "Savin Rock. It was an amusement park my grandfather owned near West Haven until 1967. I was kinda brought up there. We had pony rides, and it was just great fun."

Leo tells us that the best thing about West Haven is the shoreline. "It's got the boardwalk and old World War II music. It's so pleasant right on the water."

Leo continues, "Well, I'd have to say the best people I know are a lot of the people I've met in the First Maryland. It's like a family and we're all very close."

When Pat inquires, "Which person, living or dead, would you most like to meet?" Leo solemnly says, "Private James Grason of the First Maryland. He is who I am in our reenactments of Civil War battles. I am always Private Grason. I've read up on him and his family. They had a three-thousand-acre plantation just after you cross over the Chesapeake Bay Bridge. [Of course, the bridge was not built until the 1950s.] The little town of Grasonville is still there now, on the eastern shore of Maryland. I really admire Private Grason now that I know more about what those guys went through. It'd be great to meet him."

All three of these "Connecticut Yankees," now dressed in Confederate gray, speak earnestly about the valor with which our ancestors fought each other and the privation that they all endured so stoically. The communion of the campfire draws all of us closer together. Leo opines that getting involved in reenactment was the best decision he's made.

Pat asks Leo about his goals.

Leo laughs and says, "At my age, I'm happy the good Lord gives me my health and lets me see my grandchildren."

In response to Pat's, "What is the best thing that has happened in your life?" Leo replies, "You know, there's different things at different age brackets. In my younger years, it would be getting married and having my children. More lately, it's been the reenactments."

Pat provokes thought when he asks Leo what he'd do for an alternate career.

Leo stares into the fire for a bit, then says, "I came up the hard way, and I never went to college. All my children—three girls and one son—went to college, plus got their master's. I'd start over doing that first."

"Stay in school. Get an education," Leo offers as advice. "You may feel like it's long and hard, but you can't beat education. It's something I never had, but I know what it means."

The chill evening air and the warm camaraderie combine to accentuate our reluctance to leave, but we must.

Rhode Island, Massachusetts, Maine, New Hampshire, Vermont & Connecticut

It was a fantastic day with remarkable people and special New England autumn beauty. We were the fortuitous recipients of goodwill at every turn. Ready to rest, we got on the interstate near New London thinking we would increase our prospects of finding lodging for the night. We overshot an exit with several well-known national motel chains, and found ourselves heading north on a state road towards Norwich. We considered turning back. Then, out of the dark on our right, we saw the Oakdell Motel, an old-time motor court. Its marquee simply said, "Remember, God Loves You." We stopped for the night.

October 3, 2003, Friday
Gail Googins
Waterford, Connecticut

A pretty good frost covered our windshield in the early morning, so Scott left the engine and defroster running while he walked into the motel office to check out. A petite lady with the air of an owner pleasantly completed the paperwork and genially offered doughnuts and juice. Her positive personality was so obvious that Scott went back outside to turn off the car and tell Pat, "We need to interview this lady."

Gail Googins bought the Oakdell Motel from its original owners thirty-three years ago when her three children were four, seven, and eleven years of age. She made us feel completely welcome in the motel's small, tidy office. Hospitality seemed to flow naturally out of her.

Pat begins, "What is your favorite place in all of Connecticut?" Gail replies, "Probably right here at the Oakdell Motel! I get to meet such interesting people all the time, and I'm able to witness for the Lord. I live on Smith Cove up by the U.S. Coast Guard Academy. This is a nice area."

"We are close to the water; Mystic Seaport is nearby; this whole area draws visitors—which is good for business—and I get to meet a lot of very interesting people from all over the U.S. and Europe." We have met yet another cheerful American who loves where she lives and what she does.

Gail says, "I know in my heart that the best person I know is my grandmother, my father's mother. She taught me a lot of good. We called her 'Nana' and I, to this day, still ask myself, 'What would Nana tell me? What would she do?' When I have found myself in difficult times, I know I should listen to what Nana would say. She was so good!"

Gail tells us that the best decision she has made was accepting Jesus as her Savior, and with a serene smile she says, "Jesus is the person I'm waiting to meet."

Gail says emphatically that she has goals for the future. "It's pretty hard. At this moment, I think I'm going to do a life change, and it's kinda scary. I would really like to be able to witness for the Lord, but I'm not a preacher. I'm trying to find my way to do more. I never change my ['Remember, God Loves You'] sign out front and I know that has helped a lot of people. I've had phone calls and letters from people telling me how seeing it has brightened their day. If I could, I'd like to do some kind of educational material to present God's Good News to children. If I could start a new career, it would probably be some kind of ministry."

Gail Googins

When Pat asks, "What is the best thing that has happened in your life?" Gail ponders for a few moments and says, "That's hard to answer. I believe it was to be born into the family I was born into. They gave me great values and deep love. My grandmother [Nana] came from Finland to Troy, New Hampshire, and was part of a very close Finnish community. I'm very thankful for her strong influence for good and the closeness of our family's love."

Rhode Island, Massachusetts, Maine, New Hampshire, Vermont & Connecticut

Dear Pat & Scott,

I prayed to God that he would show me what to do with the goodwill money and he did. Last week a woman came to the motel looking for bars of soap for VisionTrust International, a non-profit corporation helping third world countries. After speaking with her . . . I knew where I wanted the money to go.

We enjoyed meeting you . . .

Sincerely,

Gail Googins

Here are Gail Googins' words of advice: "Every day, pick up your Bible and follow the instructions." It's worth noting that these words are not uttered stridently but are spoken with a gentle, grandmotherly sense of calm assurance.

Gail's amiable goodness and her good advice remained with us throughout our travels.

We cannot overemphasize how joy-filled this entire adventure progressively became. The further we went, the more positive we became about the goodwill all around us, and we told our family, our old friends, and our new friends along the road about what a fabulous experience this was proving to be. Inspired by the breadth and depth of goodwill found, we became still more enthused about finding it and spreading it.

At nearby New London, we pause to visit the U.S. Coast Guard Academy and to be reminded of the debt of gratitude all of us owe to the dauntless young men and women defending our shores and preserving our freedom.

Rhode Island

October 3, 2003, Friday
Tracy Duff
Narragansett, Rhode Island

From New London, we drove through the beautiful nautical/maritime museum town of Mystic Seaport. We have visited before and would love to linger but we edged toward Providence and our flight home. We re-enter Rhode Island at Westerly and on empty back roads, hug the lovely coast all the way across the bottom of the small state until we reach Point Judith. Try to make that peaceful drive some early autumn day.

The place names alone (Misquamicut, Quonochontaug, Jerusalem, and Galilee) fire your imagination, and the natural beauty is beguiling.

Fortified by a hearty bowl of clam chowder on the waterfront at Point Judith, we headed north along the western shore of Narragansett Bay. A small, one-story strip of small offices with an unobstructed view of the bay caught our eyes and we decided to venture in. The first two offices we tried were closed. The third was a real estate and construction firm; working alone in the office was Tracy Duff. We seemed to puzzle her at first, but as we explained the origins of our search for goodwill and the dramatic responses we have encountered, she became steadily more lively and absorbed by the idea. Protesting that she was not that interesting, Tracy agreed to be interviewed. We pointed out that our desire is not to seek out celebrities, but to highlight the good things in her everyday life and in her community.

"I was born in South Kingston, and I have lived in Narragansett since first grade," Tracy begins. "Being a native, I probably don't take full advantage of all the special spots around here. I'd have to say Narragansett Beach is my favorite place to go with my kids."

Tracy continues, "The best thing about my town is that it's not over-developed yet. But it's on its way. It's a beautiful place to live and it offers a lot for children. I love the beautiful roads and farms. Of course, it's growing here. In 1986, I worked up in Providence and by the time I got halfway home there was no traffic. That's changing."

There is a long pause when Pat asks Tracy if there is one person who stands out for doing good things. After deliberating, she says, "My brother, Jeff, is a South Kingston police officer, and he does a lot of nice things for others. He's always a good guy." What brother wouldn't be thrilled to have a sister speak so proudly about him?

Pat inquires, "Who would you most like to meet?"

Tracy thinks a bit and says, "Harrison Ford is the only person I'd like to meet that I don't know." Her tone and manner suggest that this busy working mom has not spent much time daydreaming about meeting celebrities.

Pat asks, "What is the best decision you have made?" Without delay, Tracy says, "Dating my husband." We think she is the only interviewee to say dating as opposed to marrying a spouse.

Concerning her goals, Tracy says she would love to travel more. "I said I was going to do it when I was in college. Now, I have a four-year-old, a ten-year-old, and an eleven-year-old." There is no trace of self-pity, only an unspoken acknowledgment that her three children are now more important to her than a long-held desire to travel. Tracy strikes us as being a good mom.

Next, Pat asks Tracy, "What is the best thing that has happened in your life?" She laughs and says, "There have been a lot. Let me give you one example. I had a vehicle I needed to sell, and we owed quite a bit more on it. Plus, it needed repairs. My brother suggested a place in Jamestown; two men there were going to fix it, and the next day they had it sold! Two people I had never met really helped me out, with no strings attached." Tracy is exultant, and we are delighted to get to hear the joy in her voice as she recounts this story of goodwill. "Those guys went out of their way to really help me!"

Tracy Duff

Tracy offers her thoughts on a new career, "I think every day, 'What do I wanna do when I grow up?' Only this morning I was thinking I'd like to do something that would help people more. I'd like to contribute more by helping others." We are smiling big inside, glad for the opportunity to witness the goodwill inside this good young mother come bubbling out.

Tracy Duff's message of encouragement is: "Relax more. Enjoy your family. Take advantage of all the good and beautiful things around us. Enjoy life! Money is not everything."

This is a classic example of how our quest constantly exceeded our expectations. When we pulled in and parked in front of the row of offices, we had no notion of whom we might find or what they might say. Unplanned, unscientific, random approaches kept yielding copious outpourings of goodwill. We added Tracy to our list of new friends, and her enthusiasm traveled with us to the airport in Providence, back home to Nashville, and on to states yet to be explored.

U.S. Coast Guard Academy in New London, Connecticut

Rhode Island, Massachusetts, Maine, New Hampshire, Vermont & Connecticut

MARYLAND, DELAWARE, PENNSYLVANIA, NEW YORK & NEW JERSEY

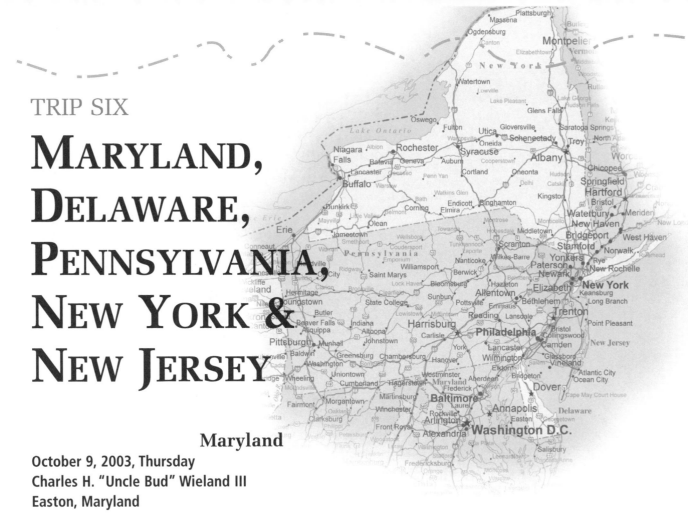

Maryland

October 9, 2003, Thursday
Charles H. "Uncle Bud" Wieland III
Easton, Maryland

On Tuesday, October 7, we drove from Nashville to Washington, D.C. The next day, Scott attended a meeting of the Board of Directors of the Spina Bifida Foundation. Real progress is being made toward understanding, treating, and living productively with spina bifida, our nation's most frequently occurring birth defect.

On Thursday morning we departed the District of Columbia and headed east, crossed the Chesapeake Bay Bridge, and reveled in the autumn beauty of Maryland's eastern shore. From Kent Island to Grasonville, we laughed and spoke fondly of Leo Scillia and his devotion to Private James Grason, C.S.A. At Wye Mills we rested our eyes on the golden, tan, and rich brown farmland and looked for goodwill prospects. Seeing a road sign for Longwoods reminded Scott that his mother spent her youth in this area, and that her oldest brother, Bud, still lives in nearby Easton.

"Why don't we see if we can interview Uncle Bud?" Scott asked.

Pat replied, "I thought we were going to pick random people."

Scott said, "Overwhelmingly, we are. And, we didn't set out this morning with Uncle Bud in mind. But he's definitely a person of goodwill and, after all, it's our book . . . let's include him if we can."

Pat agreed.

We proceeded to Easton and pulled into Uncle Bud's driveway unannounced. Through the open front door, we could see this lifelong Marylander sitting at his dining room table picking the succulent meat from his morning catch of Maryland blue crabs. What a perfect scene. This good man taught Scott as a child how to catch, cook, and eat crabs, and how to savor time together with family. He was happy to see us, but did not seem any more surprised by our visit than he might be by his next-door neighbor dropping in.

One of the world's friendliest people, Uncle Bud was delighted to hear about our goodwill quest, and he agreed to be interviewed. He continued to pick crab throughout the interview, stopping periodically to offer us delectable lumps of the prized delicacy.

There is no surprise in his response to Pat's initial question, "Is there a place in your state which you especially enjoy?" Uncle Bud says, "Easton. We have visited most of the state and that's why we're here. It has a most casual living environment and all the things we enjoy—the water, fishing, crabbing, boating. I'm not a hunter, but we have ducks, geese, and deer." Indeed, the river behind his house is full of geese and ducks all during our conversation.

When Pat asks, "Who is the best person you know?" Uncle Bud grins and says, "Man! There are an awful lot of them." We respond, "Isn't it great to know more than one!" After a moment, he says, "I have a dear friend, Joe, whose wife passed away four years ago. If you just suggest something that needs doing, he jumps in and does it. He leads a lot of good people in doing good things at places like Habitat homes, or our recycling center or at Hospice." We love hearing about the widespread volunteer spirit and community involvement all across our nation.

Uncle Bud offers another bite of crabmeat as he thinks about who he'd like to meet. "That's hard to say. I respect a lot of people for what they have done, and a lot of people—authors—who put down on paper what they have seen or thought. And, wherever I go, I talk to everybody." Having covered both celebrity and the man-in-the-street, Uncle Bud goes on to say, "I would enjoy seeing my grandfather, Charles H. Wieland Sr., again. He was a proofreader in Philadelphia, Pennsylvania, and he loved to share information. He and I gardened together. I rowed him in a rowboat. We fished together." What a marvel is our ability to remember! We feel privileged to see a good man, who helped make so many happy memories for others, recall with such fondness the memory of his grandfather.

Pat with Charles "Uncle Bud" Wieland III

The best decision he made, Uncle Bud says, was probably to marry his wife. "You know, life is a series of breaks, and that one was more meaningful. I had never really thought about getting married, then she came along."

We're grateful for meaningful breaks, too. Uncle Bud and Scott's late father, Jones Price, served together in the 1st Fighter Command at Mitchell Field on Long Island, New York during World War II. Uncle Bud introduced Jones Price to his younger sister, Kate Wieland, and thereby helped precipitate a wonderful fifty-two-year marriage. Without Uncle Bud and that introduction, no Scott . . . and no Pat!

When Pat asks, "Do you have a goal you still hope to achieve?" the tireless jokester replies, "I'm dreaming of getting one." (Translation: "I am content.")

Pat asks about the best thing that has happened in his life.

Uncle Bud mulls that one over and says, "At the time all six of my children had grown up and moved out of our house in town on Goldsborough Street, my wife got tired of wishing for something near the water. She decided to sell our house, and it went in two days! So, we decided to build down here—in our fifties, sorta late in life. But it has been wonderful living here, and I wouldn't have done it if she hadn't pushed that way."

Pat inquires as to what Uncle Bud would choose to do if given an opportunity to begin a new career. Uncle Bud responds, "I'd probably do the same as before. I enjoyed everything that I came in contact with, and I especially enjoyed meeting the public. You reflect what you expect."

Uncle Bud continues, "Life brings a bunch of opportunities. After World War II, I had a wife and two children, and making thirty-five dollars a week at the ice plant here was not enough to live on. I met a general agent [for Connecticut Mutual] in Baltimore who wanted to open an agency on the eastern shore. I took a one-year course at Purdue University—went back and forth on the train, and had a fantastic time helping folks with their insurance needs."

He pauses for a moment, apparently to reflect on a more glamorous career alternative, and says with a total deadpan face, "I really like to play golf." The pause is long enough for Scott to think, *I didn't even know he played.*

Uncle Bud continues: "The last time I played was in 1947. I gave it up to get back into gardening." It is a source of great delight to find yet another person who genuinely likes what he has done with his life.

Uncle Bud shares a message of encouragement. "Work hard, but enjoy yourself. Smell the roses as you go by; don't wait to have them piled on your grave. Don't be self-centered." He hands us more crab and adds, "It's nice to share."

Uncle Bud's well-turned phrase—you reflect what you expect—stayed with us through all our remaining states and interviews, and remains with us yet. It clarified our thinking about exactly why we had been so well-received everywhere we went. People could see in our reflection that we expected to find goodwill in them. It's a powerful thought, and still more powerful when transformed into action.

If you are out driving around looking for goodwill, and find yourself near Easton, Maryland, check out Bud Wieland. He's the real thing.

October 9, 2003, Thursday
Nancy Coleman
Denton, Maryland

From Easton, we roamed to the northeast. We hoped to do interviews in Delaware that day. Passing through the town of Denton, we saw the Provident State Bank and decided to give it a try.

Inside, we met head teller Nancy Coleman. She agreed to be interviewed but told us, in a classic Maryland accent, that we'd have to wait a few minutes as the tellers were ready to close out. We waited outside in the beautiful autumn sunlight, and Nancy came out of the bank in just a few minutes. It was an ideal day for an interview al fresco.

Nancy tells us that she is a native of Kent Island, but that Ocean City [Maryland] is her favorite place. "I can take my kids there on day trip vacations; the beach is great fun and there's lots to do," she says. "Denton is a close town. Everybody helps everybody. If you ever need help, there is always somebody there to help."

Nancy speaks with obvious civic pride. We have come upon another good place where good things take place more often than not.

Nancy Coleman

Pat's inquiry of, "Who is the best person you know?" prompts Nancy's answer, "My mother and father. They have always been there for me. Dad built my house for me."

Nancy doesn't know right away who she'd most like to meet and wants to think about it. We encourage her to take her time—it isn't a trick question. After a moment or two, she says, "I would love to meet my great-great-great grandparents;

Jackson was their name and I've heard a lot about them over the years."

When Pat asks, "What is the best decision you have made?" Nancy is resolute. "To raise my kids independently; to give them the best life I could give them."

Nancy's goal is to go to college. "I took some nursing courses in high school, and I loved it," she says. "I'd like to someday go back, go to college, and get into that field."

The best thing that has happened in her life, Nancy says, is: "Other than having my kids, coming to work here at Provident. My career choice. The people that I work with here are great; everyone looks out for each other."

That caring attitude is reflected in Nancy's encouraging words of: "Stand with your head held high. Never be afraid of what's behind you in the past and there is always love around you."

After our farewells, Nancy stepped back inside the bank and we loaded up our gear to leave. Pat reminded Scott that they did not make a photograph of Nancy. So, Scott stepped inside the bank with his camera and found Nancy in the middle of a happy group of tellers, showing them the ten-dollar bill we gave her and excitedly telling her coworkers, "They really are writing a book!"

We got a photo of Nancy and headed east, wondering what others thought about us and what we were doing. The two of us felt—and spoke—of our great sense of gladness at just undertaking this great adventure and having it unfold before us with such brilliance and beauty.

Delaware

October 9, 2003, Thursday
George Fernandez
Milford, Delaware

From Denton, Maryland, we drove east across miles of well-maintained, prosperous-looking agricultural land in southern Delaware. We carefully watch the roadsides and every little town for signs of goodwill. We reached Delaware Bay near the town of Lewes and saw no other cars or even a biker. We savored the resplendent autumn beauty in the National Wildlife Preserve. Ducks, geese, tranquil water, and cloudless sky all arranged against acres and acres of marsh grass turned gold. Near the mid-state town of Milford, we spotted a Ford dealership and decided to give it a try.

Scott told Pat, "You watch, before we get your chair unloaded someone will come up to greet us." It's an immutable law of auto sales: "Get out there and be the first to welcome that prospective customer."

Voila! George Fernandez was at our side with a quick smile and a firm, friendly handshake. He didn't seem the least bit disappointed to learn that we were not looking for a new car. He responded enthusiastically to our request for an interview and invited us to come inside and have a seat in his office.

George makes us feel perfectly welcome and his friendly smile fairly broadcasts goodwill.

Pat asks, "What is your favorite place in the state of Delaware?" With a big grin George says, "Any golf course!" We all laugh. It's a unique and happy answer. George adds, "I hold the club record up in Dover—seven holes in one." We are not golfers but we are amazed and impressed. What is the probability that one golfer anywhere will hit a little, white ball into a hole over one hundred yards away with just one stroke of the club; and do it seven times? To us that is a remarkably good thing to have happen and we are delighted to now know someone who has done it. George modestly says, "It's just the way life works."

After learning that George actually resides in nearby Dover, Pat asks him to tell us about it.

George smiles and says, "We came from Miami, I was raised in New York City, and we came to Delaware to visit relatives of my wife's. We liked it and looked all around Delaware and decided to move to Dover. We like the full four seasons here and it's really a small-town atmosphere. It's a good place for children to grow up and go to school. I've been offered jobs in D.C. and Miami, but my wife and I love it here."

George continues, "There are so many good people around here. The best is probably my best friend, Bill. When we first came to Dover, we had golf in common and a banker friend introduced us. When I had some economic difficulty, Bill offered to do whatever it took to help me out." We are glad to hear about a friend like Bill.

Then, George goes on to say, "In this community, there are so many people who volunteer to do good works in groups like the Lions and Civitans and Rotary." Just think of the multiple millions of volunteer man-hours George is referring to every year, in every community, in every state. That is goodwill.

George tells us that he would most like to meet Mother Teresa. "She gave herself up to a cause—the poor. She was a special person all the way through."

Pat asks, "What was the best decision you have made?"

George answers, "That would probably be marrying my wife. We've been married twenty-six years, and I still love her like the time we first met." This is goodwill music to our ears! Out of thousands of decisions he might have chosen to single out, George beams as he talks about the power of love and mutual commitment.

In response to Pat asking, "Do you have a goal you still hope to achieve?" George laughs softly, a bit ruefully, and says, "It was to retire at fifty, but that was not possible. So now, it's good health and a good family life."

George Fernandez

This next exchange was one of the brightest spots among all the responses we were privileged to hear across the fifty states.

For some people, naming the best thing in their life requires some extra time to collect their thoughts and frame an answer. Not George.

"Taking a typing course in high school in New York City. It was an elective my senior year," he says immediately. "Then, I tried going to college at night, but I couldn't afford the tuition. Pretty quick, I'm drafted into the Marine Corps and off to Parris Island! I'm in training and the Marines are short of admin people. So because of my special skill, typing, I get put in an admin job. If you check the list of my company from recruit training, we had a 67 percent casualty rate in Vietnam. If it weren't for that typing course back in high school . . . who knows?" George's sharing of this gives us chills and thrills our hearts as well because he tells it with such an obvious sense of profound gratitude for his good fortune.

When Pat asks, "If you had an opportunity to begin a new career, what would you choose to do?" George gives a quick laugh and says, "I'm in a new career! I was a stockbroker into my mid-fifties, but that's a game for the young. So, about one year ago, I came here to work and it's going well."

George's advice is: "Never stop dreaming, and never give up. Pray to God—He does answer you. And treat others the way you'd like to be treated."

I told the story of your visit to a customer who is very active with Jehovah's Witnesses. He told me he certainly knew of people the $10 would help. So I passed it on to them.

It was great meeting you both.

Regards,
George Fernandez

We said farewell to a new, good friend, and turned toward the north. We would recall and recount this visit for dozens of friends back home. Now, whenever we pass a Ford dealership, George Fernandez, full of goodwill, springs into our hearts again.

October 9, 2003
Betty Jane "Aunt Janey" Corkran
Dover, Delaware

The distance from Milford to Dover was only about a thirty-minute drive, and as daylight waned we hoped for one more Delaware interview. Scott suggested dropping in on his eighty-three-year-old aunt, Janey Corkran, a known quantity of great goodwill and a baker of extraordinarily delicious sticky buns.

Our arrival is met with a little surprise and a great deal of warm affection; Aunt Janey refers to us as "Darlin'," and she still possesses a wonderfully positive outlook on life. She seems thrilled that Pat wants to interview her for this book.

He begins by asking, "What is your favorite place in Delaware?" Aunt Janey says, "Oh, I would have to say Rehoboth Beach. We have had so many happy trips there ever since I was a little girl." For Scott, this response prompts a flood of joyful childhood summertime memories of fun-filled days on the beach at Rehoboth with Aunt Janey and a swarm of cousins and siblings. He recalls the cold waters and big waves of the Atlantic Ocean, the warm blue beach blanket spread on the sand, and Aunt Janey cheerfully asking each child, "Can I fix you a hot dog or hamburger, Darlin'?" She has given great joy to many.

Aunt Janey says, "Dover is a warm, friendly community with a little bit of everything. My forty-three years here have been great. I have a wonderful life with friends, neighbors, and my church. I never feel alone here, even though I live alone now."

Aunt Janey tells us that she knows many good people but, "There is one special person not living now, my neighbor, Louise Jamison. She was the first person to come see me when I moved in. We also worshipped at the same church and Louise first asked me to help with our young people. She was a deeply spiritual person, and even when faced with difficulty, nothing ever really disturbed Louise. She couldn't help talking about God, and she lived a beautiful life."

Betty Jane "Aunt Janey" Corkran

Pat asks, "What is the best thing that has happened in your life?"

With a happy smile, Aunt Janey says, "Well, it's the best things [plural]. The best decision I ever made was marrying my precious husband, Earle. I have been so blessed with a good husband, good children, and good friends. We have so much to share with others, and not just our things, our possessions. I would be happy if we could take our goodness, and God's, and take that love to others who don't know it." Once again, we experience the joy of seeing and hearing someone expressing a sincere sense of gratitude.

Pat asks, "If you could begin a new career, what would you do?"

Aunt Janey says, "I'm a little old to start a new career now!" She laughs. "I had no career in the modern sense, but I must say that I loved being a wife and mother and a homemaker. I have been so blessed. God's presence in my life has made such a difference! I have no regrets about other careers I might have had. I'd love to do more of the things I like to do—my sewing, gardening, my photo albums—and I'd love to be better at everything I do. I want to meet head-on everything that comes my way." Noble goals at any age, but particularly at eighty-three.

Aunt Janey's advice is so encouraging: "Be happy. Every day, wake up and know it is possible to reach out to others in perfect love."

My dear Scott and Pat,

I have chosen one of my all-time favorite charities—UNICEF—because hunger and malnutrition in children are their ministry around the world, and my gift plus your gift will be matched with Kiwanis International right now, hopefully saving many children.

With gratitude and love,
Janey

We took her advice and departed Dover in a state of considerable delight and happiness, grateful for her longstanding and continuing influence for good. As we rode, we discussed the fact that, even though Aunt Janey was not a totally random selection, we were especially grateful for having been able to interview her. It confirmed a structural notion about these interviews. We knew that her husband and two of her children had passed away in recent years, and that her own health had been threatened lately as well. She certainly could have chosen to focus exclusively on those negative events and spoken to us only of sadness and sorrow. Our interview did not make those realities disappear. It did, however, allow her to ponder for a few sweet minutes the reality of the positive side of life and to contemplate, as she put it, "Our goodness, and God's."

We needed to be in Baltimore the next morning to meet Ann's flight from Nashville; she was arriving for the upcoming parents' weekend at Princeton. We drove west

Maryland, Delaware, Pennsylvania, New York & New Jersey

across vast, open, moonlit Delaware and Maryland country-side, along foggy deserted roads, one night short of a full moon. The harvested fields were alight in silver and white, and we fairly glowed as well in the goodwill reflected from Uncle Bud, Nancy, George, and Aunt Janey. At eleven fifteen, we stopped for the night in Annapolis, back on Maryland's western shore. This was a grand day.

Pennsylvania
October 13, 2003, Monday
Laura Scudder
Carroll Valley, Pennsylvania

After an enjoyable weekend at Princeton with Rachel, we took Ann back to the airport at Baltimore for her flight home. From there we headed west. Our general thought was to visit Pennsylvania, New York, and New Jersey before heading home. On Sunday evening we passed through Gettysburg, Pennsylvania, and the hallowed countryside where Union and Confederate forces collided in a massive battle in July 1863. The scenes and accounts of our ancestors' bravery on both sides provoked wonder, amazement, and awed silence in most of the visitors to this historic site.

Just a few miles beyond the battlefield at Gettysburg, Laura Scudder, a Kentucky native, now lives on a lovely mountaintop with her husband Lawrence, a happy collection of cats and dogs, and an abundance of local wildlife. Twenty-five years ago, Laura and Scott served together as young lawyers in the U.S. Marine Corps. Laura always held her own in that predominantly male environment, and she always displayed a good-natured sense of humor and an admirable warm heart. She is a person of goodwill, and although our phone call from Gettysburg certainly surprised her, she responded enthusiastically to our request for an interview.

When Pat asks her about the best place in Pennsylvania, Laura responds with a big happy smile and says softly, "Exactly where I am! This really is our little piece of heaven. And it looks like lots of people want to join us." We share the joy she feels at being able to live in a place she likes the best. Laura says, "It's semi-rural, with beautiful wooded mountains. It's still a small town, full of great people from lots of varied backgrounds and we make a good mix."

Asked about the best person she knows, Laura says, "I don't know that I could settle on one single individual. I've enjoyed such a variety of contacts, I think it would have to be some blend of all the people I know and have known."

Pat asks who she would most like to meet, and Laura gives a little laugh, saying, "Pat, I live such an ordinary life, and I'm not a hero worshipper." After thus ruling out any celebrity choice, she goes on to say, "I would like to meet some of my ancestors, and especially both of my parents." We are all sitting outdoors on Laura's patio in brilliant October morning sunshine and it is delightful to hear Laura speak so lovingly of her family. She reminds us to, "Treasure your loved ones while they are with you."

Pat asks, "Do you have a goal you still hope to achieve?"

Laura answers, "I can be content if we are able to restructure our local government in a way that we will all benefit from it."

Laura Scudder

Pat follows up with, "What is the best thing that has happened in your life?"

With another happy smile, Laura says, "Pat, I'm afraid I'm gonna sound repetitious, but the best thing that's happened in my life is ending up where I am, doing what I am doing. It's like a wonderful series of accidents. I'm sure you've occasionally thought, 'What if I had started this trip fifteen minutes earlier—or later—what might have come my way?' Well, I've often thought, 'What if I had joined the Navy instead of the Marine Corps? Where might that have led? What if I had done certain things differently?' You know you could always do things better. So, the best thing in my life is that it has brought me right here . . . now."

Concerning a new career, Laura continues, "Well, I don't think I would go into law again. I have found that I really like teaching. Right now, I'm teaching swimming to a group of little kids. I think I'd like to try teaching at the college level."

Laura's message of encouragement is passionate. "Get up! Get out! Open your eyes and enjoy life! There is so much to see and do . . . and the house can be dusted tomorrow!"

Dear Scott & Pat,

I sent the $10 to Aussie Rescue Placement Helpline, a rescue organization for Australian Shepherd dogs, in which I am involved (you remember Toby, my own Aussie)....

If you all are ever this way again, do please call upon us.

Sincerely,
Laura

Our mountaintop interview concludes in sunlit beauty. We make a photo, give Laura a spread-some-good-will ten-dollar bill, and after fond farewells, we again take to the road.

October 13, 2003, Monday
Emilie Crow
Phoenixville, Pennsylvania

From the Gettysburg area, we turned eastward and followed Highway 30 across Pennsylvania's lovely farmland. The highway reminded us of Tennessee's ridge roads, whose elevations allow travelers to enjoy expansive views on either side of the road along the way. Today, we were treated to pleasant miles of neat, prosperous, well-maintained farms; overflowing produce at roadside stands; sturdy, ancient barns built on solid stone foundations; and dozens upon dozens of silos in silhouette against the autumn sky. In the Amish country, we passed handsome, black, horse-drawn carriages clip-clop-clopping along the roadways, and in a single one-mile stretch we saw three different farmers plowing in the fields with mules just as was done here more than one hundred years ago.

Just northwest of Philadelphia, we stopped in Phoenixville and interviewed a young new mother, Emilie

Crow. During the entire interview, Cory Ann, Emilie's infant daughter, slept peacefully in her car seat on the floor nearby.

Emilie tells us that her favorite area in Pennsylvania is the Amish country out in Lancaster County. "I just love the boldness of the simple way they live," she says. We concur.

"Emilie, what's the best thing about Phoenixville?" Pat asks. Emilie thinks about it and says, "It's small and quaint and reminds me of home. Everything is close by and it's easy for us to get around."

When Pat asks, "Of all the people you know, is there one who stands out for consistently doing good things?" Emilie breaks into a beaming smile and says, "I'm gonna have to say my husband, Cory. He is always looking for the good in everybody, and for good things to do for others."

We are encouraged by the warmth of her affection for her husband and his goodness, and continue with the question of who she would most like to meet.

Pat with Cory Ann and Emilie Crow

"You know, living up here around all this history has made me more interested in the presidents. I'd like to meet President Bush and talk to him," Emilie says.

Then Emilie's face lights up with a wonderful smile when she says, "Having my baby, Cory Ann, was the best decision I have made. She is just so sweet." This was another moment worthy of being captured on film so that in some future year, Cory Ann might be able to see the animated look of love she brought to her mother's face and hear the depth of tender affection in her mother's voice. It gave us great joy just to witness the dazzled gaze Emilie fixed upon her sleeping child.

Emilie says she'd like to go to nursing school and become a nurse someday.

Pat then asks, "What is the best thing that has happened in your life?" Emilie immediately says, "My family. My dad and my mom. I could not have chosen better role models than the two of them." Here again, we thought it would be nice to have a motion picture to show Emilie's parents her sincere expression of gratitude for their influence on her life. We hope these words adequately convey her loving appreciation.

Emilie sends these words of advice: "Be proud of who you are. Don't try to be somebody you are not."

Emilie's sweet baby wakes up just in time to be included in our photo.

After saying good-bye, we continued eastward, and then, in any and every direction to dodge Philadelphia's homeward-bound traffic. In the dark, we crossed a bridge close to the spot where George Washington and his troops crossed the Delaware River to launch a surprise attack on Trenton, New Jersey, during the Revolutionary War. The sacrifice and bravery of our forefathers should inspire and encourage all of us.

We made it to Princeton, briefly visited with Rachel, and rested for the night.

New York

October 14, 2003, Tuesday
Colm (CALL-uhm) McKeever
Central Park
New York City, New York

In contrast to our back roads explorations, this morning we experienced the exhilaration of joining the rail commute into New York City. The early train from Princeton Junction whisked us toward the city and provided a panoramic preview of the Big Apple's magnificent skyline. Visitors and residents alike silently contemplated the empty space where the Twin Towers of the World Trade Center once stood. In the aftermath of that evil destruction, we detected an emerging sense of goodwill. Throughout our visit on this day, we were impressed by the sustained vitality of New Yorkers. The famous bravado was still there, now in concert with an unexpectedly high level of courteous, good-hearted concern. We were treated with politeness and affability everywhere we went—from security personnel who helped us locate an elevator at Penn Station to the helpful staff at the Empire State Building, as well as from all of the bus drivers who answered our questions and helped us load and unload from their tour buses. With the kind assistance of New Yorkers, we covered much of Manhattan below Central Park South (Wall Street, Fulton Market, the Brooklyn Bridge, Battery Park, Times Square, Rockefeller Center, Herald Square, Greenwich Village, East Village, and Tribeca).

Finding the right New Yorker to interview was crucial. Our hostess and our waiter at lunch were especially kind and attentive. We would have sought an interview but thought both of them were much too busy to stop.

One tour bus took us by the United Nations Building, but our street level strolls better showed us the sea of people who came from many nations and who are now united as New Yorkers and Americans. It was a splendid sight to behold.

At Pat's suggestion, we decided to take a carriage ride through Central Park. Across the street from the Plaza Hotel, we were invited to board a carriage by the very friendly Colm McKeever. We could tell by his accent that he was not a native New Yorker. He told us he grew up living about a half hour from Dublin, Ireland, in the village of Navan. He has lived in New York for sixteen years, and he seemed delighted by our request to interview him while we rode through the park.

As Colm turns the carriage to begin our tour, he pauses as a young man of Asian descent runs toward us. He has a sack lunch for Colm, which he had obtained at Colm's request from a nearby street vendor of yet another ethnic background. What a blur of entrepreneurial activity, integrated cultures, and harmonious free enterprise!

Maryland, Delaware, Pennsylvania, New York & New Jersey

Central Park is lovely and the autumn day is ideal for such an adventure as we focus our attention on interviewing Colm.

"Central Park is truly my favorite spot in New York. I never tire of being here. It has great beauty and history and a constant variety of people." Colm opines that the best thing about New York is that, "Every nationality is represented here, and everybody is proud of where they came from. It's fascinating. Many seem to show a greater patriotism here than perhaps they might in their homeland. There are pockets of groups all across the city, in places like Queens. In Woodside, where I live, it's very Irish. We have great pride."

Pat asks, "Who is the best person you know?" Colm responds, "There is one fellow, another carriage driver, named Finear Flood. He always just does the right thing, and he's a great fellow to be around."

Colm tells us about his brother, Bryan, who was killed at the age of seven. "I'd very much like to meet him," he says. We have not counted the various answers this question prompted, but we are touched by the frequency with which people would choose to meet a loved one rather than a celebrity or historical figure.

Colm wears a big smile as he tells us his best decision was asking his wife to marry him. "We've been married five years now. I met her on Fifty-seventh Street. She's Irish." With his smile and fewer than two dozen words, Colm manages to convey a multi-faceted and beautiful response.

Pat then asks, "Do you have a goal you still hope to achieve?" Again, there is no delay in forming a response. Colm says, "I hope to own my own stables." His fondness for the steed pulling our carriage is apparent. The horse responds readily to Colm's easy hands and his soft-spoken commands. In fact, the horse handles all the work

Colm McKeever

Trip Six

while Colm enjoys his lunch, answers our interview questions, and points out notable spots in the park.

Pat's query, "What is the best thing that has happened in your life?" generates another great smile and still more twinkle in Colm's Irish eyes. "The birth of my two daughters, Alanah and Moya."

We continue to enjoy the privilege of observing the intensity of parents' happiness, triggered by thoughts of their children. The power of love is a very good thing, dear reader. If you have parents still living, take the time, right now, to let them hear from you a few words of gratitude for the love they have showered on you.

Pat asks, "If you had an opportunity to begin a new career, what would you choose to do?" After a bit of thought, Colm says, "A politician. I think I could do some good."

He'd be a wise and straightforward one, too. "Treat your neighbor the same way you'd like to be treated yourself," he advises.

Dear Scott and Pat,

I'm so sorry for not returning this sooner as it got lost during our move.

The $10 I gave to a homeless man that I've known for years at Central Park.

Fondest regards,
Colm

As we later looked back on this interview, Central Park was not in sharp focus, but Colm's friendly smile was. We remembered the person with greater clarity than we remembered the place. This was our consistent experience all along our way in these travels. We savored the scenery, and there were many days when the sheer majesty of our land made our hearts leap with joy. However, our brief, happy encounter with one kind Irish-American carriage driver in the midst of a city of more than seven million souls etched a more powerful and lasting memory.

Colm was our thirty-ninth interview and we had already begun to report to family and friends back home that we were discovering a vast reservoir of goodwill all across the country. Our joy at reporting this good news was magnified by the joy we then observed in the smiling faces of those with whom we have shared the good news. They loved hearing about the kind-hearted people we met from Ukraine, Germany, Scotland, Sicily,

Maryland, Delaware, Pennsylvania, New York & New Jersey

Ireland, and elsewhere—all of whom love living in America. Our West Virginia friend, Diane Hypes, aptly described them as, "Normal human beings living very valuable lives." Friends and family asked us to tell them more about *Looking for Goodwill* and we were encouraged by their response to our findings.

As the afternoon waned, we made our way back to Penn Station and boarded a southbound train for Princeton Junction. After a brief visit with Rachel, we moved on toward the south and east. After enjoying a pizza supper in Toms River, New Jersey, we rested for the night in Forked River. (What great place names!)

It was an excellent day, filled with goodwill. Our hearts overflowed with gratitude.

New Jersey
October 15, 2003, Wednesday
Joyce Hagen
Atlantic City, New Jersey

The Jersey shore was new territory for both of us, and our morning drive along the coast was especially pleasant. We had the roads to ourselves. As we explored Long Beach Island all the way up to the Barnegat Light, all traffic signals simply flashed yellow and we only passed one police patrol car and one other motorist. Judging by the numbers of empty beach houses we passed, we felt sure the traffic must be much heavier in season.

The wind was high and the clouds were low as we entered Atlantic City and wandered toward its famous Boardwalk. At the northern end of the Boardwalk, we spotted free parking and an accessible ramp. The remains of a Moorish-style pier which once jutted into the ocean now housed a small historical museum on one side and a small art gallery on the other. We chose to explore the gallery and met its director, Joyce Hagen.

Born near Lancaster, Pennsylvania, Joyce grew up near Penn State University and now resides in Mays Landing, New Jersey. In response to Pat's question about the best place in New Jersey, Joyce cautiously answers, "Well, I'm just not a native. We just moved here only seven years ago, so I don't know the state well yet."

Pat presses on. "What is the best thing about Mays Landing?"

Joyce responds, "It's a year-around community, as opposed to a shore location. It's much more residential, and has a good hometown feeling." She seems to feel a bit more comfortable with us, and volunteers, "Atlantic City is pretty seasonal. With conventions and casino business, on a typical summer day, we might average 130 to 140 visitors [to the gallery]. In January, it might be 30 or 40." During our visit, we see about 6 other visitors viewing the special display of beautiful handmade works by a local quilting guild.

Joyce Hagen

Joyce says, "I work in the world of art, and there are two people, both artists, who are close and personal friends of mine. Like many in the arts, they are generally more giving and more people-oriented. Both of them work in ceramic and paper, and they constantly give free workshops for school children and to all who want to learn. They are such good, generous people, and they have taught me that as an artist you must first learn who you are, so you can express yourself to others." Joyce brightly expresses her goal "to continue working in arts administration; one of my dreams is to help artists not have to always give away their work."

Pat asks, "Who would you most like to meet?"

Joyce lets out a relaxed laugh and says, "Albert Einstein. He was such a creative thinker!"

Pat then asks, "What is the best decision you have made?"

Without hesitation, Joyce says, "Having my children, my three boys. Becoming a parent taught me great lessons." She wears a proud mother's smile.

Pat follows up with, "If you had an opportunity to begin a new career, what would you choose to do?" Joyce says, "I would want to do something very similar. I'd love to develop an artists' retreat, a place where artists could both work and relax; be creative and critically and financially supported." Her positive thinking and her desire to encourage others in their creative pursuits impress us. We are also impressed with her message of encouragement: "Keep an open mind. Soak in everything you can, and then put it out there to share."

This was an important interview for us because we were able to overcome Joyce's initial uncertainty about exactly who we were and exactly what we were up to. We gained her trust and confidence, and we're glad we did. Joyce had serious insights to convey.

We ventured down the coast a bit and paused at Margate City to photograph another art form, "Lucy," the world's only elephant-shaped hotel. Someone must have had a wonderful sense of humor to build it. This is a great country. If you want to build an elephant-shaped hotel, you are free to do so!

October 15, 2003, Wednesday
David Iams
Wheaton Village, Millville, New Jersey

We turned from the coast and drove westward across southern New Jersey's rural countryside. The scenery amazed us as we passed through a portion of the Pine Barrens. Had we been dropped unawares from a helicopter into that thick pine forest, we would have thought we had landed back in rural Kentucky or Alabama.

We didn't know why Wheaton Village was highlighted in red on our map, but we were intrigued and we stopped.

Glassmaking is the focal point here, with a national Museum of Glass as well as several period shops with unique glass works of art for sale. We couldn't pick out a prospective interviewee, and we were ready to leave when we spied the Down Jersey Folklife Center. Its lone staffer was conversing with the only other visitor as we entered. We enjoyed the center's educational exhibits about this unique part of the state, and shortly the other visitor departed. Our host approached us. "Where are you fellows from?" We told him we were from Nashville, and introduced ourselves. Very gentlemanly, he introduced himself as "David Iams."

We ask if that last name is spelled I-J-A-M-S, because a former president of Pat's alma mater spelled his name in that fashion. With a twinkle in his eye, David says, "No. That is the smart side of our family." We all laugh. His quick wit has opened the door to friendship. We gladly step in.

Scott wears a black windbreaker, and David asks what the orange letter "P" on it stands for. Scott says, "Oh. My daughter, Rachel, has just started her freshman year up at Princeton." David says, "I used to go there . . . back when you could still get in." We laughed again.

We are in a very remote, thoroughly out-of-the-way place. There are no other visitors around. We have come upon a delightfully humorous and dignified New Jersey native working as a volunteer, and he is a person who radiates goodwill. Of all the places in southern New Jersey where we might have stopped, we have found just the right one!

Born at Bay Head, New Jersey, David graduated from Princeton in the class of 1958, and now resides in Port Elizabeth, New Jersey. David says, "I think my favorite place in New Jersey is on the shore, on the ocean. As they say down here, I have sand in my shoes. I find that I have to go to the ocean at least once a year and get in the water, or I will grow old and die! Port Elizabeth is also quite nice and agreeable in its own way. It's very historical. And Princeton is a favorite place as well. My grandfather was a doctor there and a co-founder of the Princeton Hospital, and my father went to Princeton, so we had relatives in town as well as in the college. It's a favorite place from years ago."

Maryland, Delaware, Pennsylvania, New York & New Jersey

"What is the best thing about Port Elizabeth?" Pat asks next.

With verve, David replies, "The wildlife! There are only a couple of hundred souls, and we are on the river, so it is wonderful for bird watching. We have magnificent osprey and blue heron." Despite his love for his New Jersey home, his mental vitality makes us believe that David would seek and find good things no matter where he might live.

When Pat asks, "Of all the people you know, is there one who stands out for consistently doing good things?" David responds, "Oh, Lordy . . . that would be a hard one! Over the years, I have met so many, it's hard to pick just one." We comment that it is a wonderful thing—in and of itself.

David continues, "I will say this. In Philadelphia, I spent fifteen years writing the society column for the *Philadelphia Inquirer*, and I was astounded at how many people who were rich and didn't have to do good things, but did anyway."

Our question regarding which person, living or dead, he would most like to meet generates a laugh. David says, "I met a lot of 'em already! In my work at the paper, I met so many remarkable people, so many who were quite distinguished." This isn't boastful. Instead, David's voice and manner reflect gratefulness. He confesses, "I wouldn't mind meeting Sean Connery . . . or Anthony Powell, the novelist who wrote *A Dance to the Music of Time*."

Pat asks, "What is the best decision you have made?" David responds without delay, "Moving down here. I found a certain peace of mind I had not known before."

David requires no extra time to ponder when Pat asks about his goals. With considerable animation, David proclaims, "I want to write 'THE BOOK.'"

David Iams

David tells us that he would like to write about how separate lives intertwine over the years. He grins broadly and expands on his plot, "You put a foolish kid like me through a college like Princeton, with other folks from dramatically different backgrounds, and follow their twisting trails." We like the idea and tell him so.

Pat then asks, "What is the best thing that has happened in your life?"

David mulls this one a bit and replies, "That's tough to say." A pause. We wonder, but do not ask: is it hard to reveal, or merely hard to decide among many good things?

David says, "I guess I would have to say getting the society column assignment at the *Philadelphia Inquirer*. I was forty-five years old and already working at the paper in an insignificant job. I felt low. Many of my classmates from school were doing well, and I felt I was going nowhere. Getting that new assignment was a great boost and a great opportunity." We feel flattered by David's openness, and we admire the thoughtful dignity with which he speaks.

Dear Pat Price:

Long overdue greetings from your guide . . . at Wheaton Village's Down Jersey Folklife Center, where you and your [dad] interviewed me. A month or so later, I realized you had enclosed a $10 bill for me to use for something good.

It took me two years to settle upon something good: the rescue mission run in Philadelphia by Sister Mary Scullion, once a fiery activist, now considerably mellowed, whom I know and like. I gave her the $10 last March at Muldoon's Saloon, a St. Patrick's Day party benefiting the mission, at which she is an honorary bartender and I the piano player.

I hope you agree it was money well spent.

Regards and keep up the good work!

David Iams

In response to Pat's question about having an opportunity to begin a new career, David tells us, "I probably should have become a college professor—there is much potential for having a good influence."

He exerts such influence with his simple and crisply spoken words of encouragement: "Don't ever give up!"

Our interview is complete. We have spoken without interruption in this quiet place, and we feel fortunate to have found so much goodwill in such a dapper, dignified, and witty package. It's also encouraging to have found another seasoned citizen who has not retreated to his rocking chair, but has instead stepped forward energetically to serve as a volunteer in his community. It's a powerful example of goodwill in action.

As we prepare to leave, David presents us with his business card, which ideally captures his irrepressible personality:

Maryland, Delaware, Pennsylvania, New York & New Jersey

DAVID IAMS

At large

We turned west by southwest to make our way home to Nashville. We reached Baltimore's beautifully transformed Inner Harbor in time for a waterfront crab cake dinner, and then reached Washington, D.C. in time to join five lanes of commuters still struggling to get home at seven thirty-five in the evening. We contemplated the possibility that at least one of them might be a government expert who spent the day drafting a directive for improving Nashville's traffic. Ironically, by that time in Nashville, most everyone was already at home and finished with dinner.

We spent the night in the mountains at Luray, Virginia. We were happy about the people and the goodwill we found in Maryland, Delaware, Pennsylvania, New York, and New Jersey, and were thankful for the opportunity to do this goodwill tour.

TRIP SEVEN

WASHINGTON, OREGON, IDAHO, WYOMING & MONTANA

November 4, 2003, Tuesday
Travel Day

We were up early to make all preparations for a nine o'clock flight from Nashville to Seattle, Washington. We pre-boarded so Pat's chair could be stowed below in the luggage compartment. A young lady on crutches also pre-boarded and stowed her crutches in the overhead bin across the aisle from our seats.

In the air, we floated freely across our majestic continent, buoyed by a sense of adventure and discovery. We streaked across thousands of miles which our pioneering forbearers had heroically toiled to cross slowly on foot or on horseback. It is not possible to gaze down upon our ferocious western landscape from a height of some 30,000 feet without feeling awed by the powerful beauty of the rivers, the forests, the mountains, and the land. Always ask for a window seat on your western flights.

In Seattle, we headed for our connecting flight to Spokane. Waiting there to pre-board was the same young lady on crutches we saw on the flight from Nashville. She smiled and asked, "Where are you guys heading?"

We introduced ourselves and explained our quest for goodwill. Laughing, we also pointed out that we had not yet decided with any precision just exactly where we would head from Spokane. Initially, we thought a clockwise loop from Washington to northern Idaho, to Montana, to Wyoming, to southern Idaho, to Oregon, and back to Spokane would be the best route. But weather reports about snow in Montana had us thinking about trying a counter-clockwise loop, with an initial turn to the south and away from snow.

On our short flight to Spokane, we learned the young lady's name is Stephanie Kuespert. A college student at the University of Idaho in Moscow, she was returning from a Future Farmers of America convention in Louisville, Kentucky. Favorable airfares brought her through Nashville. She had only injured her leg; the crutches were temporary. There was an unmistakable and unfeigned wholesomeness about her that was especially refreshing, and she was keenly interested in our search for goodwill. We wanted to interview her, although we were uncertain if or when we might pass near her campus. She trusted us enough to give us her cell phone number.

From the Spokane airport, we roamed southwest on I-90 to Ritzville, and on Highway 395 to Lind, then straight south on Route 21 to Kahlotus. This drive overflowed with unexpected beauty. We crossed vast stretches of magnificent farmland, golden rounded wheat fields contoured to gentle hillsides, then long, open stretches of flat lands. "Vast" is the most accurately descriptive word for this area, followed by "remote." There was almost no traffic on the road with us. We traveled to Lower Monument Dam on the Snake River under a pink and purple evening sky.

Our sense of freedom and adventure was powerful. We felt so downright lucky to be out there, unimpeded, taking in the exquisite loveliness of these previously unseen sights. Framed by the darkened doorway of a sturdy white barn, a lone farmer and his dog surveyed our passing. The farmer raised his hand and gave a jaunty wave, which we returned with pleasure.

In Pasco, we ate at a little neighborhood spot, where we observed some goodwill in the interplay between two older couples dining nearby. Although seated at separate tables and having no obvious connection or relationship, they talked almost nonstop throughout their meals across the gap between their tables. The topics ranged from children to doctors to travels, and each couple sympathetically and patiently listened to the other's recounting of triumphs and disappointments. On our travels, we often observed a greater tendency among the World War II generation to be excellent listeners. We aimed to emulate that good example.

After dinner, we reached the mighty Columbia River and rested for the night in Richland, Washington.

Washington
November 5, 2003, Wednesday
Pam Dougal (DOO-gal)
Maryhill, Washington

A fog bank covered the Columbia River as we departed that morning. We made our way west on Highway 14, the Washington side of this exceptionally broad and beautiful river. Across the way in Oregon, we saw the interstate highway and an active railroad line. Busy barges and boats plied the historic waters made famous by the Lewis and Clark Expedition of two centuries ago. In a span of eighty-five miles on the Washington side, we met only four cars and overtook none. We felt as though we had been given a special pass to view the mighty river and its massive gorge in the uncrowded fashion of early explorers.

Stonehenge replica

At one point, we came upon a full-size replica of England's ancient Stonehenge. We unloaded and looked around, all by ourselves.

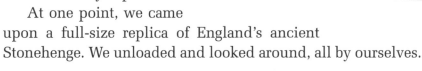

It was built by a remarkable man named Sam Hill, who is buried at the south end of the monument. Sam visited the original while serving in Europe during World War I. Successful in railroading, highway construction, banking, and regional boosterism, Sam built a mansion nearby—now a museum—and named it Maryhill in honor of his daughter. We drove over to take a look and found a mansion that would stand out in New York City. Here, it not only stands out, it sticks out. Perched on the edge of the gorge with a commanding view of the river, it is now a first-rate museum. Both the Stonehenge Memorial and the Maryhill Museum possess an air of goodwill.

Inside the museum, we met a friendly volunteer named Pam Dougal.

Pat begins by asking, "What is your favorite place in the state of Washington?" It's the perfect icebreaker.

Pam beams and responds right away, "The San Juan Islands, up between Seattle and Vancouver, Canada. It's very peaceful up there. There are modern conveniences, but it's also intimate. And the whales! It is so beautiful! My goal is to move there someday." Her unabashed joy at telling us of this place makes us want to go there.

Pam Dougal

Pam says, "The best thing about Maryhill is the culture this museum brings to the community. It has an eclectic collection that is so completely different. And the story behind it! How four totally different individuals—a queen, a dancer, a road builder, and his wife—met, and how they came together in this place." The uniqueness of the mansion and its location is accentuated by the historical fact that Lewis and Clark crossed just below this land on their return trip on April 22, 1806.

"When we moved here from Seattle, I was really lonely. The first time I rode by here, I thought it was a prison! But I came to find out about this wonderful collection of art and artifacts of local culture. Coming to work here really helped me appreciate the surroundings."

When Pat asks Pam, "Who is the best person you know?" she immediately responds with a proud smile and says, "My mom, Florence Putnam. I have never heard my mother say a single bad word about anyone! She is ninety-eight years old, and she has no evil." Hearing such good things said by one person about another inspires us. We hope to live in such a way that someday, somewhere, someone may say such good things about us.

Pam tells us that she'd most like to meet Jesse Jackson or Oprah Winfrey. "They both have done a lot to bring people together," she explains.

Her reason for admiring them is also reflected in the career she'd choose if she were to begin a new one. "I think I would try politics, try to make a difference," Pam says. "We were in the restaurant business before in Seattle; we had three restaurants. I'd like to give politics a try."

Pam pauses here to collect her thoughts, then offers some advice for us all: "Live at peace with each other. Find a way to love each other, and not be so ready to fight."

> Dear Scott & Pat,
>
> I was given $10 by you in an envelope after our visit to do something good with it. I put it away when I got home from work and only a few days ago while I was cleaning out my desk at home did I find it.
>
> That day I went . . . to do some shopping and was in a line at Safeway behind a lady and her two very polite little girls. The mother could not speak English . . . The older daughter was doing the translation for her. They did not have enough money to pay for all their groceries so . . . the cake and ice cream and soda was going back. I thought of the envelope in my purse and thought of your face and what a GREAT smile you had. I knew you would want those girls to have their treats. I gave the wave to the clerk and she let them have their items without knowing it was me. Not an earth-shattering story, but it made my day.
>
> God Bless You,
> Pam Dougal

We crossed the river and continued westward on sections of old Highway 30. Horse Trail Falls, Multnomah Falls, and Wahkeena Falls all complement the river's majestic beauty.

Racing the sun, we pressed through Portland and on out to the Pacific Ocean at Lincoln City. Boulder-strewn and tree-lined, the Oregon coastline at this time of day and year is practically empty. In places, we had the entire Pacific Ocean

Washington, Oregon, Idaho, Wyoming & Montana

and coast to ourselves. The area must be hugely popular in summer. Postcard-ready views were at every turn as we proceeded southward down the coast. The wind was high, and it was spitting rain while we savored the same stormy view enjoyed long ago by Captain Cook at the aptly-named Cape Foulweather.

Darkness arrived, and at Newport we regretfully turned back toward the east. We needed to cross the entire state of Oregon the following day. Someday, it would be good to drive that entire coastline all the way to California, or even to Mexico!

Oregon
November 5, 2003, Wednesday
Carole Kathman
Corvallis, Oregon

Leaving the chilly, rocky coves and the clusters of motels and quaint inns along the Oregon coast, we continued to drive eastward in the dark until we came upon the college town of Corvallis. Although we had no prior plan to stop here, we surveyed the campus of Oregon State University, still bustling with student activity at seven o'clock. We found a main street that reminded us of the one in Bedford Falls in the classic movie *It's a Wonderful Life*. We have friends at home named Burton, so we selected Burton's, a traditional American family-owned restaurant just across the street from local fixtures including the Regional School of Ballet, Northern Star, and the Cat's Meow.

We were greeted warmly and seated right away by Mr. Burton, the owner himself. His friendly personality infused the entire enterprise; his employees and his guests all appeared to be enjoying themselves. We overheard him tell a caller on the telephone, "There's nothing more fun than coming to Burton's."

Our meal was quite good and our waitress was remarkably cheerful, warm, and polite. Her gentle manner made us feel especially welcome, and we had a delightful time talking about the magnificent sights along the Columbia River Gorge and the Pacific Coast.

When Scott went to the cash register to pay for the meal, the teenager on duty looked over the bill and said, "Oh, you had the lovely Carole tonight." Scott said, "Yes, she really is a very lovely person." It seemed so unusual to hear a teen say "the lovely" when referring to an older person. Yet this teenager's tone of voice conveyed genuine admiration. The sincerity of the remark resonated in Scott's heart. This woman's kind spirit had indeed shone distinctively all during our dinner.

Scott returned to the table where Pat was polishing off a piece of homemade pie, sweetly recommended by Carole. "I think we need to interview this lady," Scott tells Pat before retrieving from the car the notebook, tape recorder, camera, and a self-addressed envelope with the ten-dollar bill inside.

Most other guests have already finished their meals and taken their leave; another busy day at Burton's winds down. When Carole comes back to ask if we need anything else, we tell her we are actually looking for goodwill and writing a book about our adventures in finding it. We ask if she has time for an interview.

"Of course!" is her instant reply. She eases into the booth beside Pat and we talk together as though we have been friends for decades.

Pat begins with our traditional first question regarding her favorite place in the state.

Carole says, "Here in Corvallis!" The rising inflection in her voice conveys the subtle message that Carole thinks us a little odd for not already knowing that answer. She adds, "I'm originally from Pasadena, California, went to UCLA and Pasadena Community College. My ninety-year-old father still lives in Pasadena; he had a stroke today." We tell her how sorry we are to hear that news. We are stunned to hear it, because nothing in her sweet, attentive manner betrays any of her anxiety about his condition.

Carole Kathman

Pat follows up with, "What is the best thing about Corvallis?" Carole's face glows with a warm smile as she says, "My family, my work at Burton's, my church, and all of my friends who are so caring. My husband and I came to OSU so he could work in fish and wildlife research. We had seven children in eight years—two sets of twins. [They were the first two and the last two.] We lived in campus housing for six years. I love living here; it's a wonderful place to be," she says, before telling of her husband's premature death. "We lost 'Papa Earl' four years ago. He had two heart surgeries, two lung surgeries, and had testicular cancer at age thirty-two. He had lots of medical problems, but we pressed on!" Again, we are stunned to learn of the difficulties she has faced; they did not impinge in the least on Carole's cheerful, uplifting, and hospitable treatment of us during dinner. Her fortitude is impressive.

Carole gives Pat's hand a friendly pat when replying to his next question. "I know so many good people! Mr. and Mrs. Burton have such kind hearts. They gave me work when my husband got sick and they have been right there for me, so loving and giving," she says. "My pastor, my friends, and my kids have all been so good to me." There is a little pause, then another revelation. "My daughter, Jamie, one of my second set of twins— my baby—passed away last year, and all of the children will be able to get here on Saturday to go to the Lutheran cemetery and put her ashes in the ground. Her twin, Julie, is here in Corvallis." We try to convey our sympathy as well as our sincere admiration. This polite, cheerful, gentle woman has great inner strength. The Lovely Carole has made a lasting impression on us; we will always remember her grace and her courage.

Carole says she'd like to see her mother and husband again. "Don't we always wish we could have them back? My husband

Trip Seven

was a wonderful storyteller; he loved math and science. My mom was so loving, giving, and kind." It obviously rubbed off.

Her best decision, Carole tells us with a happy smile, was: "Marrying my husband, Earl, and having all my children."

Then Pat asks, "Do you have a goal you still hope to achieve?"

With a laugh, Carole replies, "To get my house all cleaned up!" More seriously, she softly adds, "I sure would like to see my dad before he passes away." There is no hint of self-pity in Carole's voice, only tender affection.

When Pat asks, "What is the best thing that has happened in your life?" Carole again beams as she says, "Probably, getting the most wonderful parents. They raised me to be Christian, to be kind and considerate. My dad really taught me, and showed me, it's always better to give than to receive." He would be very proud of his daughter.

In response to Pat's query about her choice if given an opportunity to begin a new career, Carole says, "I love this work. But if I started something new, I'd like to volunteer to do more at church. I would help more with quilts for the inner city and for the group home."

What encouraging words The Lovely Carole offers: "Always believe in the Lord, because God is in control. Love your family and never hold grudges. We can't change other people, but we can love them."

Carole's persistent, resilient sense of goodwill embodies what we are seeking, and we load up our rental car in front of Burton's with a powerful sense of gratitude for having met her. "Corvallis" means "heart of the valley," and in The Lovely Carole we have found a kind and loving heart, whose goodness prevails in spite of sorrow or loss.

Dear Scott & Pat,

. . . It has been way over a year since you came through Oregon and stopped to eat at Burton's. You so generously gave me a $10 bill "to use for something GOOD"—and I did! I sent it to the Benton Hospice Service, Light Up A Life, in memory of my father, who died November 12, 2003.

Your $10 . . . has been a real inspiration to do extra giving this Christmas. It was fun doing gifts for our giving tree at church. Several of our cooks . . . have young children; one is a divorced dad with a boy, one of our waitresses is divorced with three little girls and she's going to school to become a nurse, so I'm going to surprise them with $10 stocking stuffers for the kids. . . .

Thanks again for the $10 to do something GOOD. Such a GOOD idea!

Love & God's blessings,
Carole Kathman

The Columbia River Gorge, Maryhill, and Pam; the Pacific Ocean, Oregon's coast; and the heart of the valley,

Carole. All in all, a fabulous day. The goodwill is out there, all around us. Carole chose to share hers with us while she was serving us, even though she was dealing with her own set of problems. We won't take for granted such displays of grace and goodwill.

November 6, 2003, Thursday
Judge Russ Hursh
Vale, Oregon

Heading eastward from Corvallis on old U.S. Highway 20, we climbed into the beautiful snow-covered Cascade mountain range and encountered our first snow. Snow plows and road crews have kept the roads passable for us and for the handful of other travelers out today. The Willamette National Forest's timber-clad mountains present postcard-perfect displays of Oregon's well-known, cool, green outdoor beauty. Less well known, at least to us, was the massive expanse of Oregon farmland we encountered as we continued eastward during the day. Huge cattle and sheep farms stretched out to the horizon, displaying their well-maintained barns and hay bales in stacks the size of an average grocery store. We marveled at the varied natural beauty of Oregon's Pacific Coast, mountain ranges, timberlands, and rural farmland. As we would do all across the country, we eagerly savored the beauty of what we saw, knowing that there was so much more out there in every state that we could not possibly see on this particular journey.

In late afternoon, we reached sun-filled Vale, almost to the Idaho state line. We unloaded and ventured into the county courthouse. In the hallway, we met a big friendly bear of a man—Judge Russ Hursh. His name was engraved in big bold letters on his big leather belt, and he had a big booming voice full of good cheer. He jovially invited us into his office and another new friendship began.

Pat asks, "What is your favorite place in Oregon?" Judge Hursh answers with great enthusiasm, "I like it right here in this area, Pat! This county has lots of sheep and cattle and 32,000 people in 10,000 square miles. I live over in Ontario [fifteen miles away], but mainly I'll tell you—you've got to bloom where you are planted!" This is wonderful. His answer both explains why he has chosen to like wherever he finds himself, and exhorts us to do the same. We determine to comply.

The judge tells Pat the best thing about his town. He laughs when he says, "Well, I know everybody. I have ten or twelve 'Hotline Hen Clubs'—folks who are retired and have enough time to tell you exactly what is wrong with the world—or, as we say out here, 'how the cow ate the cabbage.' I can get on their level, eye-to-eye, and know what's on their mind."

Judge Hursh continues, "In my life, I've had twenty good mentors. I can't really say just one person stands out as the best. Whenever I lacked expertise, I found a superstar in that area. My biggest high was getting to know Mary Kay [the founder of the cosmetics company]. She said, 'Don't ever set a ceiling on yourself. If you need help, go find people who already know what you need to

Judge Russ Hursh

know . . . go pick their brains.' I still drive the pink Caddy my wife won selling Mary Kay cosmetics, even though she has been dead five years. She was a mighty good person, Pat. And I've gotten to know quite a few. I'm sixty-seven years old now, and I've probably buried three-fourths of my superstars. I'd rather have people around that I've got to pull back on the reins, rather than try to push the chain up the hill!"

Next, Pat asks who the judge would most like to meet. Judge Hursh studiously considers this question for a few moments, then says, "Young George W. Bush [the current President]. I've met Dewey, Truman, Reagan, and Bush Sr."

Judge Hursh says that the best decision he ever made was to get out from under his dad's control and prove his own worth. "My dad put me down physically and verbally, and it meant a lot for me to stand up on my own two feet. I was disinherited over it, but it was best for me," he says.

We love this judge's enthusiasm as he talks about his goals. "I'd like to have a personal net worth of two million dollars, so I can leave a good inheritance for my three children. I'd also like to go see more of the world. Those two are a good start."

Pat inquires, "What is the best thing that has happened in your life?" Judge Hursh gives us a huge smile and says, "When Vern Wilson, Chairman of U.S. Bank, hired me on and gave me a chance to work as the field man for the bank. He opened the door and started me up the ladder. He showed me how to help people."

Judge Hursh tells us he'd start his own private bank if he had the opportunity to begin a new career.

Asked for a message of encouragement, the judge says, "Write your failures in the sand; write your goals in granite. And keep moving the goals up—don't ever be satisfied."

This positive, cheerful, encourager brightened our day and sent us on our way with a huge dose of goodwill. Darkness gathered quietly around us as we crossed into Idaho and made our way to Mountain Home to rest for the night.

Idaho

November 7, 2003, Friday
Shannon Jones
Pocatello, Idaho

From Mountain Home, we began a beautiful day's drive across the wide and often wild open spaces of southern Idaho. The speed limit is 75 mph and there was no traffic except for the truckers dutifully hauling everything from the producers to the consumers everywhere across our land. One particular truck wore the thought-provoking and truthful slogan: "If you eat, you're involved in agriculture." In this part of the country, agriculture is unquestionably the foremost enterprise. Huge potato farms join huge dairy farms, which are adjacent to huge hay farms. Although there are occasional tiny towns, these farms are in utterly remote settings which necessitate a certain self-reliance and independence of spirit amongst the farm families out here. The strength of this farm economy gave us an encouraging sense of improving strength all across the land. We felt deeply grateful for the goodwill embodied in the abundant and varied foods we enjoyed all across America. When we traveled the western United States, where the relatively recent wildness of the earth is still so evident, we were particularly impressed by how much of the land is now being cultivated and how well it is being done.

We stopped in Pocatello and visited the Museum of Natural History on the campus of Idaho State University. We enjoyed the excellent displays depicting the dramatic changes Earth has undergone through the millennia, felt especially fortunate to have been born at all, and were glad to have been alive just now to enjoy this sunny, cold Idaho day.

The historic Union Pacific depot was empty, so we stopped across the street in the recently restored Depot Grill for a late lunch. Housed amidst the somewhat faded glory of the former Yellowstone Hotel, the Depot Grill had almost a one-to-one staff-to-customer ratio when we visited, so we decided to interview one of the cheerful servers taking care of us.

Shannon Jones is somewhat rare among our interviewees in that she is actually a native of the location where the interview is taking place. She tells us the town's nickname is "Pokey" and that she recently graduated from the University of Montana at Missoula.

In response to Pat's initial question about the best place in Idaho, Shannon says, "I really like Sun Valley and Red Fish Lake. It's gorgeous! You can ride horseback, swim in the lake, sit in the sun, go for a hike, or just enjoy the people. I really like the atmosphere." Shannon bubbles with joy. We are not surprised to learn that she was a cheerleader at Pocatello High School. Her sense of good cheer definitely adds to our day.

When Pat asks, "What is the best thing about Pocatello?" Shannon replies, "I can go most places and know somebody . . . the mall, the gym, the grocery store. I have friends around me." Her smile tells us that Shannon understands and appreciates her good fortune.

Shannon knits her brow as she considers someone who consistently does good things. "That's kind of a tough one." After a moment or two she brightens and says, "Lee Mundt, my grandmother's boyfriend. She lives in Kansas and has had Alzheimer's for the last four years. Lee takes care of her. Isn't that great?" We agree wholeheartedly.

Shannon tells us that she'd most like to meet her cousins. "We are the only part of our family that came west—so all the rest are back in Georgia, Texas, North Carolina, and Kansas," she says.

Pat asks Shannon to talk about the best decision she ever made.

"Leaving to go away for college at the University of Montana. It wasn't easy to do, but I met so many amazing people and got to see a whole different side of life. I really feel good about that," she says.

Shannon says the best thing that has happened in her life is, "Having a family here that has not been divided. My sister's family is intact, too." We feel a sense of joy with Shannon as we realize how much it has meant to us as well to have a family that is not divided.

Shannon Jones

When Pat asks, "Do you have a goal you still hope to achieve?" Shannon responds, "I would like to go to graduate school and study print journalism."

Even though she does not think of her present work as a career, Shannon eagerly answers Pat's question about what she might choose to do as a new career. "I did an internship during college in public relations, and I'd like to do that kind of work."

Shannon concludes the interview with these words of encouragement: "Don't always just try to do what others expect or want you to do. Set your own goals and do things for yourself."

If we had set out to find the Depot Grill, the odds are very good that we might have missed it, and thereby missed the goodwill we found in the heart of this cheerful young woman. We feel a steadily growing sense that there is a great store of goodwill all across our land, just waiting to be found.

We make a photo of Shannon, present her with the goodwill ten dollars, and give instructions to just do something good with it. We really think we should be calling our interviewees "goodwill ambassadors," because they help to convey a spirit of goodwill out beyond our brief interactions. The ten-dollar gift we leave with each one also allows them to participate in the spreading of a little goodwill.

From Pocatello, we wandered generally eastward and reached Soda Springs as the shadows began to lengthen in late afternoon. From Soda Springs, Idaho, to Jackson, Wyoming, via the perfectly named border village of Freedom (about sixty-one miles), we passed one school bus, one car, and seven heavy-duty pickups pulling trailers full of horses. This is beautiful, wild country, and to top it off a big, beautiful moon rose over the Snake River Range for our viewing pleasure. We rested for the night in Jackson, Wyoming, where it was very quiet and fifteen degrees at ten o'clock. The weather forecast said, "threat of snow on Saturday." We were wary; we knew it would be pretty to look at and the skiers would love it, but we needed to cover Wyoming the next day.

Wyoming
November 8, 2003, Saturday
Doug DeGrote (DE-groht)
Dubois (DŪ-BOYZ), Wyoming

Five degrees was the overnight low in Jackson, and the town was still quiet when we left this morning. The drive north from Jackson must surely be one of the most glorious thirty-five miles of roadway in America. The traveler is treated to a panorama of spectacular natural beauty as the Grand Tetons vault skyward from the surrounding plains. That beautiful, wild silhouette is unforgettable! The brisk air, bright light, and majestic snow-covered heights all combined to inspire us and fill our hearts with gratitude for simply being alive and being able to feast our eyes on such sumptuous beauty. No photograph could adequately capture the transcendent grandeur of this place.

Disappointed to learn that the southern entrance to Yellowstone National Park was closed, we turned southeast on U.S. 26 and enjoyed the wild Wyoming scenery. We stopped for gas in Dubois, which appeared to consist of the gas station and perhaps a dozen small shops. Pat had wanted to do an interview at a gas station, but until now we felt that there would be too much activity going on to permit an interview. The station in Dubois was different. No other cars were there while we filled our tank. Inside, there was a small café named the "Grab-n-Dash" where we enjoyed a nice sandwich lunch. No one else came in for gas or food while we ate. The gentleman at the cash register quietly enjoyed his newspaper as we approached him. Station owner and operator Doug DeGrote (his wife fixed our lunch) readily agreed to be interviewed.

Pat asks, "What is your favorite place in Wyoming?"

Doug says, "Right here. I like these mountains. I like four-wheeling and snowmobiling. Everything about the outdoors here." He points out that the area enjoys, "A spring and summer tourist season, then sort of the 'old folks' season, followed by hunters' season, then snowmobile season."

In response to Pat's next question, Doug replies, "The best thing about Dubois is that the views here are just beautiful. We also have the largest herd of Bighorn sheep in the continental U.S., plus lots of elk and deer." He laughs and adds, "In this little row of shops," gesturing next door with his thumb, "you can buy a ten-thousand-dollar fur coat. But if you need underwear or a toothbrush, it's a seventy-three-mile drive to Wal-Mart in Riverton." We all laugh together at his cheerful acknowledgement of the uniqueness of this place he loves.

When Pat asks, "Who is the best person you know?" Doug says, "Now, that's hard to say. I know a lot of good people here. Everybody does their best. In a small town, you have to do your best." This strikes us as a very positive compliment to his community.

Doug says he would most like to meet the president, George W. Bush, and that the best decision he ever made was moving to Dubois from Minnesota.

Asked about goals still to be achieved, Doug says with cowboy stoicism, "Well, yeah. Get through this day and see what next week brings. Dubois has been real good to me—for twenty-eight years. We've done all right." There is no defensiveness in his tone of voice, only a matter-of-fact gratefulness. This is so good to see and hear.

Pat then asks, "What is the best thing that has happened in your life?" After just a moment, Doug answers, "I've had a lot of good luck and not a whole lot of bad. I'm thankful for every day."

Doug DeGrote

Asked about beginning a new career, Doug replies, "Something with no hard manual labor. I've been a plumber. This is my second convenience store. I've been sort of an entrepreneur—owned restaurants, rental units, an insulation business. I've enjoyed it all."

Doug DeGrote encourages everyone to travel. "This is a small community and a lot of people don't leave here. I say people need to see not just Europe or South America, see what's going on here in the U.S."

We feel so privileged to have not been able to drive up into Yellowstone, because our revised route brought us to peaceful, isolated, beautiful Dubois and to friendly, grateful Doug DeGrote. He loves where he lives, likes what he does, and he is thankful for every day. What an inspiring example of goodwill!

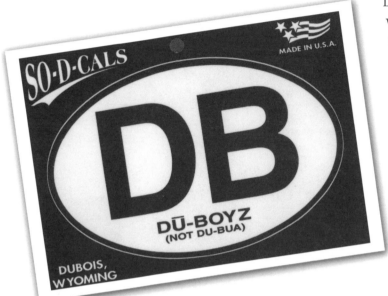

It's Dū-Boyz

With a friendly laugh, Doug gives us a black and white souvenir decal that reads "DŪ-BOYZ (not Du-Bua)," and asks where we are heading next. We tell him we don't know, and he urges us to see the Wind River Canyon.

This proves to be excellent advice as getting there allows us to see Riverton, Shoshoni, and a snow-dusted Wyoming that looks like a gargantuan iced wedding cake. This is a wild wonderland, and as Doug had told us, the Wind River Canyon is awe-inspiring.

As we drove northwest toward Cody, the evening sky was tinted with purples, pinks, and blues. After a full moon rose, we saw an eclipse. This day, place, and interview stood out as eminently worthy of admiration. Wyoming is so big, so open, so splendidly free!

Our notebook entry that night:

A day to lock away and consciously strive to permanently seal memories of the beauty we have seen. It's somewhat overwhelming to have seen the Grand Tetons, Bridger-Teton National Forest, the exquisite loveliness of snow on rock, "iced" mountain tops, fields of white, the glistening Wind River and its canyon, elk, horses, cattle, deer, hawks, geese . . . the Span of Creation . . . our "Top of the World" feelings, with majestic mountains around us in every direction. Of necessity, the people like where they are . . . it's too far to go anywhere else!

Darkness surrounded us as we arrived in the delightful cowboy town of Cody, founded by Buffalo Bill Cody himself. His daughter, Irma, was the namesake for the fine old hotel where we ate dinner, surrounded by moose, elk, antelope, deer, ram, and bison heads. An eclectic collection of modern day cowboys and their families were in town for Saturday dinner at the Irma Hotel. We saw lots of boots, jeans, bushy mustaches, and big western hats. There were also plenty of friendly nods and neighborly greetings all around. We were glad to be there.

November 9, 2003, Sunday
Matt Weber
Powell, Wyoming

It was clear and cold when we left Cody. Twenty-four miles to the north, we passed through the small town of Powell and stopped at a small roadside church, where the worship service was just beginning. Everyone greeted us with genuine warmth and we felt completely welcome; we were immediately invited to stay after the service to enjoy a potluck luncheon. We gladly accepted. We counted eighty-three worshippers and only two neckties; western attire prevailed, as did a certain western ruggedness. Public prayers acknowledged the daily challenges and rigors of life out there, and divine assistance was humbly sought. The loving wives among the congregation vividly stood out. Each held her husband's hand or gently placed her arm around his shoulder. Simple, small, but unmistakable body language that reassured, comforted, and encouraged.

It was very heartening to observe a lanky member of the congregation, whose wind-and-sunburned face bespoke a life working outdoors, stand and pray a simple touching prayer acknowledging illness, loss, and difficulty in this life, and appealing to God for a strength of spirit, a common unity, and a willingness to help each other through tough times. The service was simple and uplifting, and at its conclusion a baby-faced young man, sixteen-year-old Matt Weber, came forward to publicly and gratefully thank the congregation for helping his mother, his brother, and himself. He was soft-spoken and he only made passing

Washington, Oregon, Idaho, Wyoming & Montana

references to having gotten in trouble, but he was emphatic in expressing his gratitude to these good people for caring for his family. We were grateful to observe this pure dose of goodwill.

After a delicious lunch, we spoke to Matt. He seemed flattered that we wanted to interview him and he listened to Pat's questions with a special intensity.

The first question is about the best place in Wyoming, and Matt replies, "It has to be Yellowstone National Park. It has so many beautiful sights to see, and so much room where you are free to go."

Matt's eyes glisten a bit as he tells us the best thing about Powell. "The people here are so supportive, so caring, so loving, and forgiving." What a positively beautiful thing for a sixteen-year-old boy to say about the people in his hometown community.

Matt Weber

There isn't a moment of hesitation when Pat asks about the best person Matt knows. Matt says, "My mom, Cindy Weber," and gives us a big smile. We're encouraged to see and hear a teen-aged son speak about his mother with such tender affection. We have come to treasure good moments like these.

Pat asks, "Which person, living or dead, would you most like to meet?" Matt softly says, "My cousin, Michael. He died, and I'd like to have a chance to know him." We cannot help but be touched by Matt's mature acknowledgment of lost opportunity to know a particular loved one, and we feel that we have been exhorted to cherish each moment we have with our family and friends. We feel a stronger desire to never take for granted the time we are given to share with others around us.

Matt says the best decision he has made is accepting God and choosing to follow Him; his goal is to become a success in life, maybe a mechanical engineer.

Asked about the best thing that has happened in his life, Matt tells us, "Being born into my family—my mom and my little brother are so good—and in this place." It is unlikely, at sixteen, that Matt would have previously discussed this idea with others, and it is not the sort of thing that is taught in school. Yet, we hear again in his response the powerful impact of family and place.

Matt says, "When things go tough, [that's exactly how he says it] don't quit. And, when you work hard, good things do come."

This was a good stop, and we said our farewells with deep gratitude for the kind welcome and generous hospitality these good people showered on us.

Montana

November 9, 2003, Sunday
Justin Lobaugh
Livingston, Montana

We traveled through the towns of Belfry, Red Lodge, Roscoe, Absarokee, Reed Point, and Big Timber on deserted roads, surrounded by spectacular snow-covered mountains and meadows. What a drive! We saw dozens of herds of mule deer grazing contentedly and totally unafraid. All along the road we saw quail in considerable numbers and even a couple of magnificently beautiful pheasant. This afternoon's drive would be especially lovely on film, and we were so thrilled at being able to travel through such raw beauty. At Reed Point, Montana, we looked around unsuccessfully for an interview and were intrigued by one sign proclaiming the place to be the sheep drive capital of the world and another saying "See ewe here August 31st." Only two blocks long, Reed Point has an ancient hotel, a saloon, a few house trailers, and no other visible signs of economic activity. The sheep drive must be a sight to behold.

It was dark, cold, and damp on Sunday night when we finally reached Livingston. Clark's Crossroads was the lively and friendly spot where we stopped for dinner, and our waiter's effervescent personality brightened the chilly evening.

His name is Justin Lobaugh. He is twenty-one years old and a native of Livingston, Montana.

Justin Lobaugh

Justin tells us the best place in Montana is, "North of here about six hours, Glacier National Park. You can backpack, camp, enjoy the scenery, and you can see everything on foot. The natural beauty is just awesome. I could probably be earning more money working elsewhere, but I just love the beauty of this state." We do love meeting people who love where they live.

Jason says, "It's a little hard to pinpoint the best thing about Livingston, but I'd say it's the quiet sense of community and our proximity to beauty." We think he has pinpointed it nicely, as Livingston was the old original entrance to Yellowstone National Park.

When Pat asks about the best person he knows, Jason responds right away by saying, "My parents. I can't pick one or the other." What a loving tribute to both!

Pat asks, "Which person, living or dead, would you most like to meet?"

Jason says, "Napoleon. I could spend days and days talking to him." We would love to eavesdrop on that conversation.

Justin says the best decision he has made is keeping his options open. "At this point, I have no kids, no wife, and no house payment. I'm still free to pursue opportunities. I'm still able to go."

He laughs and says his goal is to keep out of debt.

For all of his light-heartedness, Justin's answers display a considerable depth of maturity.

In response to Pat's query about the best thing that has happened in his life, Justin says, "The way my parents raised me. I think I have good people skills and I am able to learn something new most days."

Justin tells us he'd like to own his own business. "I want to do something," he says. "I love doing."

His words of advice correspond: "Do what makes you happy, not just what you think will make someone else happy."

Justin's sunny disposition provided a great exclamation point at the conclusion of a splendid day. Our random search continued to produce such great surprises of abundant good-will in faraway corners of our beautiful country.

The parking lot was empty at our motel in Livingston; all of the cars were parked in an indoor garage. Real winter must be a serious challenge for those hardy souls who live all year up here.

We rested well, glad to be indoors for the night.

November 10, 2003, Monday
Jane Richards
Missoula, Montana
(Aldo Leopold Wilderness Research Institute
on the campus of the University of Montana)

Montana is a massive state. "Massive" is the operative word. We laughed together at the notion of trying to cover it in only one day. To make some time, we took I-90 to Bozeman and Butte, and we were treated to an exquisite panorama of immense forests, beautiful fields, wild animals, and seemingly endless mountains with their snow-crested majesty on display, and all for free.

I-15 took us to Helena, where we decided to stop. The parking lot outside the state capitol building was virtually empty, and we parked right beside the ground floor entrance.

Buffalo in the snow in Montana

Inside, we met a friendly security guard who was all alone at the information desk. The building was unusually quiet, and there was no evidence of other people on the ground floor.

On the second floor, we visited the governor's office, and the very sweet lady working there alone told us that, barring some emergency, the legislature would not be back in session until 2005. Most everyone was back home working.

This indication of rugged individualism and self-reliance seemed so fitting in this vast and awesome state. Having been settled so recently (it attained statehood in 1889), Montana reminds us of what a great accomplishment the taming of the American West really was. Inspired by the pioneers' spirit, ingenuity, determination, and good humor, "big," "open," and "free" are words that still come to mind when we speak to others about Montana.

From Helena, Highway 12 took us to the growing city of Missoula and the campus of the University of Montana. Our mid-afternoon cruise in search of goodwill was more challenging because a cold, misty rain meant we needed to seek out an indoor interview.

We spotted a small building bearing the name "Aldo Leopold Wilderness Research Institute." Because of our travels, we felt a kinship to the notion of wilderness research, and we decided to go in.

Friendly and generously sharing an easy laugh, Jane Richards is a happy native of Wisconsin. Wearing slacks and a sweatshirt, she is a totally relaxed person.

Pat begins by asking Jane about her favorite place in the state of Montana.

Jane replies, "Down in the area near Yellowstone National Park, the Rocky Mountains are glorious."

Questioned about the best thing about Missoula, Jane says, "Because of the lovely small-town feel, I think we enjoy better connection with our neighbors. And for me personally, I really like working at the Leopold Institute."

Seated at her computer monitor, Jane is surrounded by maps of Alaska and various national parks. She explains that her work involves studying the impact of visitors on wilderness places. We tell her about the joyful impact wilderness places have had on us.

As for people with impact, Jane tells us of two people with whom she works. "Dave Parsons and Allen Watson give me such great support and are always willing to help. They are very sensitive to my needs," she says. We are delighted to hear such positive things said about coworkers.

Pat asks Jane, "Which person, living or dead, would you most like to meet?"

She thinks a moment and says, "Maybe John F. Kennedy. I've always been intrigued by him."

Jane says her best decision was marrying her husband, Mick, fifteen years ago. She smiles happily and we again cherish seeing and hearing yet another person speak lovingly of their spouse.

Pat next asks, "Do you have a goal you still hope to achieve?" Jane says, "Work-wise, I am trying to get close to being a budget analyst."

"The best thing that happened to me," Jane says, "was growing up in a big family. I have five brothers and two sisters, and we had a great time growing up together."

Jane tells us if she started a new career, she'd like to do something in radio.

Pat concludes by asking Jane for a message of encouragement.

Jane Richards

Washington, Oregon, Idaho, Wyoming & Montana

Jane jokes, "What are some of my famous sayings that they can print?" We all laugh and then she says, "Grin and ignore it. Everything will be fine."

In a few minutes' time, we made a new friend, basked in her good-humored laughter, and enjoyed her friendly smile. Goodwill is all around us.

After a photo, the goodwill ten dollars, and a good-bye, we headed north on I-90 in the cold—and getting colder—rain. After our dinner stop in Superior, we drove on in the dark and dropping temperatures before stopping for the night at St. Regis. The weather forecast warned of snow. During the night, we awakened several times to listen for the sound of heavy trucks out on the highway. If they kept moving, perhaps the road would remain passable.

Idaho
November 11, 2003, Tuesday
Stephanie Kuespert (CUE-spurt)
Moscow, Idaho

A very wet snow was falling as we departed St. Regis, Montana, and climbed up I-90 to Lookout Pass. At that altitude, the snow looked about four to five inches deep, and we were grateful that, (one) there were no other cars around to dodge and, (two) there was one solid tractor trailer truck laboring slowly through the pass, leaving a relatively clear trail for us to carefully follow. We descended into northern Idaho, quickly leaving the snow behind. We enjoyed a beautiful drive around a good portion of the now-deserted Lake Coeur d'Alene. Its timber-fringed shores and cozy coves were inviting even in the off-season.

Old U.S. Highway 95 took us south through lovely countryside and down to Moscow, home of the University of Idaho. We drove through the campus, then stopped to call Stephanie, the college student whom we met on our flight one week ago. We found her apartment easily, then headed to Lefty's to enjoy lunch together.

With a pleasant smile, this friendly young woman begins the interview by telling us her favorite place in Idaho. "That would definitely be Horse Thief, Idaho. It's an old camping ground out in the mountains." (We'd love to know the local history of that name.)

Having learned that her home is Parma, Pat asks Stephanie to tell us the best thing about it.

Her bright eyes reflect her obvious civic pride as she says, "The community! Everybody knows and helps everybody. If there is one kid in town with health problems, all of the churches pray. If there's a fire, the whole community helps out. Every year, there is a time when the whole community celebrates together." It is absolutely grand to hear this young person speak so proudly, but not boastfully, of her town's spirit of community. We hope her words inspire others to work together and to build positive spirit in their own communities.

Stephanie Kuespert

Next, Pat asks, "Of all the people you know, is there one who stands out for consistently doing good things?" Without hesitation, Stephanie says, "My great-grandpa, William Shearer. He died two years ago at the age of ninety-three. As far as I know, he never in his life did anything bad. He told me, 'Whatever you do, you're going to live with the consequences—so do something good!'"

Isn't it remarkable that we "happened" to be on the same flight with Stephanie? That she "happened" to speak to us? That she "happened" to be so open and trusting toward us? And that she "happened" to have been given such good advice for all of us by her great-grandpa? This is an example of what we are diligently seeking, and we feel elated at finding Stephanie, or actually, at being found by Stephanie.

Stephanie says she would most like to meet Gordon B. Hinckley. "He's the ninety-plus-year-old president of my church. He travels all over the world and it's amazing to see how well he treats all of the people he meets," she says.

Pat then asks, "What is the best decision you have made?" With a smile, Stephanie says, "To come to the University of Idaho. I wasn't going to come, and now I'm so glad I did. I have met so many amazing people and had such great experiences."

When asked if she has a goal she still hopes to achieve, Stephanie says her goals include being a mom and a good wife; raising a good family, and being a good example. Her honest expression of such noble goals might seem out of sync with the twenty-first century magazine industry's image of American young women and their aspirations. Indeed, we would not have been at all surprised if Stephanie had told us that her goal was to be governor of Idaho. It's inspiring and thrilling to hear such a talented, outgoing young woman express her goals in terms of "goodness" ("good wife," "good family," "good example") and with a philosophical inclination toward aiding others rather than self. Noble goals indeed!

Stephanie laughs a little at herself as she recalls the best thing that has happened to her. "My family moved to Parma from Caldwell. I didn't want to move; I was eleven and in the sixth grade, and I just didn't want to move. Then, I started showing sheep and cattle and got very involved in that. I have learned a lot about hard work and self-discipline. And I have learned country life is the best!" The Future Farmers of America should put Stephanie on their Web site.

Pat asks Stephanie what she is thinking about in terms of a career. She tells us, "I have two different ideas: one would be international agri-business—world trade and marketing. Or the other would be rural sociology—how to keep small towns small but more economically productive."

> Dear Scott & Pat:
>
> I gave the $10 to Parma FFA. All the members from the chapter are donating a few dollars to buy fabric. At their next meeting . . . the chapter is going to make scarves for the residents of the Parma Senior Center. The members needed some extra money to help cover their expenses.
>
> Sincerely,
> Stephanie Kuespert

Stephanie's advice: "Stress is the spice of life. The only people not stressed are in the cemetery! Learn to enjoy life and live it to the fullest!"

This sweet, trusting young woman was such a delight to meet and get to know. Her spirit of goodwill brightened our spirits each time we thought of our wonderful journey through Idaho.

We made our way across beautiful miles of Washington countryside back to Spokane for our flight home. We drove 2,710 miles during this segment of our journey. As the twenty-first century begins, we discover the Pacific Northwest is still being tamed. It still reeks of wildness and of nature's raw power. The vast, cataclysmic changes which have taken place on earth seem so much more visible in this part of the West. You must see it with your own eyes . . . the space, the solitude, the community of hardy souls and the cruel beauty of the land. And, especially, the fascinating people of goodwill waiting to welcome you.

TRIP EIGHT
MISSISSIPPI

December 3, 2003 Wednesday
Carleen Williams
West Point, Mississippi

We left Nashville with our sights set on anywhere in
Mississippi, the Magnolia State. Driving the beautiful
Natchez Trace Parkway through southern Tennessee, part of
Alabama, and into Mississippi, on this rainy day we saw
quiet southern woods, hawks, deer, and very little traffic. We
could not help but revel in the heightened appreciation we
felt for the contrasting topography of this region compared to
our recent drives in Oregon, Wyoming, and Montana.

We love our country's variety of place names. When we
needed to stop for gas, the place we came upon was named
Okolona. Moving on, we stopped in West Point. It was still
rainy and we did not spot a likely interviewee. After dinner, we
were heading to our room through a completely empty hotel
lobby when the young manager cheerfully engaged us in
pleasant conversation.

The opening opportunities always came so pleasantly. If
we were asked, "Where are you guys headed?" our standard
response, "We don't really know" always prompted
curiosity and more conversation. If we were asked, "What

brings you here?" we immediately explained our quest for goodwill and our desire to relate the quest and our findings to others in the form of a book.

Carleen Williams, the hotel's manager, seemed intrigued by the idea, which motivated us. She was very professional and businesslike, and we assured her that we would not let the interview interfere with her managerial duties. Interestingly, during the interview, there were no phone calls to the front desk and no other customers arrived to check in. We were not interrupted at all.

Carleen Williams

Pat begins by asking Carleen, "What is the best place in Mississippi?" She says, "I like Biloxi; it has a beach and it's real nice and warm down there."

Having learned that Carleen actually resides in nearby Columbus, Pat asks her, "What is the best thing about Columbus?" She responds pleasantly, "Well, it's a nice, quiet, small place. Everybody knows each other and people are real friendly."

Carleen positively beams as she thinks of the best person she knows. "My father, Roosevelt. He wants me to do my very best and do the best with my life. I have four sisters and six brothers, and I'm the baby. And my father has been good to all of us, encouraged us," she says.

Pat asks Carleen who she would most like to meet.

She replies, "My grandmother. I didn't really have a chance to get to know her. I'd like for her to sit down and really teach me how to cook!" Carleen says this with laughter and a genuine enthusiasm for learning a skill strongly associated with her departed loved one.

Next Pat asks, "What is the best decision you have made?" Carleen responds thoughtfully, "Choosing to be a positive person. Choosing to be motivated to get back up and keep going no matter what. I don't hang around with negative people."

Carleen continues, "I would like to get my four-year degree at Itawamba Community College and my respiratory therapy license. I already have my hotel management license. I'd like to do some sort of community counseling . . . help people who need help."

Carleen smiles warmly when asked about the best thing in her life, and she tells us, "I am blessed to be alive. I am twenty-three years old and I have survived two car wrecks; every day is a blessing!" We love to hear yet another person convey such a profound sense of gratitude. Carleen's unvarnished expression of joy at just being alive for another day encourages us.

Carleen's message of encouragement reflects her father's good influence. "Do your very best. Stay away from negative people. If you work hard, you will succeed. Keep God with you always; He is your real friend. Keep your head up and keep going. Have love!"

This was a wonderful interview and we feel so fortunate to have gained Carleen's trust and friendship. After giving her the ten dollars to spread some goodwill, we tell Carleen we need to take a picture of her for our book. Hearing this, she runs into the back office, laughing. When we insist that we want a photograph of all the goodwill interviewees, she gets her purse and goes to the ladies' room to do her hair and make-up. We wait in the empty lobby, and upon her return, suggest a pose in front of a lovely painting

Carleen Williams, too

of the state tree. Carleen wants a "professional/business" shot at her desk, so we compromise and do both.

Mississippi

December 4, 2003, Thursday
Edna Cole
Columbus, Mississippi

Not far from West Point, we arrived in Columbus. There we found a small school and its poised yet lively headmistress, Edna Cole.

Edna explains that she has lived in Columbus for the past eight years to help care for her aging parents. "Columbus is a wonderful place. It has a kind of small town atmosphere. There is a very strong sense of community," she says. "Being so deeply involved in this school has allowed me to reach out into the community and really know people."

She adds, with emphasis, "The people here are just the best! For example, on Monday night we had our local Christmas parade, and everyone was there pulling together. The spirit is so good and so positive. And people recognize you!"

Pat asks, "Of all the people you know, is there one who stands out for consistently doing good things?"

Edna Cole

After a moment's thought, Edna says, "Actually, it's a husband and wife team. Max and Opal Johnson are totally involved in their community's needs, active in their church. Their children are all over the world as missionaries. They have devotedly visited my mother. They are just a great example of goodness and love. They were high school sweethearts. Both married others, then lost their spouses. They've had about five years together now; they are a wonderful team." This is more of the good news we wanted to find, and we are glad to hear about Mr. and Mrs. Johnson.

Pat asks who she would most like to meet, and Edna says, "Other than Jesus? Oh my!" She pauses. "A purely historical figure, I think, would be Thomas Jefferson. He was so diverse in his talents and interests. Biblical figures would be Jesus and his apostles."

Pat then asks, "What is the best decision you have made?" Edna says, "Choosing to follow Christ. Then, marrying my husband, Don."

Asked if she has a goal she still hopes to achieve, Edna explains, "Well, I am still very involved with the school here. I'm also a board member and we are working hard on a building program. As far as other goals, Don and I have established two businesses—a coffee shop and an antique shop—which we hope will help in the revitalization of our hometown of Millport, Alabama." This wonderful entrepreneurial spirit is so encouraging to see firsthand. All across the country, we see bold Americans like Edna and Don beginning or building onto their own small businesses; their determination and self-motivation continue to be an inspiration.

Edna smiles broadly and says, "I have been blessed with so many good things; it's hard to narrow it down to just one! I'd say the best thing to happen to me is getting to see my children grow up and be strong Christian individuals, married to godly people."

Pat asks Edna what she would choose for a new career, and Edna replies that she'd like to do something in the area of merchandising, decorating, or planning events . . . something service-oriented.

She's taking her own encouraging words to heart: "Always have a vision, regardless of how old you are. I'm fifty-five and happy to be embarking on a new endeavor. Reach out and be involved in others' lives."

Pleased with the interview, we prepare to present Edna with the ten dollars for spreading some goodwill. She, however, has a bit more goodwill to share. "I want your readers to know about some remarkable people I just saw in our local parade. All older than fifty years old, in red hats and purple dresses. One recently became a widow; one just had her hip replaced. But what strength they display! They still are setting new goals and having new dreams. We should all be encouraged by their example."

We turned for Nashville, making a side trip to drive through Millport, Alabama, to see where Edna and her

To Whom It May Concern:

Our school helps foster children in the surrounding area each year for Christmas. We obtain these names from DHS and they range in age from one year old to eighteen years old. This year we were able to provide gifts for eighty-six children. . . . At first I wondered how we could supply all those eighty-six children without having to ask people to take more than one name. . . . We still had a few names left on the list. **Mrs. Edna Cole** then came to me with your envelope and told me to put the money toward something GOOD. I immediately knew where the money would go! Your $10 provided a gift for a needy child so that he would have a better Christmas this year.

Thank you so much for including us in your project. . . . May God bless you in your efforts!

Sincerely,

Julie B. Moore

husband will open their coffee and antique shops.

Driving through the remote pine forests of northeast Mississippi and northwest Alabama, we were touched yet again by the vastness of our nation. The land is so free and so full of opportunity. Carleen and Edna are just two of many following their dreams, and they aroused in us a desire for a renewed pioneer spirit and an all-American sense of vigor.

We headed for home, determined to seek the best in every person, in every place, and in every opportunity.

Trip Eight

HAWAII (WITH A TOUCH OF ILLINOIS)

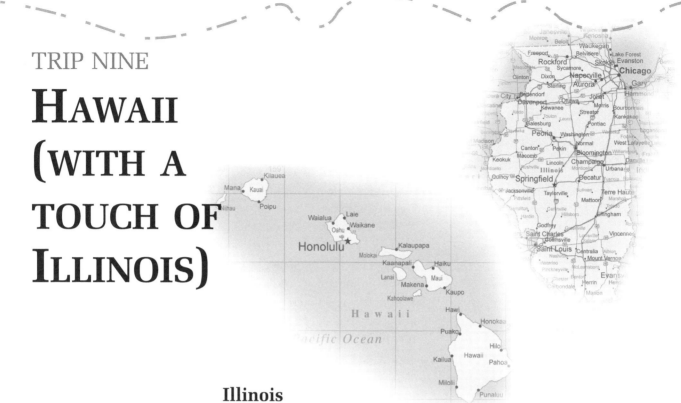

Illinois

December 12, 2003, Friday
Ray Carter
Chicago, Illinois

Months ago, Rachel said, "Dad, you've got to do your interviews in Hawaii sometime, so please schedule it when I can go, too!" On this weekend, Ann had a long-planned meeting in Chicago, Rachel's first Christmas holidays as a freshman at Princeton began, and we had saved enough air miles to all fly direct from Chicago to Maui, Hawaii on Sunday afternoon. Thus we converged on Chicago.

A dear friend in Nashville gave us the name and phone number for Ray Carter, a native Nashvillian working in Chicago. We called him, and he agreed to meet us at our hotel to be interviewed.

Pat begins by asking, "What is your favorite place in Illinois?" Ray has a great smile and an easy, relaxed manner. He tells us it's Chicago. "I love this city. Living in downtown Chicago is one of the great things about this state. It's very residential; the lakefront is preserved for all the people to enjoy; there are seventeen miles of jogging paths; great restaurants and museums. It's very stimulating to live in downtown Chicago."

Pat follows up by asking about the Windy City's best thing.

Ray says, "I think there are at least two or three. Of New York, Los Angeles, and Chicago, Chicago is the most livable. It's still midwestern in its values. It's very residential, meant to be lived in. It works. It's clean. Being from the South, I appreciate the values and the work ethic, on top of having the amenities of world-class cities." Yet another person who loves where he lives, Ray would make a fine spokesman for the Chicago Chamber of Commerce.

Next Pat asks, "Who is the best person you know?" Ray responds eagerly and with a smile, "Bob Muzikowski. He's a Chicago businessman and he gives away half, or more than half, of his income every year. He wrote a book called *Safe At Home* that tells about having worked on Wall Street then coming to Chicago. He was walking and saw kids playing ball with sticks and rocks in a run-down, rough, old section of town called Cabrini Green. Bob began building the largest Little League baseball program anywhere. Almost seventy teams now play, with real bats and baseballs, thanks to Bob. He's now building a school to help kids develop into future leaders. He's got seven kids of his own, he's a typical New Yorker–Ivy Leaguer, he quietly works behind the scenes, and he has done incredible good in this city."

Hearing Ray tell about Bob not only lightens our hearts, it makes us want to do more good things for others, as Bob has done.

Ray thinks of several people he'd like to meet. "What a choice! Biblically, who wouldn't like to have a conversation with the Apostle Paul? In American history, Lincoln and Lee, I'd love to talk to those two. From the World War II era, Patton or maybe Eisenhower. What was it like to order that many men into conflict?" Ray says. "The most enriching conversation would probably be with what Muzikowski called 'the people no one knows about,' but who are doing great things. They see a need and get it done!"

We feel a surge of joy at hearing Ray articulate what we have been feeling with steadily growing intensity. We are enjoying an unrivaled opportunity to meet and converse with real America. Allowing these good people to contemplate the positive side of life is producing a fabulous collection of good-will stories and experiences.

Pat asks about the best decision Ray has made.

Ray ponders for a bit and says, "Spiritually—responding to the gospel of Christ. Personally—career-wise, the riskiest decision was leaving my coaching position at Vanderbilt University and venturing off to seminary, not knowing where it would lead me. The people and the experience here have been so great; it is frightening to think of not having gotten to know these people." It's interesting that Ray relates his riskiest decision as his best decision.

When Pat asks if he has a goal he still hopes to achieve, Ray doesn't hesitate to reply, "To finish well. I want to understand God's purpose in my life. I want to know that moment when I can feel 'You were born for this moment,' this is the purpose for which God made me. I want to keep pursuing that!"

Ray Carter

Pat poses the next question: "What is the best thing that has happened in your life?" Ray smiles again and says, "On the positive side, leaving what was comfortable at Vanderbilt in Nashville for new challenges here. And even on the negative side, experiencing conflict with people I care about, feeling shoved out and having to figure out what's next for me has stretched me more. I might have stopped growing. All these things have helped me see that life is about more than just you!"

When asked what he would choose to do if given the opportunity to begin a new career, Ray says, "Well, I'm trying to do that now! The thing that keeps coming at me is doing a ministry of helping people gain a bigger vision of their life. It's an unbelievable adventure. I'm meeting with a number of big business leaders who are striving to understand, or discover, the call of God on their life. I want to help others go further and enlarge their vision of what God is calling them to do in this world."

Ray offers several encouraging thoughts. "One, we are made for God. People matter to God, even those who are not seeking God. Two, hear God's message—God's Word is eternal. Three, the quality of the relationships in your life means everything. Investigate—seek to know God, through Christ

Hawaii (with a touch of Illinois)

and His Word. Invest—in developing relationships with others. It's basically what Jesus says—'Love God and love people.' Love the people close to you, as well as those who can't do anything for you."

Our time with Ray was over. We felt especially grateful for what he had shared with us. Both his message and his demeanor radiated goodwill. Although the evening brought Chicago's famous chill winds along with swirling snow flurries, our hearts were warm.

Hawaii

December 18, 2003, Thursday
Rita Medina
Ka'anapali, Maui, Hawaii

The swiftness with which we flew from wintry Chicago only accentuates the warm beauty of Maui's sunny shores. Mountains, waterfalls, palm trees, warm sand, and beautiful surf would enchant at any time of the year, but uniquely so in mid-December! It was especially nice to have Ann and Rachel with us for this part of our journey, and we enjoyed a wonderful time together as a family. Everywhere we went during our stay, we were impressed by the warm, friendly spirit of our Hawaiian hosts.

One afternoon, Pat and I set out with the specific intention of finding someone to interview, but even

Sunny beach in Maui

Trip Nine

before leaving the grounds of our lodging, we met Rita Medina. She had classic Hawaiian good looks and the relaxed confidence of one who likes herself and others. Her mother was born in Hawaii; Rita was born in California and has lived in Hawaii since 1975. We were immediately aware of, and touched by, her personal warmth and kindhearted spirit. She spoke softly, always with a pleasant tone of voice. When we explained our nationwide search for goodwill, Rita reacted with sweet encouragement, and she consented immediately to an interview.

When Pat begins with, "What is your favorite place in Hawaii?" Rita responds with a sweet smile and says, "Oheo Gulch. It's in the town of Hana, and it has a lot of history for the island of Maui and the state. It also has a lot of mana, or spirit. I got chicken skin [goose bumps] almost, just being there. It is one of the last places of the real natural beauty of Hawaii; it is still pristine and untouched." Rita's genuine warmth and sincerity makes us eager to visit the Oheo Gulch.

Although our interview takes place in Ka'anapali, Rita explains that she lives nearby in the historic whaling village of Lahaina. "Lahaina is internationally known and everyone wants to go for a visit; I get to be here!" Instead of complaining about crowds of tourists, Rita celebrates being able to live year-round in a beautiful place so many are only able to visit—often only once.

Pat asks, "Who is the best person you know?"

Rita pauses and says, "That would be really, really hard for me to name just one." We let her know that we think that is a great situation in which to find herself. She goes on to explain, "There is a handful of individuals who have made a deep mark on my life."

Pat's provocative question of, "Which person, living or dead, would you most like to meet?" generates an, "Of course, Jesus Christ. That's how I feel," from Rita.

Asked if she has a goal which she still hopes to achieve, Rita gives us a radiant smile and says, "I have many. Whether they are all reachable is still in question. I try to live my life day-by-day, and I want to be the best person I can be."

"What is the best thing that has happened in your life?" Pat asks.

Rita replies, "Sticking with the church through the thick and thin all through my life. Those spiritual values have helped." Again, we are struck by the openness and goodness of the wonderful people we meet in such a random fashion and how swiftly they trust us enough to tell us such personal truths.

She says the best decision she has made is a very simple one: "Remaining humble." Such a short, sweet, and powerful response! We love her spirit.

Pat and Rita Medina

Asked what she would choose to do if given an opportunity to begin a new career, Rita responds, "It would probably be something that would expose me more to serving people. One of the gifts I think God has given me is to console people. I do that well, and would like to do more."

Besides sharing the goodwill that is within her, Rita further aided our quest by volunteering the name of another person for us to seek out and interview. We were happy to follow Rita's good advice.

Sweet Rita leaves us with: "Remember to be good to one another. It's simple to say, hard to remember to do!"

We present Rita with the ten-dollar envelope for spreading goodwill, and ask for a photograph. With a friendly smile, she immediately moves to Pat's side. This is a person we felt fortunate to have met.

December 19, 2003, Friday
Cheryl Thompson
Ka'anapali at Maui, Hawaii

Cheryl has lived on Maui for two-and-one-half years, and actually resides in the town of Kihei, on Maui's southwest shore. Pat begins our interview by asking, "What is your favorite place in Hawaii?" Cheryl replies, "The Sheraton Moana in Honolulu. We have so many wonderful memories of being there. There is a beautiful banyan tree in the back court-yard, facing the beach and ocean. It's like a lovely Hawaiian plantation home."

With a happy smile, Cheryl tells us about Kehei. "The beaches are so beautiful! There also seems to be a more natural feeling there; it's not quite as landscaped as the resort areas."

Next Pat asks, "Of all the people you know, is there one who stands out for consistently doing good things?" Cheryl beams as she says, "I am grateful to know a lot of people who have done good things that have had a world-wide impact. I especially admire Dr. Francis Schaffer and his teachings on Christianity, and particularly his emphasis on selflessness."

Cheryl clearly admires those who teach—living or dead. "Right now, if I had the opportunity, I would like to meet the Apostle Paul," she says. "I'd have all sorts of questions!"

Cheryl responds right away to the question about her best decision by saying, "Well, it was absolutely to accept Jesus Christ as my Lord and Savior. Nothing else has impacted my life that much."

Asked if she has a goal which she still hopes to achieve, Cheryl says, "My husband and I both have a great desire to reach the Third World peoples with the Gospel. We are active in our church's efforts, and we hope in the future

Cheryl Thompson

Hawaii (with a touch of Illinois)

to do some mission trips. One of our more immediate goals is just to be able to demonstrate Christ in our lives." One cannot help being impressed by the profoundly positive impact which religious faith continues to have in so many lives. We are finding the goodness inspired by faith is palpable and widespread.

Pat then asks, "What is the best thing that has happened in your life?" Cheryl laughs lightly and says, "I've had so many good things happen!" She isn't boasting; her tone suggests a sense of gratefulness. She continues, "I think it has been a combination of good things. I've had opportunities to travel the world, and meet people all over the world. It has been especially good to meet so many women who are having a positive impact." This is good news and we are glad to hear it.

> The $10 was given to Family Services (on Maui) for their food bank. Thank you!
>
> Cheryl Thompson

Queried about her choice if given an opportunity to begin a new career, Cheryl says confidently, "I'd go back to my time in mission work."

Her message of encouragement is good: "There is hope! There is truth! Take the time to seek it."

We present Cheryl with ten dollars for spreading a little goodwill. Looking through the viewfinder to take her photograph, we see a professional businesswoman from Cincinnati, Ohio, who finds herself living in Maui, Hawaii. In our brief time together, we have been the joyful recipients of her abundant gentleness and her pervasive kindness.

Both she and Rita have been wonderful interviews; their open *mana* (spirit) has added immeasurably to our enjoyment of Maui's sweet sea air, lush, verdant foliage, and warm December sunshine. We laugh as we cruise along the parkway near our beach; there is Santa Claus in shorts standing beside a sleigh drawn by dolphins instead of reindeer! Merry Christmas 2003!

Throughout our travels we wondered: Were people responding to the two of us; to the idea of a fifty-state tour; or to a one-year, essentially random search for goodwill? Perhaps it was a blending of all three? Whatever the answer may be, we were thrilled to have been received with such joy, friendliness, openness, and trust. Remarkably, no one treated us with impassivity, aloofness, or indifference.

INDIANA, ILLINOIS, MISSOURI & ARKANSAS

Indiana

January 14, 2004, Wednesday
Martha Seal
The University of Evansville
Evansville, Indiana

The new year had begun. After tidying up family, home, and business obligations, we set out around midday for a driving loop through Indiana, Illinois, Missouri, and Arkansas. We decided to examine the University of Evansville and drove through the campus. The shapes of several distinctive buildings drew us and on our second loop through the main drive, we found a spot to park and ventured in. As we crossed the campus, every student and faculty member we met (with only one exception) made eye contact and spoke to us. The unique architecture of one building in particular caught our attention and we went in. It houses the office of University Relations, and there we met Martha Seal. We explained our quest and she jovially agreed to being interviewed.

Pat asks, "What is your favorite place in Indiana?" Martha replies, "Well, I especially enjoy Evansville. I was born about sixty miles north of here in Washington, Indiana, a small-town county seat, and I moved to Evansville thirteen years ago." Pat then asks, "What is the best thing about Evansville?" Martha says, "For me, at this point in my life, it's a safe, friendly community. We have two universities, and there are educational opportunities for everyone. Anyone, of any age, can take classes. We have beautiful parks, a wonderful fitness center. It all makes for a very nice lifestyle."

Pat segues into nice people—and who Martha admires for doing good things.

Martha smiles easily and tells us, "I would say, for doing good and the right things, my mom, Alice Jean Pridemore, would stand out. She would choose the most difficult right thing rather than the easy wrong thing!" A fitting compliment for a sterling example.

Martha Seal

Martha selects Dwight Eisenhower as someone she'd like to meet. "He was president when I was born. He went to West Point, and my son graduated from West Point. In World War II and in politics, he showed true leadership. He'd be really interesting to talk to."

Pat asks, "What is the best thing that has happened in your life?" Martha thinks for a few moments, then tells us, "I had a life-changing experience when I was asked to do admission interviews for West Point [the U.S. Military Academy]. I was given the opportunity to really meet lots of interesting, intelligent, caring young Americans interested in servant leadership. Plus, I was able to meet a lot of terrific people at West Point."

When asked if she has a goal which she still hopes to achieve, Martha responds, "I do. I am currently enrolled in a master's program here at the university. More important, I want to enjoy more of life as I grow older. I want to travel and I want to see my two children and my grandchildren more often." Martha says,

"My best decision was deciding that I would have children; that I would really take care of them, love them, and nurture them."

Martha gives us her thoughts about a new career. "I really do enjoy working at the university!" she says. "If I chose something new, I would still want to serve young people somehow. That's our future . . . if we can help, we should!"

Her words of advice reflect her commitment to the young. "I would say, for anyone that's young, finish your education and experience the world before you set up housekeeping and take on too many obligations." With a friendly laugh she adds, "It's hard to give advice to young people when they know everything!"

We said good-bye to Martha and strolled back across campus. In the main administration building, we saw engraved in stone along the central hallway, "Whatsoever things are true, whatsoever things are honest, whatsoever things are just, whatsoever things are pure, lovely, and of good report—think on these things." Great positive direction for everyone, young and old alike.

Night was falling as we roamed northward; we were drawn to the town of Vincennes, Indiana, by its name. We had heard of it through the years but never visited before. We stopped to rest for the night, grateful for our safe journey.

I took a friend who is going through a nasty divorce to breakfast. . . . The breakfast was good, the company was good, and fears and challenges were discussed. She and I both felt better. Thanks!

Martha Seal

January 15, 2004, Thursday
Leo Finnerty
Vincennes, Indiana

It was a cold winter morning as we explored the old downtown area in Vincennes. A historical marker informed us that the town was named for its French founder, the Sieur de Vincennes, who arrived in the early 1700s, and was later

Indiana, Illinois, Missouri & Arkansas

burned at the stake by Chickasaw Indians in Fulton, Tennessee. Just beside the Wabash River Bridge, we spied a monument honoring the memory of George Rogers Clark. He's one of those American heroes you know you've heard of but can't quite remember what he did to become famous. An adjacent museum was warm and inviting, as was Leo Finnerty, the park ranger staffing the museum.

Leo recounts that, during the Revolutionary War, George Rogers Clark ventured to Williamsburg, Virginia, and persuaded Governor Patrick Henry to approve a secret plan to raise an army and launch a surprise winter attack against three key British forts in what are now parts of southern Indiana and Illinois. The twenty-six-year-old Clark raised an army of about 150 men, trained them himself, and led them through the icy waters of the Wabash River to gain a complete surprise and a great strategic victory over the British.

Clark was so very young to have conceived and executed such an audacious plan, and we found it awe-inspiring to hear Leo's fine recounting of Clark's bravery and the resultant heroic event in our nation's history. The story of this forefather's grit and goodwill is worth preserving and repeating. We also learned from Leo that George Rogers Clark was the brother of the much-celebrated William Clark, who helped lead the Lewis and Clark expedition to the Pacific Ocean and back in 1804.

Leo Finnerty

As there still are no other visitors to the museum, we think Leo may have time to be interviewed.

Leo is originally from Washington, D.C., and is married to a native of Vincennes and has lived here for twelve years. Leo says, "Vincennes is my favorite place in Indiana! It is the most historical place in Indiana. Living here has helped me realize my appreciation of American history. History is all around here: William Henry Harrison, George Rogers Clark, and even prehistoric Indians."

Pat asks, "Who is the best person you know?"

"That would be my wife," Leo says. "She is always helping people. She sings at three churches. She helps out at Pet Port [the local animal shelter]." With a big smile, Leo adds, "She's pretty amazing!"

Our question about who he'd like to meet generates this response from Leo: "The obvious choice is Jesus Christ. That would be the ultimate."

Leo then tells us that his best decision was, "Getting married to Nanette Grumieaux. When I met her, I met my soul mate."

Pat asks, "Do you have a goal you still hope to achieve?" Leo responds, "Well, I have lots. I guess if I narrow it down, I would like to go to Alaska. Not as a Park Service employee, just go on my own. I'd like to go while it's still unspoiled." We tell Leo we will go there at some point in our quest.

Next Pat asks, "What is the best thing that has happened in your life?" Leo jovially says, "Being born! I've been given a chance to do something with my life!" We feel, again, a surge of gratitude at having found our way to such a positive person so full of goodwill.

Dear Sirs:

It was great to be a part of your worthwhile mission. . . . I thought long and hard about the distribution of the $10. It ran the gamut of returning it to you so you could more easily continue your journey, to taking my nephew to a tennis lesson, to taking my wife to lunch, to giving it to the very poor newspaper delivery guy, and finally to including it with a card to a poor old lady here in Vincennes who has health and money problems aplenty. I sent it anonymously with a note of good cheer.

Leo Finnerty

Asked what his choice would be if given an opportunity to begin a new career, Leo tells us, "Well, I've had twenty-three different jobs, and I keep coming back to being a park ranger. I've resigned twice from the Park Service, but I must say I enjoy this work. If I were thinking of other paths, I'd choose something closer to the natural resources field, doing something to help wildlife."

Leo's message of encouragement comes from personal experience. "Keep an optimistic attitude! We have so much that we take for granted. Count your blessings at the start of

Indiana, Illinois, Missouri & Arkansas

each day—you'll be in a better mood. I've been poor, and I've had jobs . . . neither set my happiness. Stay optimistic. It helps me."

After saying good-bye to our new friend, we headed back out into the sunny, January cold. The memory of the crisp air, Leo's friendliness, and the heroism of George Rogers Clark still lingers in our minds.

Illinois

January 15, 2004, Thursday
Juanita Evans
Case-Halstead Public Library
Carlyle, Illinois

We crossed the Wabash River into Illinois and roamed across old Highway 50, past beautiful heartland farms, woods, and ice-speckled fields. Above us, the sky was a vivid winter blue with only an occasional stark white vapor trail left by a passing jet. Our spirits soared like the jet, as we drank in the lovely countryside and spoke of our great freedom and good fortune.

Just west of Interstate 57, we came upon signs for the Carlyle Dam and Lake. We had never heard of either one, so we explored. The dam was built in 1961, and the marker told us Carlyle Lake is the largest in Illinois. We have had fun with this fact ever since, as most people think of Lake Michigan as the largest lake in Illinois.

A little west of the lake, we came to the classic small town of Carlyle, with its quiet streets and neat homes. The Case-Halstead Public Library is housed in what was once someone's home. It looked inviting, so we unloaded and went inside, where we met the delightful, cheerful, and friendly Juanita Evans. We sat together at a nice reading table in a cozy front corner of the library.

Pat begins, "What is your favorite place in Illinois?" Juanita laughs and says, "Goodness! Just around here. I'm just happy to be here at home. We have covered all of central and southern Illinois; all the parks are beautiful. I've been here forty-seven years and I really like it here!" She is not ambivalent; she is certain. And we are glad to hear the lilt in her laugh and in her voice as she speaks so fondly of her home.

"I think the best thing about Carlyle is mostly that it's such a safe little community where people are friendly; you know everybody by their first name." She gives an easy wave of her hand, taking in the varied collection of people sharing the library with us, and adds, "They all have a library card, but we know them." What a positive compliment to the closeness of her community, and what an inclusive wave of her hand.

Pat then asks, "Who is the best person you know?"

Another happy laugh rolls out as Juanita tells us, "There's more than one! There's my dear family, the good people in my church, and I couldn't have a better boss than the one I've got!"

Pat follows up by asking Juanita who she would most like to meet.

"Well, I hope someday to meet God," she says. "I'd also like to see my mom and dad again."

Pat then asks our next "best" question: "What is the best decision you have made?" Juanita

Juanita Evans

repeats her sweet laugh as she replies, "Marrying my husband, Dwight, fifty-two years ago! His nickname is 'Spike' 'cause his dad was a carpenter, and as a little boy in overalls, Dwight carried a spike nail around with him everywhere he went." She laughs again with us at the mental picture she has painted.

"The best thing that has happened to me is having our two children, five grandchildren, and three great-grandchildren. Our son lives here, and our daughter lives in Grand Island, Nebraska." The look of love shines in Juanita's eyes as she

Indiana, Illinois, Missouri & Arkansas

speaks of her family. We hope her children know how much their lives matter in hers. Juanita says, "I'm going to be seventy next month—I'd like to spend more time with my family and stay healthy."

When Pat asks, "If you had an opportunity to begin a new career, what would you choose to do?" Juanita gives another happy laugh and says, "Goodness! I hope this is my last job! When I was young, my first thought was nursing. And I always thought being a stewardess on an airplane would be a great adventure."

Juanita's message of encouragement reflects Psalm 37. She says, "Trust in the Lord, and try to do His will."

When we explain and present the spread-some-goodwill envelope, Juanita removes the ten-dollar bill and says, "Save your envelope and stamp! I can tell you right now, I'm going to use it to make a gift towards our food pantry at church. It's for anybody in need of help. If you walk up there now, they'd give you some food."

Ka-boom! Neighbors, not under any compulsion to do good, voluntarily providing food for anybody in need of help. That is goodwill. We want you to know about it because we want you not to grow weary or become weighed down by negative news. There is goodwill all around you. Seek it. Share it.

We left the busy little library and loaded the car. In the afternoon sunshine, the little town's courthouse square and quiet Main Street looked almost like a classic Norman Rockwell painting. As if on cue, a nearby church's bell tower serenaded us with "America the Beautiful." It was another special moment we wish we had captured on film.

January 15, 2004, Thursday
Travel Thoughts

From lovely little Carlyle, Illinois, we wandered west on old Highway 50, then took I-255 around St. Louis with her beautiful Gateway Arch gracing the city skyline. Crossing the mighty Mississippi River, we could not help talking about

Tom Sawyer and Huckleberry Finn and feeling like, "Two drifters off to see the world. There's such a lot of world to see" (from Johnny Mercer's great song "Moon River"). We reminded ourselves of our great good fortune to be making this exciting journey.

Without a specific plan, we headed southwest across Missouri on I-44, enjoying the landscape's similarity to that of middle Tennessee: limestone bluffs along the highway, rolling rural farmland, large sections of trees and woods, and small businesses of every kind. The great American spirit of free enterprise and industriousness displayed itself for us all along the way. The radio news reported that at the top of Mount Washington, New Hampshire (which we saw back in October), the temperature was thirty-five degrees below zero, with a wind chill of eighty-two degrees below zero!

We found our way to Springfield for the night, not having felt drawn to any particular interview spot. At dinner, we talked about being in the second half of this fabulous experience. We marveled at the size and astonishing beauty of our nation and its soul. We enjoyed recalling the contrasts and similarities we had already observed, from Mobile, Alabama to Missoula, Montana; Okolona, Mississippi to New York City; and from Acadia National Park, Maine to Kapalua Bay, Hawaii.

We delighted in recalling the new friends we made, along with their smiles and encouraging words. We have been given a strong feeling of brotherhood, or kinship, by our sisters and brothers across this beautiful land. Our experiences in the first half were so remarkably uplifting that we now felt a growing sense of joyful anticipation. We were about to see never-before-seen (by us) sights and to meet new, fascinating, good people.

We experienced great joy at how easily we traveled vast distances, with no pass required, and on such good roads. They took us anywhere and everywhere.

We felt immense gratitude at being physically able to do it. Pat's strength and determination combined with his spirit of adventure make him a great traveler. Pat especially enjoyed New York City, Chicago, Idaho, and Montana. He recalled so much, and wanted to remember every single place, person,

Indiana, Illinois, Missouri & Arkansas

and event. On every return home, he always told Scott, "Thank you for the great trip." Diligently seek the abundant goodwill waiting everywhere—friends, it's out there.

Missouri

January 16, 2004, Friday
Rhonda McKelvey
Walnut Shade, Missouri

Southwest of Springfield, Missouri, we visited the Wilson's Creek Battlefield National Park and were reminded of the horrific struggles our Civil War wrought. How blessed we have been to live peaceably with each other for such a long time.

We drove south to see what—or who—we might find in Branson. It was decidedly strange to drive through such a built-up, heavily-developed place at a time of year when almost no visitors are there. The putt-putt courses, wax museums, theaters, eateries, and lodgings were all quiet and mostly empty. The town was not run-down or abandoned; we simply came to see it on a rainy day during the off-season.

From Branson, we headed north and east to follow Highway 160 across Missouri's southern edge. We wound through wooded rural countryside, and as we rounded a sweeping curve in the road, we saw a marker announcing the boundary of the Walnut Shade community. We like those lovely place names; our antennae went up. Just around another bend, we spied a small building and a sign which said, "DOGS DAY INN—Boarding & Grooming."

We pulled into the empty parking lot. We entered the building with a slight sense of uncertainty, because we were so far back in the country. We did not want to frighten (or be turned down by) the person we were about to meet. Our concern evaporated as soon as we introduced ourselves to the owner and sole employee, Rhonda McKelvey. She was friendly and made us feel welcome and at ease amidst a pet menagerie.

In the back of our minds was the thrilling thought that we had crossed the entire state of Missouri looking for goodwill, and in this remote, unique spot we not only found it, we were welcomed with such warmth that our arrival here somehow seemed to have been expected!

Pat begins by asking some questions about Rhonda's home state.

Rhonda is very direct and self-assured as she responds by saying, "This is the best place in the state. I wouldn't move from right here. I love these trees. My mom is living in New Mexico, which has lots of desert and red rock [but] I really like these trees." We will remember Walnut Shade and Rhonda's fondness for its foliage. She continues, "I grew up everywhere—my dad's work moved us all over. I was born in Sioux City, Iowa, and I went to thirty-three schools in twelve years! Right here suits me just fine. The best decision I made was staying in this area. This is where we stopped. The people here are so nice; everybody helps everybody."

Pat then says, "What is the best thing about Walnut Shade?"

Rhonda gives a quick laugh and says, "Well, it's not Branson. . . . Really, it's nice to have it close by—and we get the quiet country life."

Rhonda McKelvey

When Pat asks, "Who is the best person you know?" Rhonda ponders for just a few moments and says, "My brother. He just does good things for anybody and everybody. He's a full-time firefighter over in Branson, but I think he works harder when he's off—helping others—than when he's at work!" What a nice thing for a sibling to say!

Rhonda has goals she'd like to achieve. "I want to build some horse stables right next door and set up a horse farm. I'd like to raise Appaloosas and offer trail riding to folks visiting or living in the area."

We enjoy this independent woman, living in such a remote area, yet possessed with such enterprising spirit. Our country is strong because of the Rhondas everywhere!

Rhonda says, "I've had a lot of good things happen to me. The best would be getting to start my own business about one year ago; not having to clock in." This is not said with any hint of laziness or sloth but with genuine gratitude for having her own business—even if it means always being on the clock and on duty.

Pat then asks, "If you had an opportunity to begin a new career, what would you choose to do?" After deliberating a bit, Rhonda announces, "I don't think I would do anything different! I love animals and I like this work." This good news thoroughly contradicts frequent news reports suggesting Americans are unhappy in their work.

Rhonda encourages others to discover what they love. "Take chances. I took a chance and quit a good job to open this business . . . and I love it."

Rhonda brings out a lovely Irish Setter to join in her photograph. We wish her great success in her business endeavors.

January 16, 2004, Friday
Mike Womack
Forsyth, Missouri

East of Walnut Shade, we traversed a classic ridge road across southern Missouri hills, around well-treed curves, and came upon the small town of Forsyth. We saw a relatively new municipal building on our left. Inside, we asked for the mayor or the chief of police. The mayor was out, but the big, friendly chief, Mike Womack, invited us right in to his sunny, neat office.

Mike tells us about his town. "I really like the Forsyth area; there are so many recreational opportunities. The lakes around here are beautiful. The best thing is the small-town atmosphere. We have about sixteen hundred folks here. There's not the big city pace."

When Pat asks, "Who is the best person you know?" Mike says, "Wow. There are so many good people in this town—everyone works together." Mike continues, "I'd say Margie Berry is one of the best. She was behind starting the local Boys & Girls Club. She is a great encouragement here."

Mike thinks hard about who he would most like to meet. "I would like to meet General Eisenhower. I was in the Army for eight years, and I enjoyed Army life. General Eisenhower served this country in dire times."

Mike laughs softly when Pat asks about his best decision. "If my wife was here, I'd say marrying her!" He pauses. "That's tough. I'd say moving from Illinois to this area. I was in a large county sheriff's office for several years. It was the rat race, so we left and came here. We have a great life here—the small town, great fishing, good friends."

Mike returns to his marriage when asked about the best thing that has happened in his life. "I have a very good wife. She's very supportive and backs me up always." Another loving spouse!

Asked if he has a goal he still hopes to achieve, Mike laughs. "To hopefully hit the lottery." Then more seriously, he says, "No, really, I'd like to retire young enough to still enjoy a quality of life. I have been in law enforcement for twenty-six years, and I'd like to be situated so that if I wake up and want to go fishing, I could!"

Mike Womack

Following up, Pat inquires, "If you had an opportunity to begin a new career, what would you choose to do?"

Mike says, "I don't know if I'd change my career at all! I feel like I'm able to do a lot of good for the community in this job. Do I stop crime? Some of it is stop-gap. But the job is not just arrests. I am able to direct people to find help. I'm able to do lots of community service, especially in such a small town. You know who's having hard times, and you can get 'em help. I'm also able to have a real rapport with local kids who are now adults."

Indiana, Illinois, Missouri & Arkansas

Mike's sincere expression of fondness for his work in public service inspires us. We feel certain the people of Forsyth are glad to have Mike for a neighbor and for a police chief.

Here are Mike's words of advice for you: "Make the best of your life. Be everything you can be. Strive to better yourself."

As we turned to leave, we saw a framed black-and-white photograph on the wall near the door. In the photo, a very young Mike Womack is in a hospital bed in Vietnam. Then-commanding General Creighton Abrams is presenting Mike with the Purple Heart.

We told Mike how much we appreciated his service to our country. This is the real America . . . a man who loves his wife dearly, who knows who's having hard times in his community and gets them some help, who enjoys his friends, and who would like to do more fishing. A man who, in his youth, shed his blood on a hilltop artillery battery in a distant land but doesn't even make mention of that sacrifice during our interview. Awesome.

We wandered eastward on Highway 160 for a bit, then turned south toward Arkansas on Highway 125. This freedom to explore is so wonderful! We passed Protem and Pell, and found a free ferry which would take us across Bull Shoals into northern Arkansas.

We waited alone on the ferry ramp. It was rainy, and the serenity of the water and the woods entranced us. The only sound was the faraway purr of the empty ferry boat's motor as it crossed the water to fetch us. We spoke of the gray light, brown woods, and silver-green water; of the unusual beauty of that spot, in that moment. We thought with gratitude about how few have ever come this winding way and met such a fascinating collection of new friends in such a short span of time.

Northern Arkansas gave us long stretches of country roads (some neat, some not) and great place names like Yellville, Flippin, Mountain Home, and Cherokee Village. The communities generally varied in size from five hundred to thirteen hundred in population.

We stopped for dinner at a friendly outpost in Ravenden, where we were the only guests in the place who did not know everyone else. A little girl came in with her parents and went directly to a nearby table to say hello to her schoolteacher. At the table next to ours, a volunteer fireman was called away just as his dinner was served. He returned before we left, and a fresh meal was prepared for him. There was a great warmth and feeling of community in this small place. We were treated with goodwill, but found no convenient opening for an interview. We drove on to Jonesboro to rest for the night.

Arkansas

January 17, 2004, Saturday
Dr. Bruce Jones
Jonesboro, Arkansas

A peaceful, gentle rain nourished the earth overnight, and at breakfast we met Dr. Bruce Jones, a local general surgeon who cheerfully agreed to being interviewed.

Pat asks, "What is your favorite place in the state of Arkansas?" Bruce laughs and says, "Let's see. I'm still a transplant; been here since 1984. The places I really love are in Tennessee and Kentucky. My favorite place here would be my Arkansas hill land, about one hour from here on the edge of the Ozarks— near Imboden."

Bruce adds, "Jonesboro has a lot of friendly people, and good people. There is a good diversity of strong, active churches. This is a good place."

Pat and Dr. Bruce Jones

After emphasizing that he knows "a lot of good people," Bruce tells us, "The very best person I know would be my mom, Betty Jones. She always wants to do what's right, and she really, really wants to try to not do wrong.

"In Arkansas, I would point to our governor, Mike Huckabee. He was a Baptist minister before he ran for office. He is a moral man and he is really trying to lead on a moral basis even though it sometimes gets him in trouble."

Pat asks who Bruce would most like to meet, and Bruce answers, "Jesus Christ."

Bruce contemplates his best decision for a moment, and replies, "It's kind of an ongoing decision—to try to live my life in accordance with godly principles."

Bruce says two of the best things to happen to him were getting into Vanderbilt University Medical School, and being born into his family.

Next, Pat inquires, "If you had a chance to begin a new career, what would you choose to do?"

Bruce doesn't hesitate for a moment and immediately says, "Unless you told me I couldn't do what I do now, this is what I'd do. I love it! I want to continue to be facile and competent in surgery until it's time for me to retire." We are so glad to meet yet another American who loves his work.

Bruce's message of encouragement has several parts: "Believe in Jesus, and work hard." There is a brief pause then he adds, "And make the choice to be happy!"

After a photo and delivery of the spread-some-goodwill ten-dollar bill, we moved on to the south and east.

Dear Scott & Pat,

Gave your $10 to the NEA Clinic Foundation Medical Assistance Program. Hundreds of patients (both from our clinic and the competition) get their meds free through this program.

With kindest regards to all your family,

Bruce Jones

January 17, 2004, Saturday
Paul Miller
Marked Tree, Arkansas

About halfway between Jonesboro and West Memphis, we stopped for fuel in Marked Tree. Intrigued by the town's name, we rode around a little bit, then spotted a John Deere

Trip Ten

Equipment dealership. The parts counter was open for business, manned by a very cordial Paul Miller.

Paul seems genuinely flattered when we ask if we might interview him. He is instantly friendly, polite, and self-effacing as he explains the origin of the town's name. (Three rivers are all in close proximity to the town; American Indians marked a tree to indicate the best spot to portage canoes from one river to another and thereby save several miles of paddling.)

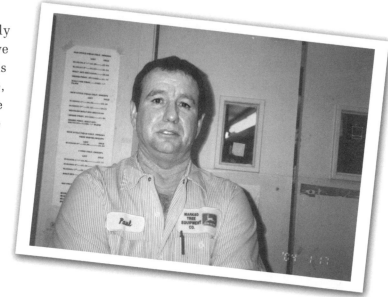

Paul Miller

Paul says his favorite place in Arkansas is up in the hills, "But I don't get to go very often. [And] I love the farm I grew up on—it's near Weona, due west of here."

Paul smiles and tells us why he likes Marked Tree. "I really like the farming people coming in here to buy parts and equipment. This is a small, quiet, farmers' town. We have a couple of factories, a grain elevator and a cotton gin, and two car dealers." He's not bragging, nor is he apologizing; he just tells it straight-out.

Paul ponders the next question—the one about the best person he knows—and says, "Well, I knew Bill Clinton pretty good . . . cooked fish for him when he was governor. But, I'd say the best person I know is my sister, Nina Hazel. She helped me through a tough divorce, helped keep the bills paid, and got me this job. She's pretty special."

There is no trace of self-pity in Paul's voice or face as he tells us who he'd like to meet. "I would really like to see my mother again. She died when I was ten years old. I'm fifty-two now. I've got some brothers and sisters that don't really remember her. There were six boys and two girls. My dad raised us. He died in 1981." His modesty and his quiet inner strength are especially impressive.

Indiana, Illinois, Missouri & Arkansas

Pat asks, "What is the best decision you have made?"

Paul responds with his decision to join the Army in 1967. "I served in Vietnam. I was in the U.S. Army, 82nd Airborne Division, out of Fort Bragg, North Carolina. I got out in 1973. One of my brothers was a door-gunner on a helicopter." We tell him that we are grateful for his willingness to serve.

Asked if he has a goal he still hopes to achieve, Paul smiles easily and says, "It's getting a little late for setting goals now . . . I'd like to see all my kids grow up, and be able to see my grandkids."

Then Pat asks, "What is the best thing that has happened in your life?"

Paul does not hesitate. "I had a terrible ordeal in 1991. I had some sort of chemical poison and almost died," he says. "I prayed to the Lord to pull me through, and then I just felt so much better, all at once. It was a miracle to me!" Paul's matter-of-fact retelling of the remarkable event lends sufficient drama.

Paul says if he could choose a new career, he'd be into computers. "I also like farming. I worked on the farm I was raised on 'til 2002."

Paul ends the interview with these encouraging words: "Have a goal. Set it and go to it! You can do it! When I went in the service, there was a lot of stuff I thought I couldn't do . . . but I did it!"

As we snap a photo and present him with the ten-dollar spread-some-good-will envelope, we ask how the equipment and parts business is doing.

Paul tells us, "The farmers have had good soybean, corn, and rice crops this year, and they are spending that money on new equipment. When things flourish in one place, they flourish in others." This heartland insight encourages us about the strength of our national economy.

> Dear Sirs,
>
> We have a young man that comes into our store almost every morning. He's unemployed and has two little girls. He has very little income. I gave him the money.
>
> Enjoyed talking with you,
> Paul O. Miller

Still more encouraging to contemplate is the abundance of goodwill we have found in the hearts of a college development officer, a park ranger, a librarian, a kennel owner, a police chief, a general surgeon, and a farm equipment partsman during this heartland swing.

Trip Ten

TRIP ELEVEN

GEORGIA &
SOUTH CAROLINA

Georgia

February 3, 2004, Tuesday

We left Nashville about thirty minutes before noon, with our eyes set on Georgia and South Carolina. Beyond Chattanooga, we jumped off into previously unexplored north Georgia via State Route 53 East, passing Fairmount, Marblehill, and Lake Lanier. Then U.S. Route 129 took us through Candler, Talmo, Arcade, and on to Athens and the campus of the University of Georgia.

All along the winding way, we searched the countryside for an inviting interview opportunity. We toured the campus and the town both before and after dinner, but we did not find exactly the right setting or person.

February 4, 2004, Wednesday
Matt Sullo (SUE-loh)
Athens, Georgia

As we checked out of our hotel, the lobby was quiet and the young man handling the front desk greeted us with an appealing air of genuine cordiality. When he asked what brought us to Athens, we explained our nationwide search. We asked if it would be convenient for us to conduct an interview with him right on the spot, and he cheerfully agreed. Interestingly, during the course of the interview, we were only interrupted by a single telephone call to the front desk.

Pat begins by asking Matt about his favorite place in Georgia.

Matt replies with a smile, "My hometown, Peachtree City, Georgia, about twenty miles south of the Atlanta airport. It's a very different community than anywhere else. It's all well-planned and not jumbled up. It's very organized with nice golf cart paths, and it's not just residential. It's a beautifully planned community."

"The best thing about Athens is the diversity," Matt says. "The city is very diverse because of the university. You have thirty-five [thousand] to forty thousand students from all over the world, with different cultures, coming to a smaller town, and they really color it. There are so many different things and different people in this town, and everyone is real nice and respectful to each other."

Pat asks, "Who is the best person you know?"

Matt Sullo

Matt eagerly replies, "That's a good question! There's lots of 'em! My mom and dad. My brother, Mark. He went to Vanderbilt and into the U.S. Marine Corps. My sister, Jennifer, lives here too, and she kind of looks after me . . . keeps gas in the car and food in the belly."

We appreciate Matt's direct reply to our question about decisions he's made. "I wasn't very adamant about going straight to college after high school. I think deciding to go ahead and move forward was important for me."

After a little deliberation about his goals, Matt continues, "The first goal that comes to my mind is mainly stability. I'm twenty-three years old, have a business management degree, and I would like to continue down a good career path, have a home, family, savings, put kids through college. Things I never thought about in the past."

Asked about the best thing that has happened in his life, Matt is philosophical. "It may be life's lessons about ups and downs. My family has gone through good times and bad, and we got through them together. At one point we didn't have much, but we had each other." Matt's wonderful insights lead to Pat's next question.

Pat asks, "If you had an opportunity to begin a new career, what would you choose to do?" Matt gestures toward the hotel desk and lobby and says, "Hospitality is a good industry. I still have thoughts about going into the military, and I also think about trying law school. I know a lot of lawyers and they seem like caring people, not just in it for the money."

He also has a famous-person goal. Matt says he'd someday like to meet the president. "Whether I was a fan or not [of the individual]. I would just like to shake the hand of a U.S. president."

Matt's advice: "I tell a lot of people this. My mom wants me to plan ahead, but life is short and unexpected things happen. So, I always say, 'Live fast and die fun.' I say do that and still achieve your goals and morals and values."

Mr. Scott & Mr. Pat Price,

I'm writing this letter as you requested to let you know what it was that I decided to do with the $10 for something good.

First I thought I could donate it to a charity. Then I thought about buying food and treats for the local pound (I'm an animal lover). There were many other ideas that floated in and out of my head. I finally settled on something that I could not only do for "good," but also spread goodwill.

I went to the grocery store and bought things to make a simple sack lunch. I made peanut butter and jelly sandwiches, sliced carrots, and [put] a small bottle of water in brown lunch bags. I was able to make about ten total (if I remember correctly). Why I did this was quite easy. You see, Athens, though it is a small city, has a large number of homeless people. So I simply handed out lunch at a local homeless spot and told them of an addiction treatment center.

Nobody can change someone else; one can only guide. Doing this helped me more than them, I think.

Your friend in goodwill,

Matt

We left Matt with a ten dollar bill, wandered out of Athens on U.S. Highway 78, and drove through Winterville, Arnoldsville, and Diamond Hill. A sign for "Old Wildcat Bridge Road" made us laugh as we speculated upon how that road came to have such a name.

Georgia & South Carolina

February 4, 2004, Wednesday
Tina Hart
Franklin Springs, Georgia

Enjoying a ride in the country, we approached a small cluster of buildings with that distinctive academic look. We stopped to read a historic marker which informed us the town was named in honor of founding father Benjamin Franklin. The campus is that of Emmanuel College.

After a brief drive-through, we came back up a hill onto the main roadway, and saw a small florist shop across the way. The sign said, "Flowers from the Heart" and there was plenty of room to park. We looked at each other and Pat said, "Let's give it a try."

So, in we went. The owner, Tina Hart, welcomed us so graciously and warmly that we felt at home right away.

Tina Hart

The flower shop both looks and smells lovely. We learn that Tina has lived in the Franklin Springs area all her life, and that her home is nearby in Sandy Cross.

Tina seems completely relaxed and at ease talking to us, like we are old friends. She has a big friendly smile and tells us, "Sandy Cross is a farming area; a real small, family-oriented community. It's quiet. We go for walks or ride horses. It's really peaceful." The serene look on her face matches the place she has so lovingly described. "We also love Lake Hartwell, just twelve miles down the road. It's so close, and we love to ski and swim and camp."

Pat asks, "Who is the best person you know?" Still smiling, Tina responds, "I'd probably have to say my mom, Carol Brown. She never meets a stranger. We kid her a lot because anything she has, she tries to give to others. For instance, if you are around when she has to take some of her prescription medicine, she'll ask if you want some of it!" Tina continues, "She is light-hearted and always spreading joy. She worked for thirty-five years in a sewing plant, eight, nine, ten hours a day. You wouldn't know they were poor." Tina's profound respect and admiration for her mother is a joy to behold and we, too, appreciate Carol Brown's goodness.

When Pat asks, "Which person, living or dead, would you most like to meet?" Tina answers immediately, "The Lord, Jesus Christ. I can't wait to meet him! The best decision I've made is to serve the Lord. That is a daily adventure! It's a joy to serve Him and honor Him every day."

Pat asks, "Do you have a goal you still hope to achieve?"

Tina mulls this one briefly and says, "I have a fourteen-year-old son, Peyton. I'd like to see him become a man of the Lord and just serve the Lord."

Next, Pat asks, "What is the best thing that has happened in your life?"

"Probably, being able to have Peyton. We went seven years and didn't think we could have children. The Lord gave him to us." A beautiful expression of joy, gratitude, and love permeates Tina's face as she speaks of the gift of her son's life.

Tina says if she started a new career, it would "probably be something like counseling in the school system. You could be a good, godly influence in thousands of lives in the course of a lifetime."

Here is Tina's message of encouragement for you: "Stay true to the Lord. Be steadfast. Put your trust in Him, and He will take care of you."

> Scott & Pat,
>
> I had been contemplating the $10 . . . and . . . thought of many things to do with it. A few days ago, after I had been asking God to send someone that could really use it, I talked with one of my customers . . . [whose] husband had walked out on her on Christmas Eve. She has been battling cancer and has two girls. . . . the bank was in the process of foreclosing on their home and they were not going to have a place to live. A neighbor had taken them to a local food bank so as to have groceries in the house. I have given them the $10 along with some extra and included a note about you both and your travels.
>
> God's Blessings,
> Tina Hart

Georgia & South Carolina

Tina's personal faith resonated gently throughout, and she was especially kind to us all during our visit. Later, in an

April 2005 telephone conversation, Tina told us that she was going back to school in order to become qualified to do counseling in a local school, just as she had hoped. She was able to sell her flower shop in three days.

Before leaving, we had Tina wire some flowers to brighten up Rachel's dorm room. Tina also very generously gave us a gospel music CD she had recorded, and we enjoyed listening to her singing as we drove on over toward South Carolina.

South Carolina

February 4, 2004, Wednesday
Mary Alice Rawson
Pendleton, South Carolina

We headed toward Clemson University so Pat could see where his uncle, Jay Price, received his master's and PhD in chemistry. At a sign pointing toward Pendleton, South Carolina, in a flash Scott recalled a home movie his father made there years ago while Jay was in graduate school. We took the right-hand fork in the road and headed for Pendleton.

This spontaneous decision was a good one. The little town of Pendleton was particularly charming. Well-maintained and attractively decorated shops were arrayed around the central square. We cruised the square twice, looking intently for an interview prospect. The photographer's shop looked interesting—but he was standing on the sidewalk out front talking with a customer. We didn't want to interrupt.

We turned off the square, drove one block into a residential neighborhood, then saw a small sign announcing "Grandma's Antiques & Things." We pulled into a short driveway between the house and the garage, and by the time we unloaded Pat's chair, a sweet little old "grandma" had emerged from the house to greet us.

Mary Alice Rawson treated us like company rather than customers and happily showed us her sizable collection of books, glassware, jewelry, and small antique pieces. When she asked where we were from, we told her Nashville and explained our decision to visit every state in the nation looking for goodwill. We told her how thrilled we were to have found so many good people with so many good things to tell. Mary Alice graced us with a beautiful grandmotherly smile and said, "The world is a wonderful place."

Mary Alice says, "I think Pendleton is the most wonderful place of all [in South Carolina]. It's small, beautiful, and everyone is so friendly. We have a diversity of shops; we try not to be 'touristy' but to be genuinely interesting. I have lived here for twenty-four years. We moved here from Mount Vernon, Iowa; it's close to Cedar Rapids." She adds, "My second choice would be Charleston. It's nice to visit, very historic, and has lots of good seafood."

When Pat asks her to name the best person she knows, Mary Alice says, "Oh my! I have such a long list! All the people at the Pendleton United Methodist Church. You see, my husband flew the B-29 in India during World War II. Late in life, he was bedfast. The doctor told us maybe he might live two months. All of

Mary Alice Rawson

the men from our church helped . . . at least three came every single day, and they did everything to help us! They would turn him, feed him, dress him, stay with him so I could run the shop. Everything! Because of their help, my husband lived another seven months. Isn't that wonderful?" We could not agree more. That is goodwill in Pendleton, South Carolina.

Next, Pat asks, "Which person, living or dead, would you most like to meet?"

Without hesitating, Mary Alice says, "Of course, I want to meet Jesus Christ. I'm waiting for that."

"Oh my," is again Mary Alice's first response when Pat asks her about her best decision. She continues, "Sometimes I think it was marrying my husband, and sometimes I think it was moving to Pendleton."

Pat then asks, "Do you have a goal you still hope to achieve?" With a sweet laugh, Mary Alice tells us, "When you are eighty years old . . . I just hope that I am fulfilling God's purpose for my life. And, if I'm not yet, I hope I catch on pretty soon!" Mary Alice is a delight!

Pat inquires, "What is the best thing that has happened in your life?"

"The birth of my two sons," Mary Alice replies.

Mary Alice says a new career choice for her would be finishing her old one. "I was in nurse's training at the University of Illinois in my hometown of Champaign. I was within five months of finishing when my husband came home from serving in India in World War II. I stopped . . . I would go back and finish that," she says softly, with an unmistakable air of determination.

Mary Alice encourages all of us with these words: "Well, I have always thought, 'This, too, will pass.' No matter where you are in life, no matter what age you are, whatever is hard at the moment, just hang in there, persevere, things will get better. 'This, too, will pass.'"

We bid farewell to this vibrant, kind, and good-hearted woman. We felt deep gratitude for taking the right fork in the road, for venturing off the courthouse square, and for finding Mary Alice Rawson. We might have missed her so easily.

February 4, 2004, Wednesday
Everett Ernst III
Table Rock State Park, South Carolina

From Pendleton, we drove to nearby Clemson, toured the university, and bought new batteries for our trusty tape recorder. We had no particular route or destination in mind as we roamed northward on quiet back roads. We made a late afternoon rest stop at the attractive headquarters of Table Rock State Park. While there, we asked the ranger on duty about the origins of a beautiful piece of handmade furniture in front of the stone fireplace.

The ranger, Everett Ernst III, is young, friendly, courteous, and informative. So we explained our quest and asked to interview him.

Everett begins, "I was born in Texas, raised in Germany, and moved to Columbia in 1991. Some unkept promises brought me to Clemson, which worked out for the best. So, I'd say Columbia is my favorite place, because that's where my family is. I'm a military brat . . . lived all over. I want my kids to really know their family. My fiancé is from Columbia, too." Everett seems especially earnest about putting down family roots.

Pat dovetails with a question about what Everett likes about Table Rock.

"The scenery," the ranger replies. "The beauty you see every day! It's so calm and relaxing with the mountain and the lake. It's a great place to work."

Everett's deep love of family shines through his answers to most of Pat's questions, especially when talking about who he'd most like to meet. "I'd probably have to say either my mom's mom—she really loved boys, and I never got to meet her—or my dad's dad. He was a mechanic, always interested in machines, and I never got to meet him. I'd love to meet either one, or both of them."

Everett Ernst III

Next, Pat asks, "What is the best decision you have made?"

Everett gives a somewhat rueful smile and says, "In twenty-three years, there seem to be so few. It was probably to start running competitively. In middle school, I was always getting in trouble—even got kicked out of school. When I went to a new school, I joined the cross-country track team. My dad, Everett Ernst II, coached me for six years. I did well, and my grades improved. My dad is the best person I know. He is one of those guys who has a heart of gold. He is always there for folks. He's basically the ideal dad."

Everett has several goals he's working toward. "My short-term goal is to get married. Long-term, I hope to have my own park [as] a superintendent. There are two parks in Columbia; I'd like to run one of 'em." He pauses, and adds, "I'd like to make it to the Olympics one day and run the marathon. The only thing holding me down is me." Noble goals and mature insight.

Everett says while one of the best things he's experienced was, "When I won my third state title in high school cross-country," he's also "grateful to have small victories every day."

Asked what he would choose to do if given an opportunity to begin a new career, Everett says, "Auto restoration, without a doubt! I would love restoring classic cars, old muscle cars."

We are encouraged by Everett's determined spirit. He says, "Keep trying. What everybody else thinks doesn't matter, keep trying!"

> Mr. Price:
>
> . . . wanted to make sure that the $10 was in keeping with what I thought your wishes to be. The $10 went to a woman who has been divorced for nine months, with no help from her ex financially, with two of their three kids. She is working two jobs to make sure her kids do not go without, including softball, camping, and hiking . . . While talking to her, I could hear the frustration of trying to provide for her kids with limited money. So your $10 went to help her.
>
> Sincerely,
> Everett Ernst

The westward drive through the night was pleasant, as traffic was light, and we talked about the four delightful friends we found that day.

We reached Nashville at 11:48 that evening, and were happy about the day gone by.

TRIP TWELVE
COLORADO

February 12, 2004, Thursday
Joe Kusumoto
Breckenridge, Colorado

Deep, soft, powdery snow covered every single thing around us, including the spectacular mountains and the massive trees. It covered us as well, as it steadily and softly continued to place a fresh layer of cool, white icing on the little ski village at Breckenridge. Pat had been invited to join a small group of young Tennesseans, all of whom live with the unique challenges of spina bifida, to participate in the adaptive ski program at the Breckenridge Outdoor Education Center. Several of our U.S. Paralympic athletes have trained here, and it was easy to see why: the natural setting could not be any more inspiring, and the BOEC instructors and facilities were absolutely first-class.

Pat and the others began their instruction early Wednesday morning, then each loaded into a molded seat affixed atop a ski. On each forearm, they wore a ski pole with a tiny, flexible ski at the bottom. These outrigger skis helped them maintain balance as they skied down the mountain with two terrific coaches.

For Scott, getting to see Pat ski was one of the most thrilling adventures in this year of travel filled with wonderful

That's Pat driving a dogsled in Colorado

experiences. Pat's great upper body strength allowed him to quickly adapt to the challenge of seated skiing, and he steadily moved higher up the mountain. He was also very fortunate to have been paired with one of the most able and encouraging coaches, Joe Kusumoto. An expert skier, Joe possesses a patient and encouraging spirit, which makes him a wonderful teacher. He and Pat easily became friends, and after he and Pat skied together all day Wednesday and Thursday, Joe agreed to sit down and be interviewed for this book.

Pat begins by asking, "What is your favorite place in the state of Colorado?"

Joe ponders for a moment and answers, "Probably out by my cabin, just north of town. I live in an old mining town called Tiger, population: five." We all laugh together at the town's size. The challenging terrain and climate help bring out more readily the joy within us. It seems that we all have a brighter outlook when we have confronted one of life's new challenges.

"What is the best thing about Tiger?" Pat asks Joe.

The reply: "It's been my home for a while, and there are just a few folks there, so you can enjoy quiet, simple living." There is a precise clarity in Joe's words that lingers in the cold air. He has not chosen the ski-bum, nightclub, jet-set life. Instead, he uses his considerable talent daily to teach and inspire many young people on the slopes. (When Scott dropped by the BOEC office a day later to say thank you to the staff, the staging room was filled with kids—but, strangely, no noise. The children's use of sign language explained the silence; yet the excited smiles on their faces meant they, too, were eagerly looking forward to going up the mountain with Joe and the other instructors.)

Next, Pat asks, "Who is the best person you know?" Joe replies, "I have to say my mom, Lola. She is always looking out for other people and caring about other people. I don't think she has a mean bone in her body!" This kind compliment is accompanied by a big, sunny smile.

Joe is a little stumped by the question about which person he would most like to meet, and with a laugh suggests, "Marisa Tomei."

Later, in a letter to us, Joe asked us to change some of his answers. He wrote that the people he would like most to meet would be his grandparents, who had passed away. "To meet them again now would be quite amazing," he said, "though I am sure I will meet them again in heaven."

Next, Pat asks, "What is the best decision you have made?" Joe thinks a moment and says, "Quitting my career in architecture and coming to work here at BOEC six years ago." We know we are not the only ones grateful Joe made that decision.

Asked if he has a goal he still hopes to achieve, Joe says emphatically, "Yes! I would like to find a small house where I could live off the land and raise a family. I hope to live a simple life—use solar power, raise a garden, have composting toilets." We believe he'll do it.

Pat then asks, "What is the best thing that has happened in your life?"

Joe says, "Probably, meeting some of the people I've met."

Joe Kusumoto

When Pat asks what Joe would do for a new career, Joe replies immediately, "I'd like to spend some time doing community development in impoverished areas. Help the Third World with sustainable design, renewable energy. Imaginative stuff like that." Joe is multi-talented, and we feel glad to have been able to spend time together with him.

His closing words are encouraging: "Just go after whatever you dream of. Keep at it! Love it!"

Colorado

In his follow-up letter, Joe named another "best thing" in his life: "Meeting my girlfriend, Tara, who you happened to meet just before you left."

Here, Joe referred to an interesting encounter we had on the following Saturday. With a few hours remaining before our ride back to the Denver airport, we looked around for another opportunity to interview someone. We sat in glorious sunshine around a warm gas log pit, enjoying the festive air and the human parade at the base of the snow-and-skier-covered mountains. People came and went—families, couples, a few singles—all dressed in a splendid variety of colorful ski costumes. Every vista was enchanting, the little town was charming, and a joyous holiday atmosphere prevailed. This helped explain why ski vacations are so popular; even if you aren't actually skiing, it's a great experience just to be alive around those who are skiing.

Dear Pat & Scott,

I did not forget about my commitment. The $10 has gone to another local non-profit called IREAD. You can check out their web site at ireadfoundation.org.

Enjoy,

Joe Kusumoto

Suddenly, from behind us, a voice called out enthusiastically "Pat!" It was Joe, on his day off, out for a stroll in the sun with his girlfriend, Tara, from San Francisco. Pat found out that Tara is originally from Maine, and that she went to college at Bowdoin. Turned out she was in class with a fine young man from Nashville whom we know well—his father and Scott used to practice law together! At times like this, our big, beautiful country felt very closely connected.

February 14, 2004, Saturday
Debbie Gaensbauer (GAINZ-bau-uhr)
Breckenridge, Colorado

This was a classic ski resort day. Brilliant sunlight on fresh, deep snow dazzled our eyes. The cold air was bracing without being incapacitating. The weekend brought a more numerous and more colorful swirl of skiers. Our unscientific observation of the national economy got an encouraging boost in this charming ski town as we took note of the not-insignificant costs associated with ski equipment: hats, sunglasses, food, coats or ski suits, gloves, food, ski boots, skis, ski poles, food, lift tickets, hand warmers, food, and lots of hot chocolate. The economy was certainly well-stimulated here.

We explored a quiet, sunny courtyard surrounded by attractive shops and complemented by beautiful views of the magnificent snow-covered mountains. Along came a lively, mature lady. She was smartly dressed, but did not appear to be headed for the ski slope. She was accompanied by a frisky, young black Labrador puppy on a leash, and the puppy instantly took a liking to Pat.

A conversation easily began, and we were immediately impressed by how articulate, poised, and pleasant the lady was. Debbie Gaensbauer cheerfully agreed to an interview.

Debbie reveals that she is originally from Minnesota, but has lived in Denver since 1969. "We now have a place up here, but Denver is still my favorite place in the state. It's a city with a lot of resources," she says. "Good theater, good symphony, beautiful outdoors . . . it's a healthy place, an idyllic place for our two sons to grow up. There are people from everywhere who have moved to Denver and are not necessarily tied to preexisting relations and commitments. They are usually far away from family, and therefore, colleagues easily become close friends. I have loved that."

Pat asks her what one person stands out for consistently doing good things.

Debbie smiles warmly and says, "That's a good question! I would have to say my younger son, James. He is a pediatrician in the Public Health Service. While he was in medical school, he worked in Nepal, Africa, and American Samoa. He now works in a clinic for farm workers in southern Washington State. Since he was a little boy, he has wanted to help in every way he could." Debbie says this in such a loving way that it doesn't sound like bragging. Her genuine maternal pride in her son's good deeds gives us joy and encouragement.

Colorado

Pat then asks, "Which person, living or dead, would you most like to meet?"

Debbie ponders for a moment, then says, "I think Simone de Beauvoir. I'm a French professor at Regis University in Denver, and she is a major figure in my academic background."

Debbie says her best decision was to go to Paris as a young college student. "The people I met, and the trip itself, shaped my life," she says.

Pat asks, "Do you have a goal you still hope to achieve?"

With a little laugh, Debbie says with flair and vitality, "Well, one is to finish a book I'm working on . . . you gentlemen are getting ahead of me!"

The best thing that happened in Debbie's life reflects a goal many could reach for. She says without hesitation, "Getting married. We've had thirty-four happy years."

Debbie smiles but has to reflect on what new career she'd choose if she had the opportunity. "Let me think about that a little bit." She seems almost puzzled at the idea of not doing exactly what she has been doing. She continues, "I'm not sure I'd change. I love teaching!" It is so nice to again hear from someone so fond of the work to which she has given herself.

Debbie's message of encouragement is spoken in flawless French: "Bon courage! Be of good courage. Hang in there!"

Debbie Gaensbauer

By this point in our travels, the book inevitably came up in most of our conversations. We were a little surprised at how eager folks—beyond our friends and family—were to know more details about our great adventure. They seemed to love hearing about all of the good people we found at every turn. Many bright, happy people expressed more than just polite interest in what we were doing, and were so vigorous in their encouragement of us. We continued to be inspired by the goodwill all around us.

Our group of joyful new skiers returned to Denver for the flight home. The BOEC provided two vans to comfortably accommodate everyone, along with all of the wheelchairs and luggage. Our volunteer driver, Rosie, was a three-time intern at BOEC with a specialty in occupational rehab therapy. The native of Melbourne, Australia, had come all the way to America three different times to help groups like ours experience the thrill of outdoor adventure. Her added dose of goodwill sent us home to Nashville with hearts full of gratitude and joy.

TRIP THIRTEEN
LOUISIANA & TEXAS

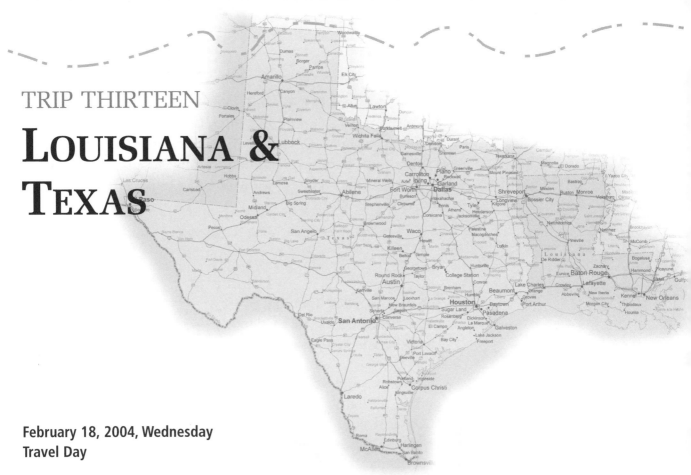

February 18, 2004, Wednesday
Travel Day

We flew to New Orleans and left the airport heading west on old U.S. 61, destination: unknown. The Deep South was beguiling, languid, and a bit mysterious, even to two southerners. We drove south through Thibodaux, Houma, New Iberia, Lafayette, and on to Avery Island, home of the McIlhenny family and their 137-year-old Tabasco sauce business. We enjoyed an interesting factory tour and the beautiful surrounding marshlands.

We soon found ourselves roaming the southernmost road along the Gulf Coast of Louisiana. Live oaks festooned with Spanish moss lined the way to Pecan Island, the Rockefeller Wildlife Refuge, and Grand Chenier. We drove long stretches of empty road with the Gulf of Mexico on our left and huge marshes, swamps, and savannahs on our right. We saw water, water, and more water; few houses; and very few people.

We looked diligently for possible interviews, but this was some of the most remote roadway we would cover in all of our journeys. We discovered a decidedly different sense of remoteness than that we experienced in the vast open stretches of the West. This was a close, almost surrounded, sort of remoteness.

On through Creole and Cameron, we turned north on State Highway 27 and drove up to I-10 at Lake Charles for the night. It seemed almost as if we had spent the day in an exotic and barely populated foreign country. We again discussed our great good fortune at seeing so much of this big, diverse country.

Louisiana

February 19, 2004, Thursday
Melissa Thibodeaux (TIB-uh-doe)
Longville, Louisiana

It was sunny and mild as we left Lake Charles heading north on Highway 171. Strip malls and shops gave way to cows and countryside. After driving a while, we passed a home with an adjoining shop. A sign near the road proclaimed: "Now open year 'round." We weren't sure what the business was, but we turned around and went back to check it out. Then we saw a sign which read "Thib's Pecan House." Set well back from the highway, the house and shop were bordered by a lovely grove of pecan trees, and the shop was filled with the tantalizing fragrance of brewing coffee, chocolate candy of all sorts, and pralines. Some places just smell so good!

The only person in view was a young woman sweeping the floor, and she greeted us warmly. It looked like she had just opened up for the day. We introduced ourselves, told her about our nationwide quest for goodwill, and asked if we could interview her. Melissa Thibodeaux gave us a friendly smile and said, "Why, sure!"

Like a lot of our interviewees, Melissa says her favorite place is where she now lives. "I was born in San Antonio and raised outside Houston," she says. "All our family is right here and we are very close-knit. We share our celebrations—or our problems. Everybody is all together. Longville is a great place to raise a family. We are close enough to town—Lake Charles or

DeRidder—but this is quiet, country living." She says this with a wonderful tone of contentment.

When Pat inquires, "Who is the best person you know?" Melissa glances out the window toward the lovely pecan grove, and says, "Let's see. It would have to be my high school friend, Leslie, in Texas. Anytime anybody has had a problem, Leslie has been there. She has always been a very giving person; she has always sponsored various children's activities. She's the best." Don't you hope someone, somewhere, glances out a window and remembers you like that?

Pat asks who she would most like to meet, and Melissa thinks a moment before saying, "That's a tough one . . . I would have to say the heart surgeon that did my dad's surgery in Nevada two years ago. It was major heart surgery, and now he's healthier than all of us!"

Melissa Thibodeaux and pecan grove

Melissa names marrying her husband as her best decision. "He's very supportive, he's a good father, and he has good morals, which is hard to find these days! We have been married three years—it's been great." Melissa speaks to us with certainty and genuine gratitude for her husband's strong traits. "Someday, we hope to move to Montana! We both love horses and hunting and so moving out there is one of our dreams!" She adds, "We have only looked at photos on the Internet; we haven't actually made a visit yet. It's in my blood, I guess. My grandparents lived somewhere in Wyoming, then moved to Texas in the late 1970s."

Melissa considers the best thing that has happened in her life. "Let's see . . . that would have to be moving to Louisiana about thirteen years ago from near Houston. I first worked in Lafayette with an oil company. It has been a major culture shock, but my life has really changed for the better! There are lots of good people here."

Pat asks, "If you had an opportunity to begin a new career, what would you choose to do?"

Melissa beams as she says, "Either a vet or a marine biologist."

Melissa's message of encouragement is music to our ears: "There is something good in everything!"

After saying our farewells, we turn for our car. Melissa kindly presents us with a small brown sack full of "Thib's House Specialties"—chocolate-covered pecans and praline candy-covered pecans. Her parting words are as sweet as the gift: "Here's something to snack on while you're traveling. Y'all be careful."

Such warm hospitality, such openness to two wandering strangers, such goodwill along an empty stretch of country road in western Louisiana. We felt grateful and happy as we drove on up the road.

February 19, 2004, Thursday
Dr. Sally Coco
DeRidder, Louisiana

Driving northward from Longville, we looked for interview prospects. We needed to get on over into Texas soon, because our flight back to Nashville would leave New Orleans on Friday evening. Feeling a little pressure, we drove slowly though the small town of DeRidder, Louisiana. Finding no one to interview, we decided to turn westward toward Texas. However, out on the west side of town, we saw a veterinarian's office just off the main road. There were no cars in the parking lot. Perhaps we wouldn't be interrupting anything. We slowed down, turned around, and drove back to the Westside Veterinary Clinic.

Inside the spacious and bright office, we introduce ourselves to Dr. Bert Coco, who, in his crisp white lab coat, looks like television's portrait of a distinguished heart surgeon. He stands in the waiting room and listens attentively as we explain our quest. Enthused by the idea, he invites us into his office.

On the way down the hall, he stops and introduces us to his sixteen-year-old daughter, Stephanie, who works on an advanced math problem as a part of her home schooling curriculum. Stephanie is not only polite, but also expresses genuine interest in our effort and asks several insightful questions about our travels and interviews. Dr. Sally Coco, charming, hospitable, and completely professional, joins us. A cat patient needs attention, so Dr. Bert excuses himself and we proceed to interview Dr. Sally.

Sally says, "We have lived here in DeRidder for twenty-five years. I would probably say my favorite place would be Natchitoches. It's the oldest town in the Louisiana Purchase territory. There are beautiful old homes, and its early French character is so lovely. At Christmastime, they have a wonderful festival of lights. It's a beautiful old town in a nice part of the South."

She continues, "DeRidder is a great place to raise a family. Our home is right next door to our office, which is very convenient. We are in a dry [alcoholic beverages may not be sold] parish, which is a plus, and faith is a very big part of our community. As a matter of fact, the *Guinness Book of World Records* says we have the most churches, per capita, of any city in the nation. I believe there are 106 churches here [and it is a small town], so this is a very religious community. The atmosphere here is very good because of that."

Dr. Bert, Stephanie, and Dr. Sally Coco

Sally thinks a moment about the next question. "I'd say one of the absolute most generous people ever is Evelina Smith. She helps everybody that comes along. She is our Registrar of voters, and her husband is a farmer right next door here."

When Pat asks, "Who would you most like to meet?" Sally smiles and instantly says, "Jesus!"

Asked about the best decision she has made, Sally says, "Probably getting married twenty-seven years ago and having our two daughters. Our other daughter, Lindsay, is a student at Texas A&M."

Pat asks the veterinarian about her goals.

"Well, I'm always working on something!" she says with an easy laugh. "My big goal is trying to be the best person I can be, and show the love of Christ to the people I come in contact with."

"I'm just blessed to be in the situation I'm in, especially when I consider the rest of the world. I was raised in a Christian home, and both of my parents always encouraged me in everything I tried. My dad worked for an oil company in Texas and everywhere. We were never in one place for more than a year. My mother was from Louisiana. They both encouraged me so much."

Sally says, "If I had to do something different from veterinary medicine, I think I would enjoy being a landscape architect. I just love the outdoors, flowers, and plants."

Here is Dr. Sally's message of encouragement: "You need to have balance in your life. Put God first, and everything else will follow. Happiness comes from within . . . it's not about our circumstances." Thoughtful words, thoughtfully spoken.

This distinctive family impresses us. Stephanie wishes us well, and we encourage her to consider coming to Nashville for college at Vanderbilt.

Dear Scott & Pat,

We have decided to match your $10 and donate it to our church's summer youth mission. The youth will be traveling to Los Angeles and volunteering in a soup kitchen in the downtown area. . . .

Best wishes!

In Christ,

Bert, Sally, Lindsay & Stephanie Coco

All three Cocos accompanied us out onto the front porch. They seemed so happy for us and for what we were doing. Sally asked, "Where are you going next?"

"We don't know!" is our answer. They all laughed. Bert pointed to the road in front of the clinic and said, "If you stay on that road for three hours or so, you'll come to College Station. You should look up our other daughter, Lindsay, there at A&M." Sally jotted down Lindsay's cell phone number for us, and they gave us a warm, friendly send-off.

What a great, almost-missed stop. We were so glad we turned around and went back. There can't be very many husband and wife veterinary clinics with a home-schooled teenage daughter on-site anywhere else in America, and it thrilled us to find the Cocos.

Texas

February 19, 2004, Thursday
Laura Richardson
Point Blank, Texas

Eighteen miles west of the Cocos' veterinary clinic, we crossed over the Sabine River and entered the great state of Texas. We have always enjoyed previous visits to this state and have long been impressed by how dearly Texans love Texas.

Soon, we stopped for a delicious barbeque lunch in little Newton, Texas, where the people were extra friendly and the biggest thing in town was the water tank. We loved their veterans' memorial in the center of town, and had a good laugh when we passed a real estate office with an empty chair on the porch beside a nice printed sign which said:

> Free Shoe Shine
> Help Yourself
> Hours: Anytime

We meandered west, enjoying the beautiful American countryside, open and free, and followed the north shore of Lake Livingston. When we saw a road sign announcing the town of Point Blank, we looked at each other and knew we had to stop. What a great place name: Point Blank, Texas! Although we were determined to find some person of good-will here, the place was very tiny and very quiet. After trying the small library and finding it closed, we drove up to a small prefab building with a sign indicating that both the constable and the justice of the peace shared it. We went in. Although neither office holder was in the office, we received a cheerful, hearty greeting from Clerk of Court Laura Richardson. She was very interested in our search for good-will and agreed to be interviewed.

Pat begins, "What is your favorite place in the state of Texas?"

Laura responds pleasantly, "I'm originally from Houston, but I love the hill country around Austin. It's just so pretty!"

Laura thinks the best thing about Point Blank is the lack of traffic. "Especially after living in Houston!" she says.

"There are really a lot of nice people out here, I just can't pick only one. People out here have time for each other." She has cheerfully praised her entire community. Even so, she picks someone famous in response to our "living or dead" question.

Laura says, "I've always been a big fan of Elvis! I'd like to meet him. I like historical people too; I'd like to meet some of the great women in history."

Next, Pat asks her about the best decision she has made.

Laura gives us a great big smile and says, "It's a continuing decision. I always decide to have a positive attitude. I can tell you the good thing

Laura Richardson

about everything that happens. When my husband was sick and we were on the way to the doctor, we were in a huge traffic jam in Houston, moving maybe ten miles an hour. I just said, 'Let's sit back and enjoy the ride!' And we did!"

Laura's joyful explanation of her continuing decision to look for the positive in every circumstance is precisely what we are seeking to do day-by-day on these journeys. We felt so glad to have come to Point Blank, Texas, to have found the library closed, to have not found someone else, but to have found Laura.

As for her goal, Laura tells us that she's been a lot of places, but there are still a lot of other places she'd like to see.

Pat asks, "What is the best thing that has happened in your life?" Laura responds without hesitation, "Getting married. My husband was from here originally, and we retired up here together. He has passed away, and I now realize I really had a good marriage! I miss him, but you've got to keep your sunny side up!" She gives us another one of her big smiles, and we respond in kind.

Asked what she would choose to do if given an opportunity to begin a new career, Laura says, "Believe it or not, I'd like to be an attorney. I once worked at a law firm, and I liked that work. If I had lots of money, I'd be a mortgage company." We are persuaded that Laura is multi-talented and that her wonderful positive spirit would serve her well in any new career.

Laura's words of advice are unique ones: "Never turn down breath spray if it's offered . . . you never know. Don't ever say, 'It's in the last place I looked' . . . it always is! And, have fun."

We received a full dose of genuine Texas enthusiasm, cheerfully administered to us without cost by this delightful lady. She displayed such abundant goodwill in her continuing decision to have a positive attitude, and in her determination to keep her sunny side up!

From Point Blank, we drove southward toward Conroe, where we found the law office of a fellow lawyer with whom Scott served in the Marine Corps years ago at Parris Island, South Carolina. Unfortunately, he was out of town, so we turned west by northwest, and reached College Station after dark. We enjoyed a pleasant dinner surrounded by college students, and afterwards, we called Lindsay Coco. Not surprisingly, she was cordial and polite, and agreed to meet us for an interview. She had an exam the next morning and a busy day, but she suggested that we could meet early at a nearby coffee shop. We agreed on eight thirty, which didn't seem too early for us. Of course, we didn't have to study for an exam!

February 20, 2004, Friday
Lindsay Coco
College Station, Texas

Texas A&M has a student body of around forty-six thousand. Many of the buildings on the spacious campus look relatively new. Bigger than most of the towns we have passed through, it appears to be thriving. Just thinking of all the meals, cell phones, clothes, and cars for forty-six thousand students made us feel positive about the strength of our nation's economy.

Lindsay met us at the coffee shop right on time. Having met her parents and sister the previous day, we were not at all surprised by her poise and graciousness. We knew she had an exam, so we plunged right into our interview.

Pat asks, "What is your favorite place in Texas?"

Lindsay thinks for a moment and replies, "Actually, I think it would be College Station. I have lived here four years, and the people are so friendly. The university atmosphere is great. The atmosphere here is really hospitable and so friendly. There's not a lot of jealousy or falsehood; everyone is pretty natural."

Pat asks, "Of all the people you know, is there one who stands out for consistently doing good things?"

Lindsay says, "That is a tough question!" After a little pause, she says, "It's probably my Aunt Evelina; she is constantly doing things for others. You could call her at three in the morning, and she'll be there for you. You never have to ask her to do anything, she just does good things all the time for lots of people."

Lindsay Coco

Lindsay chooses Condoleezza Rice, then the president's National Security Advisor, as the person she'd most like to meet.

"I admire her so much. She's a strong, Christian woman. And she plays classical piano." With a happy smile, Lindsay tells us she plays classical piano, too.

When Pat asks about the best decision she has made, Lindsay says, "Well, first, to accept Christ into my life as my Savior. Second would be my decision to study abroad in Spain last summer. Living in a foreign land in someone else's home really opened my eyes a lot. It was a great experience."

Pat inquires, "Do you have a goal you still hope to achieve?"

Lindsay pleasantly says, "Oh, yes. I want to work for a couple of years. Then I hope to go back to school for an advanced degree. I'd like to get a master's in International Relations." We won't be surprised to see this bright young woman speaking from the United Nations or White House someday.

My Bible study group had to fix dinner for a group of fifteen inner-city kids for a ministry at my church. I used the $10 to help buy the food.

Sincerely,
Lindsay Coco

"What is the best thing that has happened in your life?" Pat asks.

Lindsay laughs sweetly and says, "Oh, my gosh. I'd have to say being born into my family. My parents are so supportive, and my sister and I are so close."

Asked about her choice for a new career beyond finishing college, Lindsay says, "I'd like to be a political analyst for the Central Intelligence Agency. I'm especially interested in Eastern Europe." Her desire to give her energies in an arena of such pressing importance to our nation encourages us, and we wish her well.

Lindsay gives us encouraging words: "In whatever you do, seek the Lord first. Even if others tell you you are not going in the right direction, follow Him."

The Cocos represented our only mother-daughter interview in all of our journeys—and, like our father-daughter interviews with Roger Lee Mullins and Marcia Short, it was inspiring to note their inter-generational predisposition to radiate goodwill.

Before leaving the A&M campus, we made a quick stop at the Presidential Library of the forty-first U.S. president, George H. W. Bush. The collection highlights the positive

Louisiana & Texas

influence his parents (and his wife Barbara's parents) had on their lives. We were struck by the former president's youthful, brave service of our nation as a pilot in World War II; his return home and marriage to Barbara when he was only twenty and she nineteen; and his leadership and achievement as a Phi Beta Kappa economics major at Yale University. The presidential library also showcases his independent success in the oil business and his long record of public service. It's remarkable to know he served in Congress, the United Nations, headed the CIA, represented us in China, and served as vice president before becoming president.

An interactive computer array allowed Pat to find out that President Bush's favorite quotation was by Edward Everett Hale (1822–1909), author of "The Man Without a Country." It summarizes our quest beautifully:

Look up and not down,
look forward and not back,
look out and not in,
and lend a hand.

From College Station, we turned back toward New Orleans, traveling via I-10 through Houston, Beaumont, Lake Charles, and Baton Rouge. There was awesome traffic on the highway, especially when compared to the almost empty back roads we chose the previous day. The long drive was comfortable; this part of east Texas was surprisingly verdant, and Louisiana was so completely wet.

We talked about how we would try to convey to others this joy we felt, and the joy which other people had so readily shared with us everywhere we wandered! It was marvelous to see and feel all the goodwill. It's all around you, too.

TRIP FOURTEEN
FLORIDA

March 14, 2004, Sunday
Louis Mrachek (muh-RAH-check)
Orlando, Florida

Scott had a business meeting at Disney World, and Rachel was out of school for spring break, so we met in Orlando to enjoy the beautiful weather and varied attractions together as a family.

Scott has a wonderful friend living in the area with whom he served in the Marine Corps, James Edward Lee Seay. Jim and his wife, Sarah, were especially kind and hospitable to Scott when they were all stationed at Parris Island, South Carolina. One of the most honorable men Scott knows, we wanted Jim in the book. We called and arranged to meet Jim and Sarah for lunch and an interview. To our great surprise and delight, Jim secretly called and invited another couple, Louis and Betsy Mrachek, with whom Scott also served at Parris Island. Lou and Betsy drove from their home in West Palm Beach for a joyous reunion. Long ago, these two couples went out of their way to include Scott in their families' activities, and they made a point of sharing their enthusiasm for life with him every day. Two of the finest and most able lawyers with whom Scott has ever been associated, it was an unanticipated surprise and a distinct pleasure for us to interview both of them. We began with Lou.

Pat asks, "What is your favorite place in the state of Florida?" Lou speaks quickly and confidently, "The beach at Palm Beach. It's serene, quiet. It was narrow but now it's broad since being replenished. It reminds me of St. Simons, Georgia."

Louis Mrachek

Lou flashes a quick smile as he talks about West Palm Beach. He says he likes the weather there. "It's hot and muggy in summer, which drives off the tourists, and it's very pleasant, like spring, in the winter. There's lots of golf and tennis. It's a vibrant city with lots of cultural events, activities, and growth. We've gone from 350 to 2,800 lawyers in twenty-four years! We have lots of corporate headquarters and, therefore, lots of corporate clients. There is plenty of serious, hard-fought litigation, which is what I do."

Lou commends his wife, Betsy, as his pick for best person. "Betsy is consistently doing good things and going out of her way to do good things for people she doesn't even know, or hardly knows."

This distinguished lawyer says he would most like to meet "an athlete like Michael Jordan. Somebody I'd like to go out with, play golf with." He reflects for a moment and adds with a twinkle in his eye: "Or Mother Teresa . . . but not for another twenty-five years, at least!"

Lou says, "The best decisions I ever made were to marry Betsy thirty-six years ago, though that sounds trite; to come back from Vietnam (not going to Vietnam); and having and raising our two children, Katie and Lou. They are all you really leave. Everything else goes in a garage sale or an estate sale." It is delightful to observe such a dynamic, accomplished man so unhesitatingly acknowledge the fundamental importance of his family in his life.

Here is Lou's advice: "There is really little or no sense in focusing on tangible objects," Lou says. "They vanish. Spend time on the people around you, and with the people you love. The rest is ephemeral, passing." Wonderful insight from a wonderful fellow.

Asked if he has a goal he still hopes to achieve, Lou responds immediately by saying, "Yeah. Many. I'd like to make the pilgrimage from Paris over the Pyrenees Mountains to Santiago De Compostela, Spain, where the Crusaders brought back the body of James the apostle for burial. It's about two-and-a-half months' hike from Paris over the mountains. People have been making the pilgrimage since at least the 1200s. I'd also like to walk across England, but that's only six days or so. And, I want to live in Colorado for a while—like an old Marine friend does—and climb all the 'fourteen thousands,' all the mountains there that are higher than fourteen thousand feet. Those types of things." What an adventurous spirit! Lou's quick wit and sharp mind have not been diminished by the years. He still maintains a deep, cool inner calm beneath the intense, staccato banter.

Pat asks what Lou might choose for a new career.

Lou answers right away. "If I were unmarried, I would become a Benedictine monk, without a doubt. Otherwise, I would run a restaurant; work or cook in a restaurant. I may still do that!"

Scott & Pat,

The admonition to do something "GOOD" slowed me down in my utilization of your gift. Finally realizing that perfection is the enemy of good, my search for the perfect use leading me nowhere, I have used your gift to help fund our office's annual Toys for Tots, which brings great joy to all in our law firm, and hopefully brings equal joy to the children who receive our gifts.

Louis Mrachek

March 14, 2004, Sunday
James Edward Lee "Jim" Seay (SEE)
Orlando, Florida

Jim Seay is one of the all-time, most positive men of good-will anywhere in our experience. A graduate of the U.S. Naval

Academy, his sense of honor and duty permeate his life. He has a joyful heart and a boundless spirit of generosity. We were so glad to interview him for our book.

Jim smiles broadly at the thought of his favorite place in Florida, and says, "That would have to be my house on Christmas morning, because all our kids are there." A joyful image comes to mind at the mention of Jim's festive thought.

Pat has previously learned that Jim and his family reside in Altamonte Springs, a suburb of Orlando. He asks, "What is the best thing about Altamonte Springs?"

Jim Seay

Jim responds with a happy laugh and explains, "It's a small community, maybe twenty-five thousand people. The mayor, Russ Hauch, was a classmate of mine at Annapolis, and, at five hundred dollars, I was the biggest contributor to his campaign!" Jim laughs. "We call his wife the First Lady and have lots of fun kidding around with them. It's really a close-knit, family community."

Next, Pat inquires, "Who is the best person you know?" Jim answers without hesitation: "Sarah. She just does good things all the time. She's like a Mother Earth . . . She's nice to everybody. There's not a mean bone in her body." It is so wonderful for us to hear a husband speak so lovingly about his wife, and we especially enjoy hearing Jim's sincere use of the "no mean bone" accolade.

With soft-spoken conviction, Jim says he'd most like to meet Jesus.

Jim says his best decision was, "Marrying Sarah, November 30, 1974, on board the *Waving Girl* in Savannah, Georgia."

When Pat asks, "Do you have a goal you still hope to achieve?" Jim says, "These are hard questions!" After a moment, he says, "My goal is to continue trying to be a better person."

Asked about the best thing that has happened in his life, Jim smiles and tells us, "My kids—Henry, Annie, John, and Billy."

Jim offers an interesting choice for his new career. "A movie critic! I can't imagine getting paid to watch movies!"

Jim's words of advice are short but completely in line with his personality: "Do good!"

We part with the Mracheks and the Seays with a great sense of joy and gratitude for the smiles, friendship, and honest responses they shared.

For Scott, there was elation at seeing old and dear friends who still have joy in their hearts, who are still true to their spouses, who dearly love their children, and who are happy in their work.

Jim Seay came up with a most unique use for his ten dollars, sending out the following letter:

I have two extraordinary friends, Scott Price and Pat, his son, both of Nashville, Tennessee. Scott was a Marine attorney with me in the early '70s at Parris Island. Together they are writing a book about goodwill in America, and I was one of the persons interviewed. A part of the interview involves being given ten dollars with a request that it be used to do something good and that Scott and Pat be advised how the money is used.

I thought long and hard about how to make the ten dollars I have been given accomplish the most good. I finally decided to use it to pay the postage for letters and stamped self-addressed return envelopes to thirteen of my friends who routinely do good things. Since you have received this letter, I know you have a history of doing good things.

I would appreciate it greatly if you would take the enclosed ten dollars and put it to some good use. That use can be donation to a favorite charity, helping someone less fortunate, buying an unexpected gift for someone who deserves more recognition than they get, etc. The only "string" is that

Scott & Pat:

I am writing as a follow up with the results of the $10 provided. I have now heard from three of the remaining parties, as follows: my friend and my great friend's son, you, Pat, donated that $10 and more to the Spina Bifida Association of America; a lawyer friend gave his $10, and another $100 besides to the family of an aspiring Olympic swimmer which is struggling to meet training expenses; a dear friend in the not-for-profit sector gave her $10 to the Red Cross for Hurricane Charley relief. The only hold-out in my circle of thirteen is still trying to think of the best way possible to deploy the $10. I am sure that she will eventually make a decision, and I will communicate that to you. In the interim, based on some quick math, it appears to me that your $10 turned into a $1,920 of contributions. A pretty good return on your investment! . . .

Sincerely,

James E. L. Seay

once you have decided how to use the enclosed ten dollars, I would appreciate your jotting me a note to let me know your decision. I have enclosed a stamped and addressed envelope for your use.

You may be interested to know that I have turned the tables on Scott and Pat, since I have used $1.48 of my ten dollars to send letters and return envelopes to them. I am hopeful that I will have 100 percent participation from the group of friends I have selected, and that Scott and Pat will have a truly extraordinary listing of good things that have come from their ten dollars.

I hope this letter finds you well, and I look forward to hearing from you what good you have been up to. I also look forward to seeing you soon.

Sincerely,
James E. L. Seay

NEVADA, UTAH, NEW MEXICO, ARIZONA & CALIFORNIA

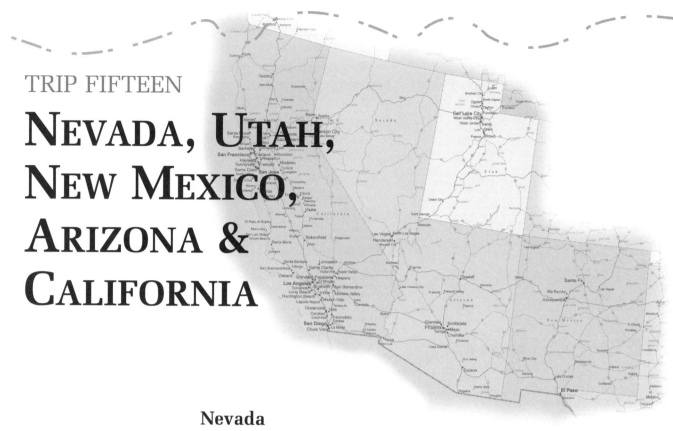

Nevada

March 23, 2004, Tuesday
Carolyn Cockett
Las Vegas, Nevada

Flying over the broad, beautiful land between Tennessee and Nevada provided another inspiring experience as we again marveled at the grit and tenacity of pioneers who made the same trip at ground level.

Brad Price, Scott's brother, was to join us in Las Vegas and help out with driving in the big southwestern states. Our flight arrived almost two hours before Brad's, so we picked up our rental car and decided to quickly look for an interview. After leaving the airport, the first big thing we saw was the University of Nevada at Las Vegas; we turned in at the first parking lot. We parked as close as we could to a building, which turned out to be the home of the UNLV athletic department. We introduced ourselves to the first person we met, Carolyn Cockett, and explained our nationwide adventure. She liked the idea right away.

Pat begins by asking, "What is your favorite place in Nevada?"
Carolyn doesn't hesitate at all and tells us, "Right here! I

love the mountains, the vast views, the colors . . . I love the ribbons of color in the rocks. I have lived in California, Hawaii, and Guam, always by the water. But this land has its own special beauty. I'm an artist, and I love these phenomenal sunsets and the desert scenery." Intriguingly, Carolyn's description never mentions the more gaudy aspects for which Las Vegas is best known.

Carolyn is open and articulate in her enthusiasm for her city. "The cost of living is the best thing about Las Vegas! If you are just here on a short trip, it can be expensive. But I haven't been on the Strip in eighteen months." We all laugh at her surefire method for limiting gambling losses. She continues, "This is a real city, with churches and synagogues, schools . . . a real city, with lots of people from all over the world. That makes it so interesting. Plus, there are lots of opportunities here; this is one of the fastest-growing cities in the United States."

Carolyn Cockett

She responds to our question about someone who consistently does good things by first explaining, "I enjoy working here because our facilities [The Thomas & Mack Center, Sam Boyd Stadium, and Cox Pavilion] are very community-oriented. I really appreciate our Director of Facilities, Daren Libonati. I enjoy watching his method. He always personally greets all of our ushers, and all of the cleaners . . . the whole 'back of the house.' I don't know if others notice it, but I do. It's so nice to see how he makes everyone feel like they are an important part of the whole team."

Carolyn's insight inspires and encourages us. You never know who's watching how you treat others.

Pat asks, "Who would you most like to meet?"

Carolyn answers, "I would have enjoyed meeting Katharine Hepburn. She was so articulate and seemed so interesting. I'd like to be that vital!"

We already think she is. We flew close to two thousand miles, rented a car, drove a few blocks, and found Carolyn. She has a heart full of goodwill and opens it up for us.

When Pat asks, "What is the best decision you have made?" Carolyn pauses for a while. "I think . . . well, I had my daughter when I was eighteen . . . I was unmarried . . . but I wanted her," she responds. "That was a good choice. Then, when I was forty, I adopted an infant from Saipan. He has been an incredible joy to me! It's like God said, 'You may have stumbled a little here and there, but I'm giving you this child as a reward.' Both of those were good decisions."

We feel overwhelming joy and gratitude—first, that Carolyn made those wonderful choices, and second, that she trusts us enough to tell us about them.

Asked if she has a goal she still hopes to achieve, Carolyn exuberantly declares, "Financial independence! Because I'm now a mother and grandmother, I want to be fiscally in the black."

Carolyn says, "Aside from my family, I have been blessed with really interesting jobs and very good friends. My friends are there for me, no matter what. It's great to have their uncompromising support and be able to truly trust them."

Asked what she would choose to do if given the opportunity to begin a new career, Carolyn gives us a big smile and says, "Something in forensics. *CSI: Crime Scene Investigation* is my favorite TV show, and I was an assistant to nine CSI agents on Guam. The work is so fascinating." We know Carolyn would do a great job.

Here are Carolyn's words of advice: "Really try to have goals, but make them attainable. Remember to recognize your small achievements, then you may be better able to move on

---

I was at the gas station . . . when a young man approached me to ask if I could help him. He said he and his wife and family had just run out of gas, and asked if he could wash my window for a couple of dollars. You had just left our office, and the $10 you gave me was "extra," so I offered to put $10 in their tank, no window washing needed. I paid for his gas and mine, and returned to my car to pump the gas.

Forgetting to get a cold drink, I went back into the station. The cashier asked if I had helped the couple. I replied, "yes." She then told me they put only $2 into their car, and took the other $8 in cash.

I guess they needed the cash more than the gas. At least, I know my heart was in the right place. It wasn't any of my business whether they needed gas, food, or drugs. I agreed to help them, so the $10 was theirs. I can only hope their heart was in the right place. The kids in the backseat looked like they could use a good meal.

Thanks, again, for the $10. Hopefully, it was used with the best intentions.

Carolyn Cockett

Nevada, Utah, New Mexico, Arizona & California

to bigger challenges. Give yourself purpose and a sense of accomplishment!" We love her good-natured enthusiasm. Then she adds, "And, don't be afraid to dream, and dream BIG! Our director [Daren] started out here as a parking lot attendant!" With a friendly laugh, Carolyn shows us an old photograph of a very young Daren standing in a huge UNLV parking lot. A caption below states, "Someday, this will all be mine!" She looks at the two of us and says again, "Dream big."

We appreciate very much the splendid dose of goodwill and the warm welcome to the southwest which Carolyn so graciously gave us. We drove back to the airport, picked up Brad, and headed directly out of town on I-15 North.

March 23, 2004, Tuesday
Gwen Olsen
Mesquite, Nevada

Our drive northeasterly from Las Vegas gave us an opportunity to wander through the vivid red rock serenity of the Valley of Fires State Park. Wild and wondrous western scenery inspired us every day of this portion of our journey.

The town of Mesquite appeared like an oasis near the Nevada-Utah border, and we pulled in at a small strip mall just off the main road through town. There was a small brokerage office which we randomly decided to visit. We met Gwen Olsen, the only person there.

Pat begins by asking, "What is your favorite place in the state of Nevada?"

Gwen smiles brightly and replies, "Right here! I was born and raised here, moved away, then moved back in 1989. I've got lots of good memories of good times here. The Virgin River makes this a nice little oasis halfway in between Los Angeles and Salt Lake City. We've got nice golf courses, no income tax, and nice weather!" Sure sounds good to us! Gwen loves "the hometown camaraderie between people. Everyone looks out for each other. My dad had twelve brothers and sisters, so we had cousins and uncles and aunts everywhere," she explains. "Everywhere we went in town, someone knew us and was looking out for us."

When Pat asks Gwen about the best person she knows, she responds right way by telling us, "I think my grandfather, Charles Arthur Hughes. Just last week, they named a local middle school after him! He was fifteen when his parents moved here. He had little formal education, only third grade. But he went out to different parts of the United States as a missionary for our church. He could remember and recite lots of Scripture . . . they called him the Walking Bible. Grandpa would tell us stories about his mission trips. He never cussed, and he had a lot of integrity. He was my hero." Pay attention! Some child who really needs a hero may be watching you.

Gwen Olsen

Pat asks, "Which person, living or dead, would you most like to meet?"

Gwen answers, "The Savior . . . and I hope to, someday!" If there can be serene enthusiasm, Gwen's demeanor displays it just now.

Asked about the best decision she has made, Gwen tell us, "That's a little hard. I'd say it was to get married and have our children. They are my most prized 'possessions'—I've got five children and four grandchildren. There'll be seven by year-end!" Happy smiles.

Beaming, Gwen tells us about her goals. "I want to be able to serve on a mission myself. As soon as I'm able to retire, I would like to volunteer to serve my church." The sweetness and tenderheartedness of this good woman in Nevada, whose future interests are not bound up in self or wealth, but rather in service to others, encourages us.

We are not surprised by Gwen's answer regarding the best thing that happened in her life. Gwen doesn't hesitate to respond. With a voice full of gratitude, she says, "Being born into the family and heritage I was born into."

When asked what she would choose to do if given an opportunity to begin a new career, Gwen says, "I'd become a school teacher for young children."

No doubt she'd tell them what she told us: "Never give up. No matter how hard it gets, never give up."

We headed out of town to the northeast, through a small corner of Arizona and into southwestern Utah. Before nightfall, we reached tiny Springdale, near the southern entrance to Zion National Park. Bumbleberry pie á la mode for dessert and a peaceful night of rest completed a terrific day!

Utah

March 24, 2004, Wednesday
Theodoro "Ted" Salazar Baca
Zican Lodge, Utah

We rose early and drove in solitude along the entire length of the park road on the floor of Zion Canyon. Morning sunlight accentuated the spectacular natural beauty of this place, and we rode in awestruck silence.

Highway 9 took us out the eastern entrance to the national park. Just a mile down the road, we stopped at a small wayside restaurant across the road from the Mukuntaweep trailer park. We were the only diners, and at the cash register in the adjoining gift shop we met Ted Baca, proprietor of the restaurant, gift shop, service station, and trailer park.

Pat begins our introduction to Utah by asking about Ted's favorite place in the state.

Ted replies confidently, "Right here where I'm at. This is the most beautiful spot in the whole state. We've got mountains, beautiful trees, big winter snows, and it's nice here in the summertime. It might be 105 degrees to 110 degrees on that canyon floor [in the park] and it'll be 95 degrees here. We've got the elevation; we're at 6,040 feet. It's nice here."

Ted smiles and continues, "I've got all my family here; my wife, my two twin sons, my daughter, and all my grandkids." Ted has a joyful, contented expression on his face. "I was born in Holbrook, Arizona, and I joined the U.S. Army when I was fifteen years old; fought in Korea." He opens his billfold to proudly show us his membership card for an organization of veterans who lied about their age to join the armed forces. "I'm glad to still be alive and have all my family here with me." We are glad he is still alive and that we found him.

Ted says directly, "If I woulda been smart, I woulda stayed in the service for twenty years—or longer. But I was young . . . I only went to the sixth grade in school, and that made it hard to even get my GED. I went to work to support my family." He's not complaining, just explaining. His hard work is evident all around us.

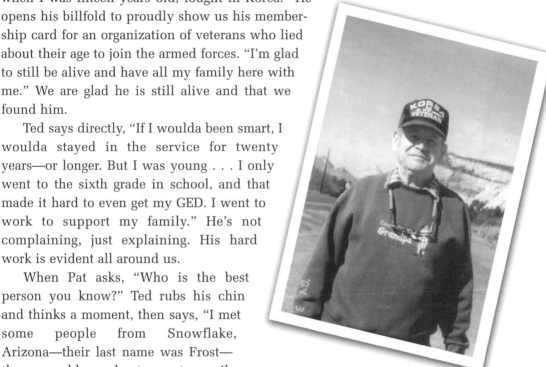

Ted Baca

When Pat asks, "Who is the best person you know?" Ted rubs his chin and thinks a moment, then says, "I met some people from Snowflake, Arizona—their last name was Frost— they moved here, about seventeen miles away. They are the nicest people I have ever met! They really helped me out mentally, and physically too. They were very kind—just fantastic really." Ted's admiration for his neighbors inspires us to be better neighbors ourselves.

A big smile creases Ted's face as he tells us who he'd most like to meet. "I would like to have met my great-grandfather, Juan Baca. He rode all over New Mexico, Arizona, and Utah on horseback. He was a freighter—an interesting man. I checked my family history and there were two captains, one on my father's side and one on my mother's side, in the Spanish Army in Santa Fe, New Mexico."

At this point Ted informs us that his middle name is Salazar. He is obviously and justifiably proud of his family heritage and of his own military service.

Pat asks, "What is the best decision you have made?" Ted smiles, points toward a lady on the other side of the gift shop, and says, "Number one was marrying my childhood sweetheart, Cecilia, in 1952. She was sixteen. Then, I'd say moving to Utah. Those two are my best."

Asked if he has a goal he still hopes to achieve, Ted says, "Yes. Retire! I'm seventy-two, almost. My birthday will be in June. My sons are coming to take over the business for me. I had a triple bypass in 1998, so I'm ready to ease up a bit." We admire Ted's vigor—in the Army at fifteen, married for fifty-two years, and still active in his business at seventy-two.

Ted gives us a friendly smile and says, "I guess the best thing to happen to me was watching my two boys being born. I was standing in the hallway, and the doctor says, 'Have you ever seen twins born? Well, you're gonna see it now!' I felt ten feet tall! That was a wonderful surprise."

This diminutive gentleman fits perfectly in the rugged, beautiful land where we found him. He is so independent, so forthright, so all-American! His words of encouragement are obviously self-learned but powerful: "If you happen to join the service, make it a career. You learn a lot, there's good housing, you get a pension. Being self-taught has been tough. Schooling is very important. I suggest that would be most important."

Uncle Brad and Pat at Bryce Canyon National Park

After taking his photograph, we stood in the morning sunshine with Ted as he pointed out the boundaries of his property and explained to us why we ought to seriously consider buying the whole operation. He was a delightful, original character.

The majesty of the American West was on display all day on this spectacular drive across southern Utah, from Zion on U.S. 89, to State Routes 12 and 22, and rainbow-colored Bryce Canyon; out Route 12 to Escalante and Boulder, where a tiny sign pointed out the Burr Trail which we took and enjoyed immensely. The long, steep, gravel and dirt roadway (trail, really) wound through the stunningly wild beauty of Capitol Reef National Park. We drove for hours and overtook no one. The oncoming traffic: four vehicles. It felt as though we were on a new planet, all by ourselves. At State Route 276, we turned south toward Lake Powell. We arrived at the lake's edge and discovered that the last ferry had departed at three o'clock. All this time we looked for interview prospects. We headed back up the highway, to Route 95, which provided us with an awesome drive through Glen Canyon and the Natural Bridges National Monument. Nightfall found us in Blanding, where we enjoyed a good dinner and a peaceful night of rest. What a glorious day!

March 25, 2004, Thursday
Fred Nelson
Mexican Hat, Utah

The morning air was clear, bright, and beautiful as we made an early start from Blanding. We drove south on U.S. 191 to Bluff, and drove west to Mexican Hat. First, we saw the remarkable rock formation which resembles a sombrero, then we came to a small cluster of businesses collectively known as Mexican Hat. We looked at several places for interview prospects, a little uneasy about the time because we also needed to cover New Mexico that day. About to move on, we spied a white pickup truck parked at the pumps of Mexican Hat's main service station. The truck's hood was raised, and one young man was checking the oil level while another pumped the gas. We were a little apprehensive about the timing, but we decided to try. We quickly pulled in and made our introductions.

Fred Nelson had a firm, dry handshake, and although he initially seemed a bit unsure about us, he quickly warmed up and smiled good-naturedly when we described the nation-wide scope of our search for goodwill.

Fred Nelson and Pat

Fred begins by telling us, "I live south of here in Monument Valley—you need to see that." He adds that for family places, he likes "the zoo in Salt Lake City. That's about seven or eight hours north from here." Big distances don't seem to faze the residents of these huge and beautiful states.

Pat asks, "What is the best thing about Monument Valley?" Fred smiles and says, "It's very quiet. There are only about 1,500 people. It's also very pleasant—short winters."

Fred says the best person he knows is his coworker, Nelson, and that he would most like to meet Benjamin Franklin. "It would be great to see how he thinks! There seemed to be so many new things in his mind. He was always inventing new things," he says. It would be fascinating to see a meeting between Ben and Fred!

"I don't know for sure what my best decision was," he says. "It was probably the decision to start working with this company." He points to the door of his pickup truck, which bears a logo and the initials SEUALG. Fred tells us the initials stand for South East Utah Association of Local Government. "We do weather-proofing improvements for low-income housing. Before I took this job, I used to have to move around a lot. I've been here three years. It's interesting work, and we really help a lot of people."

Fred laughs a little and says, "My main goal right now is just trying to finish building my home. It's a twenty-two-hundred-square-foot house and I'm building it by myself." We compliment Fred on his industriousness.

When Pat asks, "What is the best thing that has happened in your life?" we receive another sunny smile. Fred tells us,

"My wife and our three kids, ages eighteen, eleven, and nine. Having our kids—two boys and a girl—and watching them grow has been great. We just got to see our youngest win in basketball. Great fun."

Asked what he would choose if given the opportunity to begin a new career, Fred says he'd "probably be an engineer or an architect."

Fred gives this advice: "Have fun in your life, and learn, too—try to go to college."

We followed Fred's suggestion and drove through the stunningly beautiful mesas of Monument Valley, surely some of our nation's most striking scenery. Now, whenever we see advertisements set against the backdrop of Monument Valley, we always think of Fred.

Old U.S. Highway 191 took us south through the northeastern corner of Arizona to Chinle, where we saw cattle roaming freely in the streets. Highway 7 is an unpaved washboard road which took us through Canyon De Chelly, where we saw a remarkable canyon, farms, and ancient Native American ruins. On through remote, wild land, dotted with patches of snow in the shade of Ponderosa pines, we followed Highway 7 through Sawmill and Ft. Defiance, then took State Route 264 into New Mexico.

Filling up in the heart of Chinle

New Mexico

March 25, 2004, Thursday
Lola Albin
Pie Town, New Mexico

We stopped for fuel in Gallup, New Mexico, and dashed to the east on Interstate 40, which seemed as smooth as silk after the rutted, unpaved road we'd been on most of the morning. It made us feel even more grateful for those good people who went before us, putting in place the wonderful infrastructure of roads, rails, runways, and bridges. Now, people and products move about so freely and swiftly.

At Grants, New Mexico, we decided to turn southward on Route 117. The drive provided a beautiful panorama of sandstone bluffs, huge lava flows, and the graceful La Ventana Arch. We continued drifting south on C41 and A83, both of which are long, straight, deserted dirt roads. We met fewer than six other vehicles. We saw absolutely no people on foot, horseback, or all-terrain vehicles. It seemed as though we had all of wide-open New Mexico to ourselves.

Lola Albin

When we reached Pie Town at about a quarter to four, we were ready for some pie! Alas, the two cafes (separated by approximately three hundred yards) both closed at three o'clock. A former service station had been converted into a small gallery. It was closed. A note on the window gave a phone number to call if we saw anything of interest. The only other building we saw was the United States Post Office. It was open, and we introduced ourselves to the only person on the premises, Postmistress Lola Albin. She seemed a bit cautious about us, but this wasn't surprising. Pie Town is tiny and very, very remote, and we were complete strangers who just walked in. Nevertheless, she agreed to be interviewed.

Pat begins by asking, "What is your favorite place in the state of New Mexico?"

Lola says, "Probably right here. I was born in Socorro, but this is my home."

Pat asks, "What is the best thing about Pie Town?"

Lola smiles, ever so slightly, and says, "It's nice and quiet; not many people."

We ask what the population of Pie Town is and she says about sixty. That would tend to keep things pretty quiet.

Next, Pat asks, "Who is the best person you know?" Lola ponders a moment and replies evenly, "Most people are good, don't you think?" Our experiences would have us agree.

Pat continues with, "Which person, living or dead, would you most like to meet?" and Lola answers that she's "an Alan Jackson fan. I'd like to meet him."

Lola tells us the best thing to happen in her life was, "The same as my best decision—to get married and have a family. I've been married thirty-two years, and have two children. One boy and one girl."

All of Lola's answers are short and direct. She would be well-cast in a Western movie as the reticent cowgirl. We are surprised at her sudden burst of enthusiasm when Pat asks what career she'd choose if she could begin anew. "If I was young, I'd become a dancer!" she declares. "Not ballet . . . it'd have to be lively!" We're delighted that she reveals this glimpse into her personality.

Here, direct from Pie Town, New Mexico, is Lola's message of encouragement: "Be honest. Be yourself. That's the best you can do."

This interview stood out for us because the setting was so totally remote, and because Lola seemed to gradually realize that she could trust us and open up to us. It seemed a fine triumph of goodwill over doubt.

We headed west out of Pie Town into the golden setting sun.

March 25, 2004, Thursday
Jacqueline "Jackie" Geng
Quemado, New Mexico

High, open plains stretched out endlessly beside us as we made our way west on U.S. 60. This western panorama provided a splendid show in the setting sun. Quemado consists of a tiny cluster of buildings, one of which is the El Serape Café. We were ready for dinner, and the El Serape provided a bountiful and delicious southwestern repast. After dinner, we strolled across the empty street to Allison's Motel looking for goodwill. We hit the jackpot.

The motel office was also the living room and world headquarters of its sole occupant, Jackie Geng. She exuberantly spelled it "G-E-N-G" as she introduced herself with a friendly smile and a warm handshake. There were plants growing everywhere in the lobby, and Jackie told us, "My husband drinks aloe vera for his health." In her living room, the TV was on for company (Regis and *Who Wants to Be a Millionaire*), and her knitting waited beside an easy chair. Jackie's sunny disposition would make her a successful hotelier in any setting. We felt fortunate to have just walked across the street and found her. There were no signs of any guests, and Jackie seemed glad to have visitors.

Pat and Scott enjoy the American West

As we begin our interview, she tells us that Mark Twain was her great-great uncle on her mother's side, so writing was in her blood. She later tells us that Samuel Clemens (Mark Twain's real name) is the person she would most like to meet.

A big smile lights up her face as Jackie tells us about her favorite place. "My ranch! We've got 320 acres [half a section] in Mangas, a house and a dog, and, well, we bought a three-wheel Honda that I just love to ride! I might take four or five hours to do my fences. It's just great!"

"Quemado is a small, little town with very friendly people," she continues. "We came here because people were so friendly, and we like this little place. For the first time in twenty years we'll close on Sunday to take our first vacation. We're going to see Las Vegas. We're usually open 365 days a year. You can't really afford to hire any help, so we just look after everything ourselves." We see a wood stove in the living room, a nice fireplace, and colorful blankets on the sofa. We ask Jackie about winter business. She tells us she has hunters who are regular customers, and that she keeps the place open no matter what—even if the temperature gets below zero. We'd love to see this ebullient pioneer woman on her three-wheeler.

Jackie says that the best person she knows is now dead. "Her name was Jeddy Davis and she lived in Old Town. She did a lot of good for people in this town. I miss her. She was a homesteader—came from Texas! She drove four horses and a wagon here all the way from Texas. Her husband was scalped by Geronimo."

Another friendly smile covers Jackie's face as she says, "Moving here to New Mexico from Illinois twenty-seven years ago, on July 2, 1977, was the best thing we ever did. That last year we were there, for six weeks straight it stayed below zero, and my husband was in a bad accident. We needed a warmer, drier climate. It's so nice here."

Jackie Geng

Jackie says she'd like to see all the states in the U.S. "I haven't been able to travel much because of the work here. My husband went to San Diego in 1978–79 to do catering work, and left me here with two hundred chickens and thirty-five pigs!" Her laughter makes us all laugh. "I'm ready to travel some."

Pat asks, "What is the best thing that has happened in your life?" With a happy laugh, Jackie tells us, "Having my children. I bore five and adopted four!" It is a remark she must have made many, many times, and she said it to us with genuine joy. Jackie adds, "Five of the nine are in Mesa, Arizona. They are all great children—they arranged our trip to Las Vegas."

When we inquire as to what she would choose to do if given the opportunity to begin a new career, Jackie emphatically says, "Be a nurse!"

Asked for advice, Jackie says, "I'm sixty-two years old. Just live each day the best you can—you never know what's going to happen tomorrow!"

Dear Scott & Pat,

My . . . daughter has a friend with three children, who doesn't have much money. The children wanted to get their mother something for Mother's Day, so I gave [them] the $10 [from you] and also gave $10 from me. [My daughter] also put in another $10 . . . Thank you.

Jackie Geng

We were thoroughly elated by the people and places this day had brought our way! Fred Nelson in Mexican Hat; Lola Albin in Pie Town; and Jackie Geng in Quemado. Each one is special, yet all are bound by a common thread of goodwill.

We reached Eagar, Arizona, and rested for the night . . . eager to see the new day and seek more goodwill.

Arizona

March 26, 2004, Friday
Patty Young
Williams, Arizona

On this day, we needed to cross the state of Arizona, and Pat chose a northerly route along I-40. We left Eagar at 6:38 that morning. On Highway 180, we enjoyed a beautiful drive through the Petrified Forest National Park, and had it all to ourselves. The morning sunlight accentuated our subsequent enjoyment of the Painted Desert, then we pushed westward. Just before reaching Flagstaff, we stopped at Walnut Canyon National Monument, home to cliff dwellers more than eight hundred years ago. It was an enchanting site, and we enjoyed contemplating the varied lives which must have passed through this place before our arrival.

West of Flagstaff, we got off I-40 and onto famous old Route 66, which brought us to the cowboy town of Williams, where we ate lunch and strolled around. We saw a building off Main Street with a small sign indicating that a court was located within. We went in but found the judge occupied. Retreating down the hallway, we saw a small seamstress shop, empty except for the seamstress/owner, the delightful Patty Young.

Patty is seated at her sewing machine, unfinished lunch beside her, and a tiny TV on for company. No one interrupts our pleasant visit. We tell her about our search for goodwill in all fifty states and ask if we might interview her. "Fire away," she says genially . . . and keeps sewing.

She has a great, husky laugh, and even though busy, she seems to really enjoy having us stop in. Before Pat can begin asking questions, she tells us, "I've got five daughters, so I feel like I've been sewing all my life." We learn that she was raised in Riverside, California, bought land in Williams in 1983, and moved there for good in 1990. A friend came to visit once, and while shopping with Patty saw the empty space that is now Patty's place of business. She persuaded Patty to start her sewing shop.

With a big laugh, Patty says, "I've been in business here for eleven years now! No phone, no computer, no credit cards. I just wait for folks to walk in . . . and they do! If you do a good job, word of mouth will spread your reputation in a small town like this. It also helps to keep regular business hours. Lots of folks from California think they can come here, open a business, and in six months be a millionaire." She rolls her eyes and laughs heartily.

Patty Young

We immediately love Patty's business savvy, strong, positive nature, and entrepreneurial spirit. She tells us she was a parts manager for an auto dealer in San Bernardino, California, before moving to Williams, and it is obvious that she has good business sense to complement her friendly personality.

Pat asks, "What is your favorite place in the state of Arizona?" With a quick laugh, Patty says, "Home! I don't really 'go' too much. I go to the Grand Canyon with my relatives whenever they come to visit. It's beautiful, and I like that IMAX theater up there. Other than that, I'm not a 'goer' . . . I'm here from nine to five. Moving out here from California was our best decision. We paid off our ten acres, and that led to this!" Patty is a backbone-of-America working woman, independently doing her job and doing it very well. "I have met a lot of nice people in my work. I learned to sew from my mom on an old treadle sewing machine. That kept our hands busy and kept us out of trouble!"

When asked to explain the best thing about Williams, Patty sews a little while and says, "You really get to know people here. It's more like the old days . . . everybody knows everybody. It's not so security-conscious." She's not bragging, but expressing sincere gratitude; it's great to hear it in her voice. She continues, "I know everybody . . . it's so nice."

Pat asks, "Who is the best person you know?"

A little more sewing, then Patty says, "That's kinda hard to know. Everyone in their own way can do good things. Around here, we've got good police officers, good teachers, good hospital workers; the American Legion owns this building and they give lots of grants and scholarships. There are so many good people—just open your eyes!" Patty's answer exquisitely restates what we have been seeing.

When we inquire about who she'd most like to meet, Patty says, "I can't think of anybody famous I'd want to meet." Pause. "I would like to see my oldest daughter; she was killed in a car wreck." Love of family trumps fame once again.

Patty says her goal is to stay healthy. Then, with a quick laugh, she adds, "Just stay alive . . . I'll be sixty-nine on my birthday." She seems considerably younger to us. Then, beautifully, she adds, "Pat, I have had a hard life, but I've had a good life." With the simple eloquence of a western pioneer, this lovely spirit makes the profound point that hardship and goodness are not mutually exclusive.

Asked about the best thing that has happened in her life, Patty smiles and says, "Just having my six kids. My first husband left with a girlfriend and left me with five kids. So, I worked a long, hard job—ten o'clock a.m. to two o'clock a.m. It was hard, but I did it!" We want Patty to come to Nashville and help write some country music lyrics. She has lived a life of triumph over adversity.

Pat then inquires, "If you had an opportunity to begin a new career, what would you choose to do?" Patty has a good laugh and says, "Stay at home! I'm too old to start something new!" After a moment's reflection she adds, "My original 'want,' back in high school, I wanted to be a nurse. In sixth, seventh, and eighth grades, I worked for the school nurse, Catherine Edwards, R.N. I just thought she was great!"

To all teachers and nurses and coaches and parents out there who think you may be laboring away in relative obscurity—keep up the good work! Someone is watching, and they also think you are great. They will recall your name, deeds, and example when they are sixty-nine. Patty has illuminated a powerful truth for all of us: Someone, somewhere is going to remember you. What will they recall? Goodwill or ill? You get to choose!

As you might expect from a mother of six, Patty has a good supply of sound advice: "Be honest; don't give up; set a goal; plan for the future; and if you can, save five cents out of every dollar."

She adds, "Don't be afraid to work; it's good for your body and your mind."

Patty stops, and gestures toward the hallway. "Sometimes, a teenager leaving the courtroom down the hall will stop and ask me to give him ten dollars to help pay a speeding ticket . . . I say, 'Get a job!' Work is good for you." This goodhearted mother concludes with the exhortation to "Learn something every day!"

We didn't want to go, but we had to. Patty gave us such a great dose of resilient goodwill, we knew we would always remember that great laugh and her determined spirit of goodwill.

We pushed further west.

March 26, 2004, Friday
Roger Swenson
Kingman, Arizona

After the wide-open spaces of western Arizona, we found Kingman to be an interesting urban hub. We meandered through the streets enjoying the cool, quiet feel of the place and the small, tidy homes. We found ourselves in an old-timey looking neighborhood where, we later discovered, Clark Gable and Carole Lombard were wed. At the crest of a small hill, we came across an official-looking building where we met Kingman's pleasant city manager, Roger Swenson.

Pat begins the interview by asking, "What is your favorite place in the state of Arizona?"

We are not surprised at all when Roger responds by saying, "Kingman! When I thought about moving, I talked with my wife and we realized just how much we both love it here."

Pat asks, "What is the best thing about Kingman?"

Roger says with a laugh, "It's easy to get to. It's quiet. There is only one stoplight on my way to work! And I have made more friends here in eight years than in twenty years in Oregon. There are lots of good people here."

Of those good people, who would Roger select as a stand out?

Roger chews on this one and says, "Doing good things . . . Wow! There are a lot of people doing that here. This is a very volunteer-oriented city. The community spirit here is so heavy!" It's good news that he can't choose just one.

Asked which person he would most like to meet, Roger replies, "Oh golly!" He pauses. "Franklin Roosevelt. His leadership in the Great Depression and the Second World War. He lived in such an interesting time."

Roger Swenson

Trip Fifteen

Pat asks, "What is the best decision you have made?"

Roger laughs and says, "Several! One was marrying Linda sixteen years ago. Two was moving to Kingman. Three was hiring Toni Weddle as our new city clerk. And four is: staying out of the way 99 percent of the time!"

On goals, Roger says, "There's a lot of stuff I'd like to work on with the city. We have new, more explosive growth, so we're wrestling with those challenges: water resources, power, how to improve our services. There's lots of good things to work on."

"What is the best thing that has happened in your life?" Pat asks.

Roger breaks into a big smile and replies, "Knowing my dad, Russ Swenson. He was a pretty good egg. I didn't know it for quite a few years!" We feel privileged to witness such a genuinely fond tribute to one's father.

Pat asks, "If you had an opportunity to begin a new career, what would you choose to do?" Roger laughs and says, "Wow! If I could live two lives and compare them, it'd be fun to have been able to work in the private sector, alongside my thirty years of public service."

Roger confesses his encouraging words are not original, but says they're true: "Don't sweat the small stuff . . . and 99 percent of it is small stuff!"

He is upbeat and good-natured, and we are very glad we found him. He introduces us to Toni Weddle, the new city clerk, and tells her about our adventure. She asks where we are heading next and, as usual, we respond by saying, "We don't really know!" We explain that we have no set itinerary, but we do want to reach California tonight.

Toni suggests we take old Route 66 west to see the old mining town of Oatman. "The mines are closed, but the donkeys from the mining days are

Dear Scott and Pat:

With patience, I knew that an opportunity would arise that represented a good investment of the $10 you left in my care. A couple of weeks ago, I noticed a woman that works at a local convenience store . . . paying her utility bill, and "digging" for enough money to get caught up. I know her from the store where she works. She is recently divorced with kids at home and is attending the Community College to get her AA degree, so money is tight.

I went to my office, got the $10 bill, placed it on the counter, and said, "This isn't from me!" and walked away. I explained the story to her on my way home that evening. "It allowed me to pay my electric bill, too!" was her comment.

. . . thanks for brightening several days here in Kingman and making me a part of it.

Sincerely,
Roger Swenson

Nevada, Utah, New Mexico, Arizona & California

still roaming the streets of town," she says. That's something we don't want to miss, so we take her advice.

It's hard to imagine Route 66 was once "The Mother Road." It's wild, twisting, and often without guardrails. All across the desert we continued to see beautiful, wild, rugged mountains. Oatman was worth the drive. We crested Snob Hill and entered a tiny town packed with shops, busy bars, and streets full of donkeys and donkey poop! Incongruously, the last shop on the edge of this out-of-the-way town was a bookstore.

At sundown, it was eighty-one degrees in the desert and the air felt soft. At Golden Shores, we crossed the lovely Colorado River and entered California. We slept in quiet Needles, California, remembering Patty Young, Roger Swenson, and all the goodwill we had found so far.

California

March 27, 2004, Saturday
Ruby Newton
Baker, California

This tremendous day began in Needles, California, with a majestic sunrise and soft, balmy air all around. As we loaded the car, we noticed on the motel balcony above us a young man with Asian features and a huge smile of pure joy on his face as he filmed the scenic views sprawling beautifully below our hilltop location. He seemed so intensely happy to be here and to be capturing the immense, wild, free landscape with his video camera. We departed at 6:31 A.M., wondering if this was his first daylight glimpse of the American West; we were happy that his enthusiasm for the day and the place rivaled ours.

We drove west on I-40, laughing at the idea of trying to cover much of California in a single day! Sixty-two miles west, we turned north on a simple park road, which carried us through the heart of the Mojave National Preserve. By our continuing good fortune, we came to the desert at the ideal time of day and at just the perfect time of year. The light, and the air, the tiny desert flowers, and the awesome openness of this wild place all converged to make our hearts leap for joy. A mission-style railroad depot at Kelso stood completely empty, although some effort was underway to renovate it. A train idled on the track, bearing perhaps two dozen U.S. Marine Corps tanks. We saw no one at this eerie spot, so we pushed on northward past a gargantuan lava flow and a vast soda lake.

Interstate Highway 15 borders the northern edge of the Mojave, and we stopped for a late breakfast at the small town of Baker. On the desert's edge, it looked like a Hollywood movie set. The parking lot held gleaming motorcycles and a nice collection of convertible sports cars. Inside the restaurant, we joined America for breakfast: young, old, Chinese, Mexican, Indian, German, black, white, long hair, and crew-cut. The American tapestry was exquisite. The noise was joyful, and the contrast with the desert's solitude and silence could not be more compelling.

After eating, we cruised up the main street and found Ruby Newton, a Mojave Desert Ranger, all alone in a small visitor's center. Guess where she lives? Kelso, the small railroad depot we passed through when crossing the Mojave. Her gentleness and warmth were immediately evident.

Pat begins by asking, "What is your favorite place in the state of California?"

She laughs and says, "Well, California is such a big state! It's hard to say. I have come to love the desert here, but I also love the seashore—as I was raised on Lopez Island in Washington state." What a contrast!

Ruby answers immediately that the best thing about Kelso is: "The view of the Providence Mountains to the south. I also enjoy the Kelso Dunes; they're the third highest in the U.S." Ruby explains that Kelso was once a town of two thousand during World War II, a busy train stop for water. The change from steam locomotives to diesel spelled the end for Kelso during the 1950s.

When Pat asks Ruby to name the best person she knows, she says, "Oh my," and pauses for a moment. Then, with a sweet smile she says, "Probably my father. He was just a wonderful person: honest, kind, and smart!" Happiness and pride appear in her face at her memory of her good father.

Ruby says she thinks she would like to meet Mother Teresa. "It sounds like she was a wonderful woman," she explains.

Pat then asks, "What is the best decision you have made?" After a moment's thought, Ruby replies, "I suppose it was deciding to marry my children's father. Because of that, I have a daughter who's thirty-two, a son who's thirty, and another daughter who's twenty-two." She adds, "Having those children—being a mother—is the best thing that has happened in my life."

Asked if she has a goal she still hopes to achieve, Ruby enthusiastically responds, "Yes! I'd like to move into the medical profession—emergency medicine. I always wanted to be a nurse."

Ruby's message of encouragement is firm: "Just go for your goal and never give up! And start earlier."

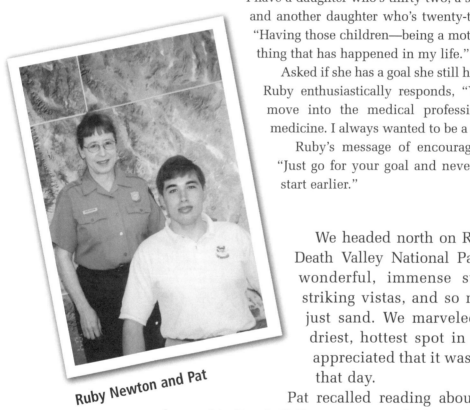

Ruby Newton and Pat

We headed north on Route 127 toward Death Valley National Park and found a wonderful, immense surprise, full of striking vistas, and so much more than just sand. We marveled at the lowest, driest, hottest spot in the U.S.A., and appreciated that it was not hot at all on that day.

Pat recalled reading about a historic inn located in Death Valley, so we sought it out. It was a magnificent oasis: palm trees, fountains, gardens, and a lovely swimming pool, all truly in the middle of nowhere. It was remote, even by twenty-first century standards. We would love to meet the bold soul who was brave enough to build such a splendid place in such a deep desert area in 1927!

We had dinner on an open rooftop and talked well into the night beneath a dazzling display of diamond-like stars in the black velvet desert sky.

Trip Fifteen

March 28, 2004, Sunday
Dr. Herman Neijens (NANZ)
Furnace Creek, California

We rose early to savor the desert dawn. The silence was massive and awesome. After breakfast, we packed up, not certain where we would find another California interview, but knowing we needed to make our way toward Las Vegas for our trip home the next day.

As we checked out at the front desk, a distinguished-looking older gentleman standing nearby struck up a conversation with Pat. He used a handsome walking cane, and motioned with it toward Pat's wheelchair, "I use one of those at home," he said with a friendly smile and a distinctly European accent. Pat introduced himself and quickly learned that Dr. Neijens lives in Amsterdam and works as a pediatrician at a university hospital in Rotterdam. Having long ago decided that we would accept goodwill wherever we found it, we explained our quest to this good-hearted visitor from the Netherlands. He sat down on a nearby sofa; his Dutch wife, also a physician, sat beside him on the arm of the sofa, giving a steady stream of encouraging smiles and gentle pats on his arm throughout the interview. They were a lovely, loving couple.

Dr. Neijens spends a good bit of time talking about his wife. He takes her by the hand, and with a boyish grin, tells us meeting her was the best thing to happen in his life. "When we married, it was the beginning of a new life for me!" Explaining why he considers her the best person in his life, Dr. Neijens says, "She is such a person of feelings, and we have such trust." He casts a fond glance her way.

Dr. Neijens also tells us that he enjoys several places in the U.S., and even lived in Boston for a six-month sabbatical. "You have such a wonderful country; there are several places we love. I would say our favorite is Boston. It's a very stimulating city with good universities. For us, as Europeans, we like the city life, and because our interests are in academic medicine and science, it is very interesting in Boston. We enjoyed New England, and also San Francisco, New York City, Seattle, New Orleans!" He names each city with rising inflection in his voice and with a happy twinkle in his eyes. Dr. Neijens and his wife have thoroughly enjoyed their visits to a variety of U.S. locales.

Speaking thoughtfully, he tells us, "In my professional life, there are others who were great landmarks for me. Several of my teachers in high school and in medical school." He looks directly at Pat and adds, "Try to find persons who can teach you by the way they are living." It is so inspiring to see this good man give such excellent advice in such a grandfatherly fashion.

Dr. Neijens tells us he'd like to see his father again. "He died very suddenly at the age of sixty-two. He had worked hard; he set up a company, and he facilitated letting his children go to university. I would have liked to deal with certain topics with him."

Dr. Neijens says his best decision was: "To study medicine. I have such a pleasure in medicine! It includes the human factor, plus engineering."

Dr. Neijens continues, "What I have tried to do—besides medicine—is develop a number of other interests. My goal now is to do a little less in my professional life, and do other things. So, I am serving on the board for a zoo in Rotterdam. Nature interests me very much, along with history, philosophy, reading, collecting books, and travel. Try new things, learn new things!" His exhortation inspires us.

Dr. Neijens enthusiastically says he'd choose to be an architect if he weren't a doctor. "It fits me well . . . I like imagining how to do this [motioning to the lobby walls, floors, and ceiling] better. At friends' homes, I like to imagine how to design their home better. My wife says 'No!'" They laugh together, and we feel grateful he included us so comfortably in this revelation of his secret career.

He encourages everyone to be optimistic. "I see it in my patients. If they are negative, they go [sic] worse. I can tell you, I have a serious, complicated disease. I'm fighting it the last ten years." Except for the walking cane and his mention of using a wheelchair back home, we would not have described Dr. Neijens as anything other than cheerful and robust. Until this point in the interview, we did not know he was ill.

With another happy smile directed at his wife, he adds, "We take the positive things in life—the good! She has made every day worth to live [sic]."

Drum roll, please. In a remote California desert hotel lobby, a Dutch doctor struck up a conversation with Pat, and brought to us another remarkable dose of goodwill!

The interchange with Dr. Neijens remains brightly painted on our memory . . . his grin, his taking her hand, and the joyful tone in his voice as he says, "The beginning of a new life." Nothing else stands out in our memory; we remember no other activity in the spacious lobby or at the front desk, nor do we even remember glancing out the large windows at the desert scenery. We cannot recall the color of the sofa or anything about the floor covering. For the few minutes of the interview, we sat close to Dr. Neijens and his wife and just listened and watched them carefully. Looking for goodwill reemphasized for us the wonderful

The Doctors Neijens

benefit of really, intently looking at and listening to the person with whom you are speaking. Look and listen diligently, as though you may never have another opportunity to see this face or hear this voice again. Your eyes and ears will capture on the wonderful canvas of your mind a lasting portrait of that new friend.

Leaving Furnace Creek, we followed Route 190 to Stovepipe Wells and the Sand Dunes; Death Valley deserves another visit someday. Highway 374 took us over Daylight Pass at 4,316 feet and into Nevada. We drove down the beautiful Amargosa Valley toward Las Vegas and our flights home. Nevada, Utah, New Mexico, Arizona, and California. Beautiful places, well-spent days. Carolyn Cockett, Gwen Olsen, Ted Baca, Fred Nelson, Lola Albin, Jackie Geng, Patty Young, Roger Swenson, Ruby Newton, and Herman Neijens. A magnificent cross-section of memorable faces, open hearts, and abundant goodwill!

Iowa, Nebraska, Kansas & Oklahoma

Iowa

April 6, 2004, Tuesday
Russ McGlothlen
DeSoto, Iowa

Jet aviation represents a marvelous advance. We awoke in Nashville at four thirty, reached the airport at five forty, and before eight thirty, we were on the ground in Kansas City, Missouri to begin a loop through Iowa, Nebraska, Kansas, and Oklahoma.

I-35 took us northward into Iowa, where we jumped onto back roads through Truro and into Winterset, birthplace of John Wayne. We toured his home and looked for interview prospects. Finding none, we wandered north on U.S. 169 through beautiful farmland. As we neared I-80, we stopped for fuel. Next door was an antique mall. We went over and were greeted by the owner, Russ McGlothlen, who told us he collected antiques for more than twenty years before he began to sell any. We wondered how he chose DeSoto for an antique mall, as it seemed so remote. Russ said he always wanted an interstate location, and the quietness of the area disguised the fact that we were only fifteen or twenty miles from Des Moines. He told us that he used to actually live in the shop, but now lives in Des Moines.

Russ tells us his best decision was: "To start this business! Back then they said, 'If you don't have a job, create a job!' . . . Well, I did it! I turned my whole collection into this place. I'm not making a great deal of money, but this is something I really wanted to do."

We are so delighted to sit in tiny, quiet DeSoto, Iowa, listening to a friendly voice speak about our incredible freedom to try! Russ warms to the subject. "I'm sort of a pioneer out here. I could've done something drastic, like auction off everything on eBay. But, people like the place . . . the feeling." He is correct. We particularly enjoy being there. "I just need them to find some things to buy!" He glances out the front door for a moment or two and says, "I'm going to stay with it."

Russ McGlothlen

When Pat asks about his favorite place in Iowa, Russ says, "In this business, I travel a lot. My car has 360,000 miles on it. I'd say I enjoy the state as a whole—no one single place is the best to me. I have favorite routes I enjoy driving; there's a grotto which is unique . . . I'm fifty years old and I've only been there once. And I really like the Mississippi River; it's fun to antique up and down the river. I suppose the river is probably the place I think of as the best. You know, Iowa means 'beautiful land' in the Indian language. I just love driving out in the country, looking at old houses, thinking about the antiques there and how they got there."

Russ continues, "I think the best thing about Des Moines is that the community is all trying to come together to make it a better place. There are new corporate offices, new construction, and lots of renewal." We like this encouraging news from the heartland. He adds, "As a boy, I had to dress up to go downtown. My parents didn't have a car 'til I was in fifth grade, so we walked to the store for groceries. That was a real quality life. In Des Moines, we're going to try Family Day on Sundays, where everyone just walks wherever they need to go."

"I would have to say Carolyn Peterson in Des Moines is the best person I know," Russ says. "She is always willing to help someone, even when she has nothing! She would always be first to help and the last to leave!"

A van arrives to pick up several items, and Russ apologizes for the interruption. He offers us a soft drink and goes to help load the van. We browse inside and out. Somewhere, Frank Sinatra singing "I've Got You Under My Skin" plays softly. The sunshine is gorgeous. A big piece of farm machinery pulls over onto the shoulder of the road out front to politely allow a motorist to pass. The nearby fields await the plow, but it is just not quite spring yet.

When Russ returns, Pat asks who he would most like to meet.

Russ thinks a moment. "I suppose John F. Kennedy. I was in fifth grade when he was assassinated. It seemed he was doing something good. I think he would have been a greater man if he had lived. I'd also like to meet Jerry Garcia of The Grateful Dead. I'm a big fan," he says.

Asked if he has a goal he still hopes to achieve, Russ responds, "I think, having a good life, having fun in everything I do. I'm always working; I'd like to get a new truck; I need better capitalization, so I've thought of adding a deli to help generate more cash. I told the ladies next door [at the gas station] 'Pray for me, so I can stay in business.' They must have . . . business picked up right away! If I had a better van, I could sell at markets more profitably. I need to be out there buying and selling more merchandise. I like talking to people, being nice to people, and learning from people."

Pat asks, "What is the best thing that has happened in your life?" Russ laughs when he remembers, "Probably when I got to be sixteen and got my driver's license. It seemed like such a big thing to me. My mom took two friends and me to Indianola, and we all got our driver's licenses together. That is a happy memory."

Asked what he would choose to do if given an opportunity to begin a new career, Russ responds, "Law would be interesting. I've seen 'em in action. I always liked watching Perry Mason. It was interesting to watch the courtroom activity." He pauses, then adds, "I suppose, if you were starting over again, everyone, if they could do it, would like to go into medicine."

Russ gives thoughtful advice when he concludes, "Ask yourself the hard question: 'What do you think is the importance of life? Why do you do what you do?' Do what you think

Iowa, Nebraska, Kansas & Oklahoma

is right, even if others don't agree." After a pause and a smile, he adds, "Be nice."

We liked his perspective, and we identified with Russ's fondness for the entirety of Iowa. Many have asked us which state we liked the best. It is too difficult to select just one state; it is the transcendent, wonderfully varied beauty of all the United States of America, and the people therein, that thrilled our hearts most.

April 6, 2004, Tuesday
Rosa Clemsen
Elk Horn, Iowa

From DeSoto, we drove east and up to Johnston on the northern edge of Des Moines, hoping to find a family we met years ago when Pat was competing in the Junior National Wheelchair Championships. Unable to find them, we turned westward on straight State Route 44 and sailed across the majestic land under spacious skies.

In tidy, tiny Elk Horn, we were drawn to an authentic Danish windmill and the Danish Immigrant Museum. In late afternoon, we had the place to ourselves. The well-arranged and well-displayed collection of Danish immigrant possessions, photographs, books, clothes, china, and more is impressive and will be of great assistance to future historians. We were fascinated to find it out in such a remote spot. What hardy, hard-working folks these ancestors were; how fortunate we all are that they poured into the great American melting pot.

We met petite Rosa Clemsen, a museum volunteer full of vitality and enthused about our nationwide quest for goodwill.

Pat begins by asking, "What is your favorite place in the state of Iowa?" Rosa's eyes twinkle as she smiles and says, "Oh wow! The Loess Hills. There are no others like it except in

China! It's wind-blown soil from off the plains that's been piled into small mountains. They are so unusual. We like to go visit there."

Asked about her favorite good person, Rosa says, "Oh my! I can't name names." She is so joyful as she continues, "There are so many." After a moment she says, "My mother, Johanne Jensen, was a very special woman. She was a Danish immigrant . . . kind and good. She was ninety-eight years old when she passed away two years ago."

Pat's next question is about the person Rosa would most like to meet.

"These are difficult questions!" Rosa says. "I'd say the royalty of Denmark: Queen Margrethe II. She is the Protector of our Museum."

When Pat asks, "What is the best decision you have made?" Rosa gives a

Rosa Clemsen

sunny smile. "To marry my husband! We've had fifty wonderful years together. We have lived on the same farm southeast of here for fifty years. We were married on April 18, fifty years ago, at the Elk Horn Lutheran Church." Once again, we feel a surge of pure joy at finding another very happy soul who loves her spouse and remains committed to their union.

Asked whether she has a goal she still hopes to achieve, Rosa smiles and says, "I think, probably, I have met my goals. I have been to visit Denmark four times! So, we've succeeded." Her tone of voice conveys feelings of gratitude and contentment, not complacence.

Pat asks, "What is the best thing that has happened in your life?" Rosa gives a pixie laugh and answers sweetly, "I was fortunate to have twin daughters! I was very, very ill and they survived. In all, we were blessed with five healthy, healthy babies."

Asked what she would do if given an opportunity to begin a new career, Rosa tells us, "I couldn't take nursing—whenever

Dear Scott and Pat Price:

The $10 will go to the youth program at Elk Horn Lutheran Church. For the past four years, thirty-some youth and four adults set out to do mission work in the inner cities. They spend one week doing mission work—goodwill!—and this summer they will be going to the Appalachia area in West Virginia.

The youth work with at-risk kids, homeless youth, and adults; [do] cleanups in the inner city; renovate buildings for low rent; [volunteer at] nursing homes, homeless shelters, food pantries, AIDS clinics for the homeless, ... expressing their Christian faith wherever they may be!

They hold many fund-raisers during the year to help pay for these trips, and they volunteer all their services.

What a way to show their goodwill!

Sincerely,

Rosa Clemsen

I went to the doctor I'd have to go with my sister!" Another pixie laugh. "I've been a secretary with an engineering firm . . . in a new career. I would like to teach." We would love being in her class.

We're struck by the universality of Rosa's message of encouragement: "Show lots of love to all people, and work to keep peace in the world. Show your faith in God."

As we say our farewells, she tells us *Velkommen*, which is Danish for welcome, and *Mange tak*, Danish for many thanks.

This was such a wonderful experience—to glide across remote Iowa farmland and came upon such a lovely, positive person, in just the right setting for an uninterrupted interview.

After a delicious dinner at the Danish Inn, we wandered north, west, then south to Omaha, Nebraska. In the lingering twilight we saw the campus of the University of Nebraska at Omaha and the massive headquarters of Mutual of Omaha, long-ago sponsor of *Wild Kingdom*.

We found a place to stay for the night, and counted ourselves among the most fortunate of all people to have been able to visit Russ in DeSoto and Rosa in Elk Horn, and to have seen the massive beauty of midwestern farmland all around us all day.

Nebraska

April 7, 2004, Wednesday
Kenton Rowe
University of Nebraska, Lincoln

It was a short drive to Lincoln from Omaha, and we decided to peruse the university town. It looked newer and prosperous, with a variety of shops, stops, and restaurants. The spacious and well-signed campus even had free parking near the State Museum of Natural History. The exhibits were fascinating and enlightening. Who knew elephants, rhinos, and camels once roamed northwestern Nebraska? Several groups of grade school children enjoyed the museum with us, and we decided an interview was not likely.

Outside, we strolled back toward our car and spied a young man studying alone on a freshly mowed lawn. We hesitated, undecided about whether to interrupt his studies. We decided to plunge ahead and introduce ourselves. Kenton Rowe possessed quintessential midwestern wholesomeness and all-American good looks.

Originally from Grand Island, Nebraska, about ninety miles away, Kenton tells us he recently spent eight years working as a safety engineer for Water Pik in Fort Collins, Colorado, overseeing Occupational Safety and Health Administration (OSHA) compliance and workers' compensation for six hundred employees. Now, he attends school to become a physician's assistant.

Pat asks, "What is your favorite place in Nebraska?"

Kenton says, "Actually, the most beautiful area is the Platte River Valley, about halfway between Lincoln and Omaha. In the fall, the trees and the valley are especially beautiful."

Kenton says the best thing about Lincoln is the people. "The people here are just . . . what you see is what you get. They are not superficial, and not so concerned about possessions. People here are more real." He says this with appealing earnestness.

Kenton tells us about his wife, Karen. "We've been married two and a half years," he says. "She's a nurse at a nursing home. She graduated last May, and was working in pediatrics at a very large hospital. Now she's in geriatric medicine. She has had a huge impact on people's lives; several in their last days. She has really helped families and individuals during times of great need. Marrying her was the best decision I ever made," he says with a smile.

Kenton says his goals include finishing P.A. [Physician's Assistant] school and starting a family. "I wasn't a stellar student before, but now I recognize what I can do. I have been taking some tough classes, and I just found out I have ADD [Attention Deficit Disorder]. If I had earlier found out about ADD and prepared myself better, I would like to have gone to medical school. I have a great advisor, and a wonderful wife. I'm getting there." Great attitude!

Kenton Rowe

Kenton says he'd like to meet Robert E. Lee. "I really admire his leadership qualities. I'm not a sports hero follower. So many of them have fans for their sports prowess, but no personal qualities worth emulating. Lee had so many great leadership attributes."

Kenton smiles broadly as he talks about the best things in his life. "My wife has been a great influence on me for good," he says. "And my parents were missionaries in Ecuador, South America. I spent three years in high school in Ecuador. Their influence on me was very positive."

Kenton says, "From my past experience, it seems like too many people just go through the motions in life, then end up in jobs they hate, not doing their best. Actively live your life. I would say pursue opportunities for helping others, and work on improving yourself." After a brief pause, he adds, "I would say actively follow God, but I'm afraid not many in our world want to hear that." If only he knew how often God was mentioned positively by people we met during our quest for goodwill!

We said farewell, and Kenton headed off to class. We loaded up the car and headed west. Among the twenty-three thousand students enrolled at the University of Nebraska, we found just the right one!

April 7, 2004, Wednesday
Bob Spencer
Aurora, Nebraska

From Lincoln, we drove west on I-80, then south on U.S. 6 to Milford. We liked the name and the fond memory it evoked of our interview with former Marine George Fernandez in Milford, Delaware. We sought, but did not find, an interview prospect in the Nebraska version of Milford, so we continued northwest on I-80 to Utica, and west on U.S. 34 to York and Aurora, looking, searching, seeking. At this point, we had discovered eighty-seven astonishing people of goodwill and been inspired by their words. The sheer beauty of the lands through which we wandered so freely enhanced our confidence that we would find goodwill in people all around us—and that included Nebraska!

At this time of year, Nebraska is golden. To drive alongside magnificent farms is not only a feast for the eyes, it is an eyewitness news report on the great strength of American agriculture. We saw no run-down places. As we slowly drove through Aurora, we spotted a simple metal building with a sign which said, "Plainsman Agricultural Museum."

We went in and met Bob Spencer, a volunteer guide. We were the only visitors, and Bob gave us a fascinating tour of the museum's vast collection of antique farming equipment. A retired farmer, he possesses great mechanical aptitude. His lifetime of actual farming experience shone as he patiently explained all of the intricacies of the fabulous old machines. He was very grandfatherly and we enjoyed the tour immensely. At its conclusion, he asked what brought us to Aurora. We explained what we were doing, and Bob agreed to participate.

Pat begins with, "What is your favorite place in the entire state of Nebraska?"

With a hearty laugh, Bob says, "My recliner! As you get older, you can't travel as much, so you like what you got! I really enjoy being in my shop at home; I can do metal or woodworking." This cheerful, good man is straight-talking and rock solid.

Bob thinks a moment, then remarks, "My granddad came to Aurora from Sweden, and my dad was born in 1888 on the farm where I still live, five miles northeast of town. We have a lot of peace here." We think, in a flash, of Inna Kourdeltchouk in Versailles, Kentucky, on our very first day of our journey, and her sweet, joyful expression of gratitude for the peaceful nature of her community. Bob's simple statement reinforces Inna's observation.

Bob continues, "The folks here do hundreds of hours of volunteer work. Everybody pitches in. I do this [museum work], and I do other work with our youth, volunteer at the hospital, promote local business. We are a small community, but we are light-years ahead of lots of other places."

Pat asks, "Who is the best person you know?"

Bob says, "Wesley Huenfeld. He started this place and gave over two hundred thousand dollars to help build it. This was his dream."

Next, Pat asks Bob who he'd most like to meet.

Bob glances out of the window of the small office area where we are seated. Except for the steady "tick-tock" of the big office clock, there is total country silence. No other voices, no cars, buses, trains, or planes. Only the clock's steady notation of time's passage. Bob shifts in his chair and says, "Well, there's a lot of 'em. I would enjoy meeting some of the old prophets of the Scriptures. You know, there was an outstanding sermon by Jonah; he converted a whole town! There's an abundance of people I'd like to meet; someday, I hope I'll meet them," he says.

"And, I've always been fascinated by mechanics and science. The trouble is, I run out of brain power! I open *Scientific American*, and I'm over my head. I'd like to meet some of our great scientists." We'd like to just be the waiter at a dinner for Jonah, Bob Spencer, and Albert Einstein!

When asked about the best decision he has made, there is another bit of total country silence until Bob replies, "Well, maybe I haven't made it yet!" No one else has given this response.

Bob goes on to say, "I've enjoyed having my family; I married a good wife—forty years ago. I was an old goat at thirty-six when I got married. Joining my church was a good decision, too."

Pat asks, "Do you have a goal you still hope to achieve?" Big smile, and Bob says, "Getting up tomorrow morning!" We all laugh. Bob says, "That's getting increasingly difficult . . . but I do it."

Bob then says, "Well, I suppose the best thing to happen to me was being born of good parents. I wasn't taught to be a crook. I wasn't taught to be dishonest. They taught me what they knew, which was a lot! By comparison to most countries of the world, I'm an extremely rich individual. Compared to folks around here, I'm not. But I have so much to be grateful for." And such a wise perspective!

Bob Spencer

Queried about what he might choose to do if given an opportunity to begin a new career, Bob responds enthusiastically, "I always thought it'd be interesting to be a machinist. Those that can get it down to a thousandth of an inch, I have great respect for. I'd also like some job where you could roam around the world, and I also would like to fly an airplane—be a fighter pilot. I was too young for World War II, and I never had a body of competitive quality. I was classified 4-F because I lost my thumb."

Bob's advice: "Hard work is a great teacher. I feel sad that jobs of repetition don't exist for youth today. When I was a youngster, we scooped grain all day. Or, we would dig a half-mile of post holes or shovel manure. You didn't like that, but you did it. And, you never used the expression 'bored' . . . that would mean even more work! Yes, I'd say hard work is a great teacher. It taught me well. I was able to farm a little less than a section [a land unit of 640 acres, or one square mile] and I thought I was a big farmer. That's not big by today's standards."

We thank Bob for the excellent interview, make a photo, and present him with a spread-some-goodwill ten-dollar bill. As we prepare to leave, Bob motions toward Pat's wheelchair and asks, "How'd you get hurt?"

Pat says, "I was born with spina bifida."

Bob says, "I'm sorry," in a straightforward expression of support.

Pat simply says, "It's OK," acknowledging that spina bifida is part of his life, but it is not all his life. The air is laden with mutual respect.

From Aurora, we drove west on I-80 to Grand Island and turned south on old U.S. 281. All along the way, we saw handsome farms and neat farmhouses, green hills and pastures, barns, large equipment, and thousands of cows; we passed through a few spots of cool rain and cool air. The majesty of the land was awe-inspiring.

Just south of Red Cloud, Nebraska, we crossed into Kansas. As in Iowa and Nebraska, we were treated to the spectacular beauty of pheasants along the roadside with their dazzling red, gold, green, and brown plumage on display. Often during this afternoon drive, we could smell the earth, that noticeably different smell of newly turned fresh soil. At times, we could definitely smell the cows, too.

Just a few miles into Kansas, we saw a small sign which directed us to the geographical center of the forty-eight contiguous states. We found the small stone monument and made a photo. No one else was there.

We wandered eastward a bit and found a classic steak house for dinner. It was totally isolated and very clean; had a happy, comfortable crowd of diners and excellent food and service; and, in the middle of mid-America, had lots of watercolor paintings of coastal Maine for sale. There was a great spirit in the place.

On to the east, we found Belleville, Kansas, and stopped for the night.

Kansas

April 8, 2004, Thursday
Judge Adrian A. Lapka
Minneapolis, Kansas

A peaceful spring morning greeted us as we drove south on U.S. 81. Curious to see Minneapolis, Kansas, we traveled through that classic small town. We were intrigued by a sign for Rock City, because Rock City is a major attraction in Chattanooga, Tennessee.

As we drove out the country road from Minneapolis, we saw a small office beside an airstrip, with a sign which said, "AG-BY-AIR." Hey! We hadn't interviewed a crop duster. We stopped, but found no plane and no people. Through the window, we could see a newspaper unfolded on a table beside an open box of doughnuts. There was also a baby crib! Was the pilot a woman? Was the baby up there flying with her?

We waited a few minutes longer, then drove on out to see Rock City. No one was there, and we casually examined the unusual rock outcroppings that appeared to have been dropped onto the Kansas countryside from outer space.

Rarely in these travels did we double back over roads we had already driven. However, we really wanted to check out "AG-BY-AIR" again. We did, but we again found no one at the deserted airstrip.

Back in Minneapolis, we made our way to the Ottawa County Courthouse and went into the first courtroom we found. When the judge concluded his docket, Scott approached the bench, introduced himself, and explained the purpose of our trip.

Judge Adrian Lapka adjourned court and invited us to join him in his chambers. We learned that he is a native of Great Bend, Kansas, and that when he first became a judge, twenty-seven years ago, at the age of twenty-seven, he was then the youngest trial judge in Kansas. He made the highest score on the state exam for lay (non-lawyer) judges, and in that capacity hears small claims civil cases and misdemeanor criminal cases.

Iowa, Nebraska, Kansas & Oklahoma

Pat begins by asking, "What is your favorite place in the entire state of Kansas?"

Judge Lapka says, "Oh boy . . . Lake Kanopolis, between Ellsworth and Salina. I like being around the water, and fishing and camping. It gives me a nice way to separate from my courthouse work. You better have a diversion, or else you'll have ulcers!"

Judge Adrian Lapka

Judge Lapka brightens even more and speaks with enthusiasm about his home. "The people here in Minneapolis really care about the community. We have a great VFW, and a large Lions Club. Both invest time in community development. We have a very active Chamber of Commerce. We have Love, Inc., a charitable organization to feed the poor. We also have a We Care center for used clothing for the needy. You can see, this is a very close-knit community, and it's organized to really care about the citizens. Every month, there's a fund-raiser somewhere for something. I fell in love with this community thirty-two years ago because of the community spirit!"

When asked about the best person he knows, Judge Lapka quickly says, "I can't answer that . . . no one single person, because there are so many good people here in our community, and they all really help people. Folks here are aggressive in helping!" With a laugh, he says, "If I'm forced to narrow it down to one, I'd say Judge Gene Penland was the biggest, most positive influence early on as far as my career."

Judge Lapka deliberates a little about who he'd like to meet. "Living or dead . . ." Pause. A glance at Scott and a nod toward Pat. "Boy, he asks some tough questions!" Pause. "Thomas Jefferson. I would like to ask how the Constitution really came about. Who kicked who in the seat of the pants to get things done. The history!"

Judge Lapka says, "Making Minneapolis my home was the best decision I ever made. I'm now getting ready to retire, but I plan to stay here. I equally want to give back what the community has given me. I'll be president of the Lions Club next year, and commander of the VFW next year. I'm a member of the Masons. Those groups all help the community. I want to give back. The people here have given me twenty-seven great years as a judge."

Pat asks, "What is the best thing that has happened in your life?"

With a great big smile and a lilt in his voice, Judge Lapka answers, "It happened in February! I got remarried, and we took a honeymoon cruise to the Bahamas! We loved being on that ship! And there was two inches of ice on our SUV at the airport when we came back." He chuckles happily at the memory.

Asked what he might choose to do for a new career, the judge responds, "The computer scene; no question about it. Make 'em, sell 'em, troubleshoot . . . that would be my new field."

Judge Lapka offers some encouragement. "Have honor first and everything else will follow, in all aspects of your life. If you have honor, you won't have to worry. It kept me alive in Vietnam."

After taking his photograph, we present Judge Lapka with a spread-some-goodwill ten-dollar bill. He removes the money and tells us, "Save the envelope. I'll tell you right now, I'm giving the money to Love, Inc. It'll help feed the poor." We like this man of action. After thanking him for his cordiality and his time, we return to the road.

We made one more stop outside town at "AG-BY-AIR," but there was still no one there. We still wonder about that baby crib and who's doing the flying.

Iowa, Nebraska, Kansas & Oklahoma

April 8, 2004, Thursday
Darlene Schroeder (SHRAY-duhr)
Goessel (GUESS-ul), Kansas

From Minneapolis, we followed Route 106 to Route 18 to U.S. 81 to I-135 south to Elyria. We were fabulously free! The farmland almost vibrated as springtime bloomed all around us. Our road atlas highlighted the Mennonite Heritage Museum in red, so we decided to go look. One really had to want to get there, as it was in a distinctly remote and out-of-the-way part of wide-open Kansas.

We took U.S. 56E to Route 15 South to Goessel. It was tiny and quiet; an enclave, really. The museum was easy to spot; we parked and went in. We were the only visitors on the essentially self-guided tour, with both internal and external exhibits. The museum showcased an excellent collection of Mennonite family artifacts and household and farming history, and it reflected their traditional dignity, kindness, and God-fearing/God-loving heritage. A small group of Mennonites left Ukraine in 1874 as part of the vast flood of European immigrants who sought (and found) religious freedom and a better life here in America.

Darlene Schroeder guided us through six historic buildings relocated to the museum complex for preservation. She told us she grew up in Tabor, which is three miles south, one mile east of here, and that she and her husband, Jerry, now live right across the section, one-half mile west of the church. The big open land of Kansas promotes distance description in miles rather than city blocks.

"What is your favorite place in the entire state of Kansas?" Pat asks.

With a cheerful laugh, Darlene says, "Home! I enjoy gardening and I love the nature on display here. I look at other places too. As far as tourist places, I like Prairie Rose Wranglers at Bentley, Kansas, northeast of Wichita. They have good country music and barbeque. I also like to go to our state museums."

Darlene smiles and says, "Goessel is a pretty neat place! There is no liquor store. We have a good school system and wonderful elder care. It's a caring place." Speaking about this rare island in mid-America makes her beam. "The first Mennonite Hospital is now our retirement home, and we have a good library and a cooperative grocery store."

Pat asks, "Who is the best person you know?" Darlene pauses, then replies, "Justina D. Neufeld. She is a refugee from Russia who had a tough life. She has written a book, *A Family Torn Apart*, telling about her life. She, and it, are so inspiring!"

Darlene says, "There are several people I'd like to meet. Ever since I saw the movie *The Sound of Music*, I thought it would be wonderful to meet Maria von Trapp. I would also enjoy meeting Tasha Tudor. She's a children's author; she wrote and illustrated her books in the '80s. She lives like the pioneers did; she has animals and lots of beautiful flowers. I have done some writing, and I so admire her work."

Asked about the best decision she has made, Darlene replies, "Accepting Jesus as my Savior." Like so many of the people we have found in our travels, Darlene's quiet response and gentle manner reemphasizes the significance of personal faith all across our nation.

Pat then asks Darlene about her goals.

She gives a little laugh and says, "I have many; I don't know when I'm going to get them all done. I would like to do more photography, more gardening, spend more time with my six grandchildren, and improve the museum. I want to help more people come here and learn about our heritage."

When asked about the best thing that has happened in her life, Darlene says, "Well, as far as travel, we made a trip to Europe that I will always remember. My husband sings in the Kansas Mennonite Men's Chorus, and they were invited to go to Germany, Switzerland, and Holland to sing. Spouses got to go too, and we had a wonderful time. We saw where Menno Simons (the sixteenth century leader of

Darlene Schroeder

the Anabaptist movement, out of which the Mennonite movement grew) preached."

Next, Pat asks, "If you had an opportunity to begin a new career, what would you choose to do?" Darlene responds right away, "I wanted to be a teacher, but we didn't have the money for me to go to college. If I could, I would get qualified to work with children, to teach and help them."

Here, from the heartland, Darlene provides encouragement. "Enjoy every day; make the most of it. You have this day only; yesterday is gone and you don't know if you'll see tomorrow. Love this day—live this day!" Marvelous insight.

> Dear Scott and Pat,
>
> Thanks for the $10 bill. The Kansas Mennonite Churches have an MCC (Mennonite Central Committee) Sale every spring. My husband and I had pledged to sponsor one of our friends who was entering the 5K walk to help raise money for MCC. The $10 you gave was combined with our donation to help "mend a broken world." . . .
>
> Thanks again for coming and may God bless you.
>
> Sincerely,
>
> Darlene Schroeder

We slowly drove out of peaceful little Goessel; little children played in the schoolyard and senior citizens rocked in chairs on the sunny porch of the retirement home. This was a good visit to a good place.

We took Route 15 south to Newton, I-135 south through big Wichita. To avoid a toll road at Haysville, we took U.S. 81 south through rolling, green land; taller wheat; more cattle and birds; very few people in cars; vast vistas; and a sea of soil. We passed an appropriate roadside sign which read, "One Kansas farmer feeds 128 people, and you!"

We crossed into Oklahoma at Hunnewell, and continued to drift further south. Neither photographs nor motion pictures could capture the amazing feelings of elation generated by driving at your own pace through this fair land. Throughout our journey, at the end of a long day of driving and interviewing, instead of fatigue, we felt joy and gratitude. We were locking away beautiful memories of special people and special places, and of the journey together.

After a delicious barbeque dinner in the historic old town of Guthrie, we drove a little further south and stopped in Edmond.

Oklahoma

April 9, 2004, Friday
Nancy Bargo Anthony
Oklahoma City, Oklahoma

The trip from Edmond to Oklahoma City was a short morning commute for us. We circled the imposing State Capitol building, and found our way to the nearby offices of the Community Foundation of Oklahoma City. We imposed on Executive Director Nancy Anthony and obtained her genial consent to be interviewed.

Concerning her favorite place, Nancy says, "Well, since I'm not from Oklahoma, I may have a different perspective than a native. Oklahoma City is where I live; obviously, I'm very fond of it. We have a cabin at Lake Fort Gibson, south of Tulsa. Our kids have grown up going there in the summer. That area has a lot of more typical small town Oklahoma, and it has been good for our girls to see that aspect of Oklahoma life. It's more like rural Oklahoma. If you need something fixed on a Saturday afternoon, the place may well not be open. It's been good for our kids."

Nancy pauses a moment, then continues. "This area was settled by those who did the Land Run—and oh, the land they came to! The climate extremes; the wind and rain; it'll be hot as blue blazes one minute, and hailing the next. It gives you a great appreciation of how the pioneers persevered and persisted. In the cities—not just in Oklahoma City—it's hard to get the real flavor. Most larger cities have a Chili's or a Just For Feet . . . there's been somewhat of a homogenization. When you get outside the city, you begin to get a real feel for a state. That's why I'm particularly fond of the Lake Fort Gibson area." We smile inside as Nancy neatly summarizes what we found to be true in our back road explorations.

Pat asks, "What is the best thing about Oklahoma City?"

Nancy smiles and replies, "It's the kind of a place where opportunity is what you make of it. There's not a commitment to a particular class of people. It's a very open kind of community. There are not real distinctions made because of religion, ethnicity, etc. It's very open," she says. "You know, it was just in 1889 when the Land Run occurred, and Oklahoma just became a state in 1907—we're not even one hundred years old yet! My

Iowa, Nebraska, Kansas & Oklahoma

Nancy Anthony

husband Bob's grandparents came in from outside. The state is still open; there is a great sense of opportunity, and a real pioneer spirit. It's very entrepreneurial, very independent, and very much a free market state." She's a persuasive voice for Oklahoma.

When asked, "Who is the best person you know?" Nancy says, "That's an interesting question. I would say, among the best, we have a volunteer here at the Foundation, Martha King, who was originally a nun and taught in a Catholic high school here for years. I don't know the circumstances, but she left the order and started Neighbor-for-Neighbor, a way for people in the faith community to offer food and household goods to people in need, and also help with emergency and utilities assistance. She operated it on a shoestring. Then, World Neighbors, which was founded here about fifty years ago by a group of Methodists, hired her to help Third World people learn how to do things, not just make financial gifts, but teach how to *do* . . . it's a Peace Corps-like organization. Then, she retired again."

Nancy says, "After the bombing of the Murrah Building, 178 children lost one or both parents, lost their financial and emotional support systems. Lots of financial support flowed in. So Martha King came in and handled this. With her help, we put together a significant support system for those kids to help monitor and stabilize their lives. She still, after nine years, comes every week. She's one of those people you can count on. She's always positive. She sees a need and fulfills it. She doesn't try to do everything, but does what she can do. She's very saint-like." We were glad to learn about Martha King's powerful influence for good.

Pat asks, "Which person, living or dead, would you most like to meet?"

Nancy says, "That's another interesting question. I haven't thought about that in a while. I'd say someone like Theodore Roosevelt—out there on the edge, willing to do what is right."

Nancy thinks about the next question for a moment, then says, "One of the best decisions I've made came after the bombing in 1995. There was lots of controversy, as lots of money was flowing in here, and there was no real plan for how to best utilize that help. The Foundation had to decide if we were going to step up and do something. There wasn't anybody else doing it. It impacted my life and my perspective on other things. We could've just divided up the money evenly—same amount to everyone—but we stuck with the idea of looking for the real needs. Some individuals needed more. That decision weighs on my mind. We did the right thing. We took some criticism at the time, but now we are praised for it. And, it has given us lots of new opportunities. After 9/11, New York City saw us as a model."

The goals she hopes to achieve constantly evolve, Nancy says. "Now, I'm eager for my children to get out and do well in the world. So I want to support them in their goals. I've been here eighteen years, and sometime in the next ten, this organization needs to evolve beyond me. So, another goal would be to have a seamless transition here; to have the organization respond well to change, and transcend what I have to offer." Nancy's attitude is selfless and forward thinking. And good.

Thinking of the best things in her life, Nancy says, "I have been fortunate in so many ways . . . the family I have and the family I grew up in. These are incredible blessings, and they have provided me with such wonderful opportunities and support."

Pat asks, "If you had an opportunity to begin a new career, what would you choose to do?" Nancy says, "I think I would like to do something with my skills so that I could help people directly. Here, I can direct funds to groups and to people that then give help to people directly. I think I would like to be directly involved in the way I was when I coached softball for eight years. I was able to interact with those girls and really get to know them and influence them. Those who have a direct impact—I covet that.

"There is a whole lot to be said for being patient," Nancy advises. "Some things do come with time and experience. Opportunities will evolve over time. Now, patience is different from being docile or lazy. Sometimes, you have to patiently work toward a goal. Just don't be discouraged if it doesn't come as fast as you want!"

Nancy is a uniquely energetic combination of intelligence, dynamic action, and goodwill.

We had lots to think over as we drove north on I-35 to the I-44 turnpike, through Tulsa, up Route 66 to Claremore, where we visited the Will Rogers Memorial Museum. We found no interview prospect, but we loved learning more about Will Rogers, his enormous wit, and his common touch. His most famous quote: "I never met a man I didn't like," resonates with us. On up Route 66 into the country of northeastern Oklahoma, we passed through Vinita and Narcissa, then took Route 69 to Miami.

April 9, 2004, Friday
Jan Browning Stepp
Miami (My-AM-uh), Oklahoma

Northeast Oklahoma reminded us a bit of Arkansas on this drizzly Friday afternoon. We drove around the little town of Miami, looking for goodwill; we needed to be back in Kansas City by the next afternoon to fly home. On almost all of our travels, we enjoyed good weather conditions, which was very fortunate because rain adds extra challenges for a wheelchair. Along the main drag, we saw what once was a service station with a nice big bay to pull under out of the rain. A sign said "Cremer Monument Co." A variety of headstones and stone markers were arrayed across the empty driveway where gas pumps once stood, and inside we saw a woman working alone at a desk. In the gathering dusk, we wondered if our arrival would make her uneasy. Determined to reflect what we expect, we plunged in, all smiles.

Our concerns were whisked away immediately. Jan Stepp welcomed us warmly and responded with great enthusiasm when we explained our nationwide quest for goodwill. She really encouraged us quite a bit before we even asked for an interview.

Jan tells us she spent about thirty years in Tulsa, her favorite place in Oklahoma. "It's a beautiful and very family-oriented town. My husband died eight years ago, and I've lived nine miles south of here, in Fairland, the last two years. My dad lived there, and I came to take care of him. When he died, my brother helped out so I could stay in Fairland, I liked it so well. I love the country." Despite the loss of both husband and father, Jan is positive and upbeat.

When Pat asks what is best about Fairland, Jan laughs merrily. "If you like small towns . . . Fairland is for you! There are about nine hundred people," she explains. "When you live in this area, you don't just live in that small town—whether it's Miami, Vinita, Grove, Fairland, or Quapaw. You live in the area. They each have different things to offer."

"Who is the best person you know?" Pat inquires.

Jan says, "That's a toss-up. I could not possibly pick only one." She continues, "Of course, there's my father; he was fantastic. My sister is above fantastic, and my brother is just wonderful. They are all outgoing, helpful, kind people. I can't say enough good about them."

"There are so many people I'd like to meet that I have a hard time naming just one. I find most people are very interesting." That's evident in how she treats us.

Jan Browning Stepp

"There are movers and shakers who stand out, but there are good people all over." We tell her that our desire to illustrate that truth has been a major motivation in our quest.

Jan smiles when Pat asks about her best decision, and says, "Moving down here. I was born here and lived here 'til I was

Iowa, Nebraska, Kansas & Oklahoma

seventeen. I had a wonderful life in Tulsa with my husband. We traveled a good deal." Her eyes speak of happy memories. She continues, "But around here, the peace, the solitude, and the people—at this stage of my life, it sits well with me."

Speaking of goals, Jan tells us, "Since my husband died eight years ago, I have enjoyed developing a new me. I've been awakening, and learning to do things on my own. And when you come out on the other side of that process, it feels like a big achievement!" We are so encouraged by this good-hearted woman who has not allowed personal loss to overwhelm her.

Jan beams when asked about the best thing in her life and says, "There are so many good things in my life: marrying my husband, moving down here, finding this place, having wonderful relatives. I've been blessed by not just one thing . . . it all comes together." A beautiful sentiment, beautifully expressed.

Next, we ask Jan what she might choose to do if given an opportunity to begin a new career. She responds, "I would probably do something in the care-giving area; be a nurse or a doctor."

Here is Jan's message of encouragement: "Completely have a positive attitude. Stay young-thinking. Go in positive and upbeat and happy; it influences others. I think that's the way most people want to be, but they kind of forget how." We are delighted to hear good advice with which we completely agree.

As we took her photo and explained the purpose of the spread-some-goodwill ten-dollar bill, Jan continued to encourage us. She was glad we were doing it, and wanted it to go well. We were grateful to have found her in this out-of-the-way place. We bid her a fond farewell and drove into the night to Baxter Springs and then took I-44 to Joplin, Missouri. We would drive 218 miles to the Kansas City airport and fly home to Nashville on the following day.

As we gazed out the window of the airplane at thirty-one thousand feet, we shared a rush of contrasting memories:

- Just two weeks ago, we were in the still, dry, brightly sunlit Mojave Desert; today, Missouri was windy, cloudy, and rain falls on ponds, lakes, rivers, and streams.

Trip Sixteen

- The flat, calm, even serene, prairie spaces of Iowa, Nebraska, Kansas, and Oklahoma in April quietly unveiled spring's arrival; half a year ago, in November, the jagged, snow-covered, indescribably wild Grand Tetons of Wyoming seemed to shout at us with lusty vigor announcing the approach of winter.
- The two capes we visited: Cape Foulweather, Oregon, and Cape Cod, Massachusetts.
- Hustling, bustling, vibrant Chicago, and quiet, out-of-the-way DeRidder, Louisiana.
- The dry, sandy smell of Death Valley, California, and the moist, pine-scented sea air of Acadia, Maine.

We have experienced wonderfully and wildly varied scenes whose natural beauty is surpassed by the spirit of goodwill we have found in people everywhere.

TRIP SEVENTEEN
TENNESSEE

April 20, 2004, Tuesday
Randall Pardue (Par-DOO)
Nashville, Tennessee

Though we have traveled thousands of miles looking for goodwill, we wanted to include one person close to home. Randall Pardue works at Lipscomb University, just two miles from our house in Nashville. In addition to his professional work, he consistently and cheerfully visits the sick, shut-ins, lonely, the bereaved, parents of new babies, and a host of people in need of a lift. He consistently does good things. He constantly spreads goodwill.

Randall tells us about his favorite places in Tennessee. "There are several that I think are especially beautiful. Reelfoot Lake in west Tennessee, where the eagles nest, is absolutely breathtaking. I'm also very fond of upper East Tennessee— Johnson City and Kingsport. East Tennessee State University has one of the most beautiful settings for a school in the whole United States. The colors in the mountains, especially in the fall, are very special to me. The beauty in nature reveals the hand of God."

Randall continues, "Nashville is one of the best communities in the world to raise a family in. We have lots of churches,

Christian schools, and some of the best people I have ever met anywhere; they are wholesome and friendly. It's like the old fella says, 'There are good people everywhere—we've just got the biggest number in Tennessee!'"

Asked about the best person he knows, Randall says, "If I were just to pick one person who has had a positive influence on vast numbers of people, it would be Willard Collins. As a preacher, he baptized more than ten thousand people! He served as vice-president and as president of Lipscomb University, where he had a great influence in the lives of young people and faculty members. I can't think of anyone who has done more with the talents God gave him," Randall speaks fondly. "He remains humble and loves everybody, and he always gravitates to the low man on the totem pole . . . the people most likely to be overlooked by others. Willard seeks them out and relates to them. He shows genuine love and concern for people."

Pat asks Randall who he'd most like to meet.

Randall says, "Obviously, I would love to have been around in the days when Jesus walked the earth. Not just to see His miracles, but to observe the relationships He built with people—how He did it. You know, He saw more in Zaccheus than others did. I would like to have witnessed their meeting."

With respect to his best decision, Randall says, "Besides marrying my wife, Terry, it was deciding to become a Christian. I had encouragement, and had people pointing the way; I'm certainly grateful for that. Accepting is the beginning point; then go on and use what God has blessed you with."

Randall Pardue

Asked if he has a goal yet to be achieved, Randall replies, "Number one is for me and my family to all be reunited in heaven. Personally, I would like to be remembered in the way Willard Collins is: as a person of goodwill, an encourager of others, and as a person who used his talents for the benefit of others."

With a big happy smile, Randall talks about the best things he has experienced. "Oh! The births of my three children and the recent birth of my first grandchild. That's the most exhilarating elation one can have. I know I'm not the only one to get to experience that joy. When you have your children, you are so unexperienced, it's hard to know or appreciate the blessing God has given you. When you are older and wiser, with a grandbaby, you see the great potential that is there to do good."

"If I chose a new career, I would probably go into the ministry," Randall continues. "I never saw myself in that way before, but in the last ten years—with encouragement from Willard Collins—I have done more, and have enjoyed it. It has opened so many doors of opportunity to do good."

Randall shares these encouraging words: "Never give up! Always look to the future, and know that God has a plan for your life; you were created to accomplish certain specific things. Keep pressing forward; keep getting better."

Randall's positive spirit of goodwill is even more inspiring when you learn a little more about his youth. His mother abandoned the family when Randall was young. When Randall was a teenager, his father went to jail. Encouraged by a kindhearted teacher, he did not turn to mischief or self-pity, but instead completed high school, and with a group of friends, joined the United States Marine Corps.

In very short order, he found himself in South Vietnam on a flight

Pat and Scott,

Never have I given as much time and attention to the use of a $10 bill as I have to the one you gave me. Perhaps, it was the instructions to do something GOOD with the money that has caused such consternation. I am reminded of the parable of the talents and want to use this gift in a way to bring greatest honor and glory to our Lord Jesus, not to simply give it to the lenders (bankers) for a modest return.

Finally, I have decided to add a little more to the pot and send an inner-city child to camp this summer through the Y.E.S. (Youth Encouragement Services) program. These youngsters will be taught Bible classes each day, will enjoy three nourishing meals per day, be surrounded by Christian counselors that will model Christ for them, and experience a week of great fun and excitement. (None of which is part of their normal routine.)

Thank you for encouraging me to take stock in new ways to be useful in His kingdom.

In Him,
Randall

Tennessee

to the embattled Marine combat base at Khe Sanh, in the mountains just south of the North Vietnamese border. Although vastly outnumbered by two North Vietnamese Army divisions, the U.S. Marines—and young Randall Pardue—withstood as many as a thousand shells and rockets a day, along with repeated infantry assaults. The valor displayed by young Marines like Randall during the siege of Khe Sanh deserves our everlasting gratitude.

Randall came home, went to college, and then to work, pressing forward with his life. He made no mention of these trials in the course of our interview. He doesn't dwell on them or use them as an excuse for anything. Instead, he lives as a devoted husband and father, a valued employee, and a community leader. He writes encouraging notes, makes phone calls to boost spirits, and visits, visits, visits. He is always doing good things. What a fine man.

April 24, 2004, Saturday
Robert Stroop
Red Boiling Springs, Tennessee

We so thoroughly enjoyed exploring the back roads in our travels across the nation that we wanted to do the same in Tennessee. We set out from Nashville on this day and followed old Route 70 north up through the classic small towns of Rome and Carthage, then north on a variety of backroads. We drove through pure middle Tennessee hills and countryside. Cordell Hull Dam and Lake were serene and beautiful, and it seemed as though we had the whole lovely earth to ourselves.

Just a few miles below the Kentucky border, we came to Red Boiling Springs, a peaceful little community where visitors once came for mineral baths and "curative" waters. Three very old hotels remain along the main road, and our preliminary cruise took just a few minutes. We determined that the Donoho Hotel was open because there were a few cars parked along the side under massive shade trees. A ramp had been added at one end of the great, two-hundred-foot-long Old South front porch, so we unloaded and went in.

An older lady and gentleman sat in rocking chairs on the front porch, and they greeted us warmly as we passed. Inside, we learned that the Donoho was established in 1914, and that President Woodrow Wilson once slept here. A small ladies' group was meeting in the front parlor, and, seeing no other interview prospects, we went back out onto the big front porch.

The couple in the rocking chairs greeted us again, commenting on the beautiful weather. They were Mr. and Mrs. Robert Stroop of Murfreesboro, Tennessee, which is about forty minutes southeast of Nashville, and they happened to be the new owners of the Donoho Hotel. Robert had a couple of checkbooks in the breast pocket of his shirt, and he wore a baseball cap bearing the logo of a Murfreesboro car dealer. We asked if he was a Tennessee native, and he told us he was born March 26, 1927, at Halls Hill, eight miles north of Murfreesboro.

As his wife, Pauline, listens with a sweet, albeit bemused, smile, Robert tells us, "We came into this place in an unintended manner. I'm semi-retired, own some rental properties, and at a seminar in Nashville I met a fellow who had the listing to sell this place. He told me all about the history and all about the 'healing' waters, and we drove up here last May just to see it; we climbed in through a window because the place had been closed down since October. Well, I told Pauline about it and we made the deal."

We ask if either of them had any prior hotel experience. They laugh and Robert says, "Not other than staying in them." He notes that he was able to use his own rental property maintenance crew to fix up the Donoho with 225 gallons of paint, new plumbing, new wiring, new heating and air conditioning, and a new roof.

We are absolutely knocked out by the youthful vigor and enthusiasm of this seventy-seven-year-old entrepreneur, who proudly tells us he hails from seven generations of farmers. He also talks about getting along easily with the local folks in Red Boiling Springs. When he wanted to add an outbuilding behind the old hotel, he spoke with the mayor about any building

Tennessee

permits that might be required. The mayor replied, "Just stay on your own property!" There is plenty of goodwill in this quiet, friendly place.

We explained our ten-and-a-half-month quest, and the Stroops wanted to hear about some of our experiences. We obliged, then asked Robert if we could interview him.

Pat begins by asking, "What is your favorite place in Tennessee?" Robert laughs softly and says, "I guess right now it'd be Red Boiling Springs and Halls Hill. I divide my time between the two. Rutherford County is a great place to be in business and to raise a family. The location is just great! We are close to Nashville, which is nice, and yet we have almost everything you could need in Murfreesboro. We have a great school system, an excellent road system, and all you need for a good lifestyle."

Robert smiles as he remembers his father, a man who Robert says was always doing good things. "My father, Homer Stroop, would be ninety-nine years old this year. He died not long ago. I always looked up to him. He had a great sense of humor. He was in the hospital when he was ninety-five, and he loved Hardee's biscuits and gravy, so I took him some. He was putting salt and pepper on it when the nurse came in. She got all excited and said, 'Mr. Stroop! You can't eat all that salt!' My dad just smiled at her and said, 'Ya'll got any ninety-five-year-old doctors around here?'" We all enjoy a wonderful laugh together and savor such a memory.

When Pat asks who he'd most like to meet, Robert says, "Well, I may sound repetitive, but it would probably be my mother. She died seventeen years before my dad, and there are many things about her that I still miss." We aren't tracking numbers, but family trumps fame once again.

Next Pat asks, "What is the best decision you have made?" There is a pause while Robert thinks. We hear the sound of a nearby brook and a bird's song, and nothing else. No radio, no traffic. The peaceful tranquility of the place is itself cause for joy. Robert answers, "Being baptized into Christ at the age of twelve."

Speaking of goals, Robert says, "I would like to live out my life well and grow to know folks. I would like to enjoy good health so as not to suffer at the end. And I hope to live a life that will give me everlasting life."

Pat then asks, "What is the best thing that has happened in your life?" Robert responds, "Well, I was in the U.S. Navy in World War II. I survived, and I suppose that it something I'm very grateful for." He is a classic, understated member of that glorious World War II generation, to whom the world owes so much.

Robert laughs again at the thought of a new career and says, "This might seem unusual, but I'd prob-

Pat with Robert Stroop

ably be an airline pilot. I have always been fascinated by flying. I have several friends who went that route, and they have great stories to tell!" At seventy-seven, he's still adventurous.

Robert leaves us with words of encouragement. "Live a life that you are proud of. You can't change what you have already done, but strive to do the things that will make you proud; that will serve you well."

Red Boiling Springs is one of those places you will not just happen to drive through, but it is worth seeking out if you are ever close by. Sit for a while on the broad front porch of the Donoho Hotel and relish the serenity and goodwill.

Tennessee

WISCONSIN & MICHIGAN

Wisconsin

April 28, 2004, Wednesday
Bruce Jondle
Columbia Park/Lake Winnebago, Wisconsin

Spring's progress encouraged us to push into Wisconsin and Michigan in our search. We were not at all tired of traveling; the preceding forty-four states provided such an astonishing abundance of good people and goodwill that we were eager to explore anew.

This morning's early flight transported us to Chicago, then we quickly drove up I-290 to I-94 beyond Milwaukee. Old U.S. 41 was lightly sprinkled with traffic as we wandered northwest. Hunger beckoned us off the road at Lomira, where we found thirty-three other guests enjoying lunch at Susie's Homecooking restaurant. It was twelve forty local time, and it was a happy crowd. We cruised the small town of 2,233 souls after lunch, but found no prospects. On to the north. We looked closely at Fond du Lac. We loved that name, but could not locate someone to interview.

From Fond du Lac, we took Route 55, which hugs the eastern shore of Lake Winnebago. Near Pipe, we turned down a side road, which dead-ended at the lake beside Columbia

Park and a lighthouse tower. The park was totally deserted, but at the water's edge we saw a solitary man in a wet suit with a board for windsurfing. We scanned the lake . . . there were no other windsurfers in sight. Actually, there was no one else in sight anywhere! We saw opportunity and introduced ourselves.

Lighthouse at Fond du Lac

Wisconsin native Bruce Jondle was originally from Menomonee Falls. He has lived in this area for twenty-three years, and right now he is trying to warm up a little bit before going back onto the water. Bruce says he loves to be anywhere on Lake Michigan. He speaks with brisk enthusiasm. "I really love Door County—the peninsula that sticks into Lake Michigan near Green Bay." Lake Michigan is indeed like an inland ocean, and as such it dominates both the geography and the populace.

Pat asks, "What is the best thing about Menomonee Falls?"

Bruce grins quickly and says, "It's a pretty good village. It has a great library that is part of the Central Wisconsin System, so you're able to get any book in the state. With fewer than twenty thousand people, it's a nice village, really."

Bruce ponders the best person he knows. He says, "I would probably say my brother-in-law. He has the strongest principles and is willing to express them. I don't necessarily agree with him, but I admire his willingness to get involved."

Pat asks, "Which person, living or dead, would you most like to meet?"

Bruce answers, "That's a tough one; I never thought of that. In the overall scope of history, I'm really into ancient Greek history, so I'd probably choose Socrates as my number one pick."

Pat asks Bruce about the best decision he has made.

Bruce laughs cheerfully and says, "That's a toss-up. Certainly getting married was one. I've had a good long marriage. Or, getting into windsurfing and whitewater kayaking."

Asked if he has a goal he still hopes to achieve, Bruce replies, "Not really from a career standpoint, there's no big management ambition. I'm an engineer, and I enjoy doing what I'm doing now." We find it particularly encouraging that Bruce seems to thoroughly enjoy both his work as an engineer and his adventurous windsurfing hobby.

Contemplating a new career, Bruce flashes a happy smile and says, "The way things have turned out, I don't think I would've done things differently. I can't say I really envy other professions." He thinks again. "Well, maybe professional wind-surfing in Hawaii or Aruba!" There's plenty of Wisconsin wind, but the air is definitely brisker here than in Aruba. Still, a tone of gratitude prevails in Bruce's voice.

Bruce tells us, "My children are the best thing that has happened to me. I have two girls, one, twenty, and one, seven-teen. They are bright spots in my life."

When asked if he wants to offer a message of encourage-ment or words of advice, Bruce replies, "Well, I don't place a very high value on my opinions. When I say, 'This is the way it is,' I often find out I could have been wrong!" We admire his humility.

After making a photo and presenting a spread-some-goodwill ten-dollar bill (which Bruce puts in his car), we watched him reenter the lake and zip away on his windsurfing board. How easily we might not have driven down this side road. Or how easily we might have arrived a few minutes earlier or later at a time when Bruce was not on shore warming up. What an interesting way of finding a person of goodwill.

We followed the shoreline northward, then headed east toward Lake Michigan on U.S. 151.

Bruce Jondle

April 28, 2004, Wednesday
Scott Stevens
Two Rivers, Wisconsin

From Lake Winnebago, we roamed toward Lake Michigan, passing through Manitowoc. We loved the name, but didn't find an interview. Just up the shore, we came to Two Rivers, a small, exceptionally quiet town. The lake seemed as vast as an ocean, and we slowly cruised along the shore, seeking an interview. Off on a side street, we saw a neat metal building with only one car in the parking lot. It was a small church, but the door was locked. We thought perhaps a custodian was inside cleaning.

As we turned back toward our car, the door opened. A very friendly Scott Stevens shook our hands and invited us in. Various people must come by the building with some frequency looking for help, as Scott looked quite surprised when we explained that all we were seeking was goodwill.

Scott Stevens

Scott tells us that Two Rivers was his hometown. "I went away," he says. "The Lord led me back."

Pat asks, "What is your favorite place in the state of Wisconsin?"

Scott replies, "Door County. It's the most beautiful place, north of here about an hour and a half. The peninsula sticks out into the lake. It's the 'door' from the Great Lakes into Green Bay; it's a real interesting place. Some folks call it Devil's Door because so many ships sank in the swirling current at the mouth of Green Bay."

Pat asks, "And what is the best thing about Two Rivers?"

Scott smiles warmly and responds, "It's small, and full of good people. We have a strong community. And, being right on the lake makes it like being on oceanfront property. Our size is nice; a little under thirteen thousand."

Next Pat inquires, "Who is the best person you know?"
Scott contemplates for a moment, then says, "There are so

many! I don't know if I could name just one, there are a lot. At least six names pop right into my head—family members, several friends. They've all been good influences on me. Number one would be my mentor, Charles Welch. He has a kind heart and a wise spirit. He was a great aid in my growth as a young minister. He's a kingdom-minded man; he loves everybody, even bad people. He finds the good in them!" It is a delight to hear one human speak so highly of another.

Without hesitation, Scott says he'd most like to meet King David. "He royally screwed up so many times—he was a good man who got knocked down, acknowledged his mistakes, and got his life right with the Lord," he says.

When asked about his best decision, Scott says, "Going into the ministry eleven years ago. I was twenty-eight when I first became a Christian. I had been a nominal Catholic—Christmas and Easter—I was an alcoholic. The Lord called me into the ministry at age thirty-four. Obeying that call was my best decision. I have several goals I hope to achieve. Some are real personal and hard to share. One is, I don't want to hang my hat up forever in Two Rivers; there are lots of people out there in need all around the world. My wife and I have talked about doing mission work together."

Pat asks, "What is the best thing that has happened in your life?" Happy smile. Scott says, "Meeting

Dear Pat,

When you left, you gave me that $10 bill and told me to do something good with it, I felt a little like one of the servants that Jesus spoke of in the parable of the talents found in . . . Matthew 25:15–30. I wanted to do the most unique thing I could to see the greatest return. I considered our local food pantry and a couple of other worthy institutions, all of which I knew would use the money properly and for a good cause. For some reason, I felt restrained from doing that and continued to hold onto the $10. . . .

We had in our church with us a missionary to El Salvador, Cathy Killoren. . . . She has set up medical missions in areas that traditional relief organizations have refused to go because of the dangers involved. . . .

After she gave her presentation to us about the medical missions' work, I suddenly realized where the $10 was going. She told us that she could buy $100 worth of medicine for about $10 through drug relief organizations. . . . We also multiplied that $10 by eighty for a total of $810 and told her to use it for whatever was the greatest need. $250 went to an orphanage, $260 went to medicines, and the last $300 went to purchasing other supplies. . . .

I want to thank you for trusting me with the money you left. I also want to thank you for getting me to look for a good place to invest the money. There are so many people out there who have needs that we just don't see until we start looking.

God Bless You,

Scott Stevens

Wisconsin & Michigan

my wife. We have been married twenty-four years and we have two boys, twenty-two and twenty."

We ask what he might choose to do if given the chance to begin a new career.

Scott replies, "Maybe, go back into retail. I liked working with people. But I don't think I'll go back. I like this."

"Try not to sweat the little things," Scott encourages. "Too many people get all high-strung about little things. When I feel sorry for myself, I try to recall the lines, 'I cried because I had no shoes. Then I saw a man with no feet.' People need to do that exercise. As the Apostle Paul says, 'I have learned, in whatsoever state I am, therewith to be content.'"

We bid farewell and left quiet Two Rivers, talking about the fascinating variations of goodwill we found in such diverse locales.

We passed through Two Creeks and moved north into the oft-mentioned Door County. To our eyes, the uniqueness of the area was that there were big, handsome farms like we saw in Pennsylvania or Nebraska, but they appeared to be on the ocean because of their proximity to massive Lake Michigan. The contrast of farmland and vast inland sea was strikingly beautiful. At Algoma, we turned west on County Road 5 and drove toward the sun as it set over Green Bay. What a beautiful day we were given!

Near the campus of the University of Wisconsin at Green Bay, we stopped for dinner and enjoyed listening to the accents of our waitress and our fellow diners. Short, clipped words. The conversations around us were about figure skating, hockey, and the possibility of snow on Sunday. We knew we were up north.

The sun didn't completely set until almost eight o'clock, so we drove north toward the Michigan border along the scenic western shore of Green Bay.

We stopped for the night in Oconto, Wisconsin. As we unloaded in the motel parking lot, two twenty-something young fellows from the Upper Peninsula of Michigan (the "U.P.," as they say) greeted us with cheerfulness. As we entered the lobby they said, "We can't wait to get into that pool!" Their first question to the desk clerk was: "Is there any place in town where we could find shorts or a swim suit?" Their accents were fabulous and accentuated by youthful enthusiasm.

Michigan

April 29, 2004, Thursday
Susan L. McCarthy
Escanaba, Michigan

"The Wisconsin shore" was not a phrase we had heard, but we had the good fortune to see it firsthand in the morning sunlight as we drove up U.S. 41 from Oconto to Marinette, and into Michigan at Menominee. Highway 35 runs as a long, straight forest road alongside Green Bay and Lake Michigan; on display are well-kept houses, cute cabins, lots of cedar trees, and beautiful water stretching away to the eastern horizon.

Escanaba had the look of a regional hub, a sort of jumping-off point for the Upper Peninsula of Michigan. We drove around slowly, on the lookout for goodwill. Pat spotted a local office for Congressman Bart Stupak, who had been very supportive of the Spina Bifida Association of America. We parked and headed for the office, glad we wore sweaters that fine spring morning.

We introduced ourselves to Susan L. McCarthy, the congressman's longtime local aide. On learning our home base was in Tennessee, Susan told us that because of her dad's work, she had lived briefly in Memphis. We also learned that she is actually a native of Escanaba, and that the word "escanaba" means "flat rock."

She pleasantly agrees to our request for an interview, and Pat asks her to talk about her favorite place.

Susan has a friendly smile and tells us, "I actually like it right here. I have lived away from here, but there is just something about living along the Great Lakes that you miss when you are living elsewhere. I drive along the lakeshore coming to work each day, and I've found whenever I live inland, I miss the water." We delight again to find a friend who enjoys living where they live.

Susan McCarthy

"The people in Escanaba are friendly; we try to take care of each other and our visitors. Plus, the weather isn't so severe as further north on the U.P. It's just such a pleasant place to live."

Susan says, "I know a lot of good people who I would consider standouts in terms of taking care of their family and their neighbors. I am very fortunate to have so many acquaintances and friends." We wholeheartedly agree.

Next, Pat asks, "Which person, living or dead, would you most like to meet?"

Susan thinks for a moment and sighs lightly, then says, "I just couldn't narrow it to just one. One would be Jimmy Carter; I especially respect what he's done since he was president. Number two, I always admired Anwar Sadat."

Pat momentarily stumps her by asking what was the best decision she has made.

Susan responds, "Wow, that's a tough one! I don't know that I have one . . . it was probably to get as much education as I could. I worked after college, then went back to school twelve or fifteen years later in a different field."

Susan says there are things she still needs to do. "You know, sometimes we work to meet obligations. I hope my next job will be for free. I am still putting that together," she says. "I was premed in college, and later I went back to study and get an accounting degree. Then I went to work in the political field. I'd like my next job to be back in the medical field."

In a new career, Susan says she would "like to do a little work along the line of reflexology, something in the health field . . . some type of alternative medicine."

Pat asks, "What is the best thing that has happened in your life?"

Susan quickly responds, "There has been so much! These are life questions!" She continues, "I'd probably say, when the student is ready, the teacher appears. At the times I've needed help or guidance, that's been true for me. It could be a book, or a friend, or an event. I've been very fortunate in that respect." She ends with these words of encouragement: "Be kind to one another."

Glad our path had brought us that way, we said farewell and wandered out of town.

April 29, 2004, Thursday
Sharon Tesch
Christmas, Michigan

We headed north on U.S. 41 through quiet forest land that was still a bit silver and gray, on the verge of spring. At Trenary, we took Route 67 north, then traveled east to Munising. In front of us was mighty Lake Superior, the largest body of fresh water on Earth. Its 31,700 square miles cover an area larger than the state of South Carolina. Pat said, "This is the 'North Coast' . . . now we have been to all four coasts of the United States!"

We drove westward along Highway 28, hugging the beautiful shoreline and stopping often to marvel at the big blue lake.

Perched right on the shore, straddling Highway 28, was the little village of Christmas, Michigan. We slowed down; there must be some goodwill here. Rachel was almost a Christmas baby, so we stopped to mail a card to her bearing the Christmas postmark. Nearby, we saw a gigantic Santa Claus sign adjacent to—what else—a Christmas shop. We had to go in.

Sharon Tesch greeted us with a joyful "Merry Christmas" and a big, friendly smile. She was so cordial and hospitable, we knew right away we had found just the right spot on the U.P. She asked for advice on how best to make her shop more accessible, and she bubbled with enthusiasm about our search for goodwill.

Sharon tells us she is a native of Grand Rapids, and that she is related to both Johnny Appleseed and Harriet Beecher Stowe. She moved to Christmas two years ago, and bought the shop in October of 2003; the grand opening was on the day after Thanksgiving that same year.

"I have to say, since I moved up here, I love the entire U.P. The Pictured Rocks, the Tahquamenon Waterfalls, Sault Ste. Marie, all along the Upper Peninsula. No single town or spot, but the whole U.P.," she says.

Sharon continues, "The people in Christmas are really friendly. Being from Grand Rapids, a big town, I have enjoyed everybody knowing everybody up here, and how everybody helps anybody that needs help. There are around five hundred people here, and we're close." She displays comfort and assurance in her voice and a happy twinkle in her eyes. Out the shop's window and across the road, sunlight sparkles and dances on the blue waters of Lake Superior. This certainly feels like a good place. We wonder what it must be like at Christmastime.

Sharon Tesch

When Pat asks, "Who is the best person you know?" Sharon answers right away, "My husband, Jack!" She laughs—it's really more of a happy giggle—and says, "I can't help it!" It's wonderful to see her express her affection so joyfully. She continues, "He stood behind me in making the decision to buy this business; he helped with the remodeling, the decorations, the sign. He helps with everything. He's even growing a beard so he can play Santa! Marrying him has just changed my life so much for the better!" We are so glad we found this good, loving woman, and that we get to hear her speak of her love.

Pat moves forward by asking, "Which person, living or dead, would you most like to meet?"

Sharon says, "Oh, gosh! I suppose I've always thought of being back in time with the disciples and Jesus and Mary Magdalene."

Asked about her goals, Sharon says, "As I am getting on into life, my only real goal is to make enough of a success of the store to be comfortable. I'd like to have the health to do the things we enjoy doing. We stay busy with our church and we enjoy doing volunteer work."

Sharon cites traveling as some of the best things she's done. "I guess I would say my trips to Europe and especially Ireland a couple of times. It was just beautiful. I met so many wonderful people."

When asked what she might do in a new career, Sharon laughs at us and says, "I just started a new career!" We all laugh together. Sharon continues, "Actually, since I met my husband, this is my third career. I was an administrative assistant in the Art Department at Aquinas College in Grand Rapids. Then, I went into road construction. I drove big off-road dump trucks, rollers, and loaders. Now, I'm running this store." What an intriguing mixture of talents and an obvious will to work. Sharon definitely doesn't fit into any traditional economist's pigeonhole!

Pat concludes the interview, as always, by asking for words of encouragement or words of advice.

Sharon looks at Pat with another friendly smile and says, "Now, I will get a copy of your book, right?" We are flattered that she wants one. Then she says, "Be true to yourself, and follow your heart. And trust in the Lord."

Dear Pat and Scott,

It was so nice to meet you both, I cannot tell you what an impact it was for me. . . . Trying to decide what to do with your *Looking for Goodwill* gift was very difficult. There are so many programs in the area that could use help. In deciding, I also did some praying and asked God to guide me.

This last spring and summer the senior youth group at our church had done different things . . . to raise money for everyone to go to a youth rally in Florida. They all worked hard and in the end everyone was able to go, with very little out-of-pocket money from those parents who could afford it. No member was left behind; all were able to go. I contributed your "goodwill" to the youth for their rally.

I also wanted to let you know I followed your advice on how to put my handicap ramp in. It works much better than what I was thinking. We have had many compliments on it. You must come again and check it out.

Love and Peace in Christ,
Sharon Tesch

We made a photo of sweet Sharon and gave her a ten-dollar bill. Somehow, we just knew she'd use it well. We said good-bye and pushed on to the west alongside the Fourth Coast.

At Marquette, we stopped for a snack at what Scott thought was a pastry shop. There, we learned that a "pasty" was a U.P. specialty; ours was a sort of sealed beef-stew sandwich. Hadn't had one of those before. We turned south onto I-95,

Wisconsin & Michigan

acknowledging that we needed to be in Chicago by the next day for our flight home. It was a country drive all the way to Iron Mountain through beautiful, rural America. Two-lane highway, small villages, little traffic. U.S. 141 took us south into Wisconsin farmland and back to Green Bay, where we picked up I-43, still southbound.

We got off the interstate at Newton just to explore. We drove down Lake Shore Road, enjoying the lovely homes perched on the high bluffs overlooking majestic Lake Michigan. We glanced back up the coast and admired the beautiful curve of the shore. It was a pretty place.

Up ahead, in the front corner of a yard, there appeared to be a pyramid of cannon balls. We slowed, wondering what battle took place near here. Closer examination showed they were bowling balls! We had a great laugh and still wish we had stopped to find out the history of that particular pyramid.

We simply followed the shore until we reached Sheboygan, where we ate dinner at a downtown harbor-front redevelopment. Across the way, we saw a huge resort project under construction, and we talked over dinner about the many risk-takers we have met on these travels all across our nation. Sharon's Christmas shop and the Riverfront Hotel project in Sheboygan differ in scale, but each bespoke an optimistic entrepreneurial spirit.

We also continued to note the phenomenal nationwide show of support for our troops overseas. American flags and yellow ribbons decorated many a mailbox, front porch, or roadside tree everywhere we went, especially in the country. Lots of businesses had added the prayer "God Bless America" to their signage. These are important individual expressions of gratitude for our collective comfort and security.

It was seventy degrees when we strolled the docks at six o'clock. While we ate dinner, a big storm suddenly blew in off the lake, and by eight o'clock it was forty-two degrees!

On the Chicago side of Sheboygan, we found a place to rest for the night. We felt very good about what we found in these two spacious states. We would not soon forget the

Wisconsin farmland, the cows, or the coast, nor would we fail to remember the unique and independent air of freedom we breathed beside Lake Superior and all along Michigan's Upper Peninsula.

MINNESOTA, NORTH DAKOTA & SOUTH DAKOTA

Minnesota

May 10, 2004, Monday
Travel

We were up and at 'em at five forty, in the airport by seven fifty. Our flight was delayed, so we read and talked about our feelings of great anticipation as we drew near our fiftieth state. This loop would take us to Minnesota, North Dakota, and South Dakota. We wondered a bit (but not to the point of worry) about how to schedule Alaska.

At two twenty-five, we loaded our rental car in Minneapolis, Minnesota, choosing first to angle westerly across the vast black farmland on Highway 12. We encountered lovely small towns, like Maple Plain and Cokato. There were lakes everywhere, making the landscape more beautiful.

In tiny Darwin, we were the only visitors stopping to see the World's Largest Ball of Twine (by one person)—17,400 pounds worth! Francis A. Johnson worked on it from 1950 to 1979. Wish we could have interviewed him.

Pushing west on Highway 12, we looked for prospects in Atwater and then in Willmar, a classic small-town railroad hub. We turned north on U.S. 71 and stopped in Sauk (pronounced "sock") Centre for dinner at the old Palmer

House Hotel, built in 1901. We were enchanted by pressed tin ceilings, old photographs, cigar boxes in a glass case in the lobby, and a fascinating collection of handwritten stories by guests and workers about their encounters with ghosts in the old hotel. We looked hard for a goodwill prospect, and drove by the boyhood home of Sinclair Lewis before heading northwest into the sunset on I-94.

May 11, 2004, Tuesday
Jim Augdahl (OG-doll)
Brandon, Minnesota

It was cool and overcast when we set out at 7:33 a.m., and we cruised into the town of Brandon in time to see small groups of children walking to school together. Three bicycles were parked in front of the school; we noted with pleasure that they were not locked. Other than that activity, the town was completely quiet; we saw no other car moving as we circled the center of town. Across the street from a huge grain elevator, looking through the window of the local barbershop, we could see a lone barber sitting in the barber chair reading a newspaper. We thought our timing might be good, so we went on in.

Jim Augdahl had a quick smile and greeted us with a strong handshake. We introduced ourselves and explained our search. Jim told us his first appointment wouldn't arrive until nine o'clock. He had time to talk. We started with a question about his favorite place.

Jim thinks a moment, then says, "The place I probably enjoy most is up on the North Shore around Duluth. The scenery along the Great Lakes and in the parks is really beautiful."

"I like Brandon because of the small-town environment. We're in an area where there are a lot of advantages. Alexandria is just twelve miles east of here for groceries, shopping, all the big stores. So we have all the big-city conveniences in a small-town environment. I was born here and grew up here, on a farm. I went to Brandon High School, then moved to the Twin City area and worked there for about twenty-five years in a defense plant making gun mounts and missile launchers for the U.S. Navy. About ten years ago, I retired and moved back to Brandon, and began to cut hair. I'm loving it!"

Pat inquires, "Who is the best person you know?" Jim smiles and says, "That is a good question! I guess the Good Lord . . . and my dad, Lloyd. He's the nicest person I know. He's ninety-two and my mother is ninety-two. They both live in a nursing home in Alexandria."

Jim says he would enjoy meeting one of the more interesting people in the political arena. "Maybe John F. Kennedy," he says. "He made a big impression on a lot of people in a short time. Everyone alive at the time remembers where they were when he was assassinated. Not too many others have made that kind of impression."

When asked about the best decision he has made personally, Jim says, "Probably getting back into this small-town environment, leaving a job after twenty-six years where I worked in a plant with eight thousand workers. Making the move back up here was tough, but it was a very good move on my part. It's nice to not have to deal in the tough world." Gratitude fills the quiet barber shop.

Pat then asks, "Do you have a goal you still hope to achieve?"

After reflecting for a moment, Jim says, "Well, at the age of sixty-one, I think my goal is to cut hair here for a few more years, and cut back on my hours and just enjoy my last years of working. My dad was a farmer, on land that's been in our family for 127 years or so. There's been an Augdahl on that farm a long time; my sister lives there now." He clearly relishes his family's connection to the land, and comments on the influx of newcomers: "Seventy percent of my business comes from folks who have relocated here."

Jim's best things: "I was married for forty years and we had three girls, one boy, thirteen grandchildren, and one great-grandchild! And I'm grateful for being able to enjoy them! They all live in the Twin Cities area."

Asked what he might choose to do if given an opportunity to begin a new career, Jim says, "Hmm. At age seventeen, I would have worked a little harder in high school. See, I grew up on a farm and that's all I knew. So I concentrated on the farm work. I probably could've worked harder and went on to college and chosen a more stable area such as education or physical therapy. I could've made it a little easier on myself. I would take a better look at the path I chose," he says. "I'm not complaining. I did work hard, and I did well."

His encouraging words reflect his experience. "Work as hard as you can. Do the best you can. Treat people the way you want to be treated. Never lie." That is sound advice, straight from the barber's chair in Brandon, Minnesota.

We gave Jim the spread-some-goodwill ten-dollar bill, but we got so interested in the photos he was showing us of his family that we forgot to take his picture.

May 11, 2004, Tuesday
Steven Janssen
Fergus Falls, Minnesota

Steven Janssen

From Brandon, we wandered northwest on Route 82 through brawny countryside. We liked the name Fergus Falls and we cruised around the streets there three or four times, just looking.

Thunderstorms and a cold rain complicated our search. We went into a distinctive-looking old municipal building, the city hall, but did not find a likely prospect. We cruised Main Street once again and spotted a photographer's studio. We investigated and were rewarded with the pleasure of meeting genial Steven Janssen. He responded enthusiastically to our

Trip Nineteen

explanation of looking for goodwill and thoughtfully rearranged some furniture in his studio so we could comfortably conduct an interview.

Steven pleasantly tells us about several of his favorite places. "In this area, I love our lakes. We have open water all winter, so we get geese, ducks, swans—it's beautiful!"

Pat asks, "What is open water?"

Steven explains that the water going through the power plant gets heated enough that it doesn't freeze over. He continues, "My other favorite spot would be Itasca State Park, about one and a half hours north of here. It's the source—the headwaters of the Mississippi River. You really should see it if you get the chance." We hope to do so on a future visit.

"To me, Fergus Falls is a great place to work and raise a family. We have enough commerce to support the community; we're only one hour to Fargo and three hours to Minneapolis, so we're close to city opportunities. But we are very much out in the country. The people here are real great." Steven speaks with sincerity and energy; we are delighted to find another person who loves where they live!

When Pat asks, "Who is the best person you know?" Steven answers right away. "There's a gentleman here, Merril Enstead, he's now retired. He's a past national president of Kiwanis. He's not a young man any more, but he is a real go-getter! He is always doing good things!"

Dear Scott & Pat:

I think it's great that you guys not only have the idea for this book but are actually pursuing it. It is also very cool that a father and son are working on this project together.

As for the $10 you asked me to do something good with: Of course, there are many charitable organizations that could use the money, but I wanted to do something original. As I told you when you were here, I have a daughter who will be graduating from high school in a couple of weeks. Last night she had her very last band concert. We are very fortunate to have an outstanding group of teachers in our schools. We are even more fortunate because most of the students realize the quality of their teachers.

It has become a tradition for the kids to give Mr. Iverson, their band instructor, a small gift at the last concert of the year. This year they presented "Mr. I." with his dream car, a 1965 Mustang. How cool is that?

Only one problem, well actually, several problems. The Mustang has been neglected. It is in much need of body work. It doesn't have an engine or transmission, and I'm sure there are more problems that we don't know about.

So I have [contributed the $10 and] also kicked in a few dollars of my own to go to the "Fix Up Mr. I's Mustang" fund. You should know that the money is going to a man who cares very much about our young citizens. The world is better because of all of the young people he has influenced over the years.

Sincerely,

Steve Janssen

When Pat asks who he would most like to meet, Steven ponders for a moment, then says, "The standard cop-out would be Jesus, but the truth is I'd like to meet Him. That's a tough question. I think it'd be great to meet Abraham Lincoln; he really changed the nation."

Pat queries, "Do you have a goal you still hope to achieve?"

Steven smiles easily and responds, "Well, it's a vague one . . . I'd like to eventually retire early enough to really enjoy it and to be comfortable."

Having told us his best decision was starting his family, Steven says, "The best thing to happen to me is when my children were born. I have two really great kids, a daughter, seventeen, and a son, fourteen. My daughter is about to go away to college, and I know we'll miss her even though her school will only be about an hour away." His earnestness is encouraging.

When Pat asks about beginning a new career, Steven gives another smile and says, "I always wanted to be something in aviation. Maybe get my pilot's license. I think I would enjoy that."

We welcome this good advice and the positive spirit in which it is given: "Being an owner of a small business, I would say there are good times and tough times . . . hang in there. Things tend to work out!"

We photographed the professional photographer and gave him a ten-dollar bill, urging him to do something good with it. Among all the shops in Fergus Falls, we found the right one.

Steven was our one hundredth interview, and only a few more remained. It was remarkable to us that we felt absolutely no sense of impatience or eagerness to get to the end. We recognized what a rare experience we were having. The spirit of these people and their abundant goodwill was just amazing! We would be happy to go on for a second loop.

North Dakota

May 11, 2004, Tuesday
Zineta (ZEE-net-tuh) Imamovic (Ee-MOM-oh-vitch)
Fargo, North Dakota

It was near midday and overcast when we came to Fargo. Most everyone has heard of Fargo, maybe because of the movie by that name. But not many people have really been there, including us, until now.

On the corner we spotted a building with a sign which said, "Center for New Americans. Serving Refugees and Immigrants." We looked at each other and knew we had to check it out. Something good was bound to be happening in a place with a name like that!

At the front door, we met Zineta Imamovic, a native of Bosnia who escaped that war-torn country almost ten years ago. While her accent was quite strong, her English was very polished. She bubbled with enthusiasm as we explained our search, and she gave a boost to our spirits when she said, "You guys are just great! What you are doing is great!"

Zineta tells us that Fargo is North Dakota's biggest city, and that she loves being here. "It's a very, very nice city to raise a family. It is a quiet, safe, peaceful place to live in. One of the most beautiful places in the state is Medora. It's a lovely place to rest and vacation. You should see the Roosevelt Park there."

When Pat asks about the best person she knows, Zineta says, "Wow! There's a lot of good people in the United States . . . I just can't choose! There are so many kind people I've met, especially here in Fargo. People are so friendly it feels like home! I hate to say just one!" She laughs. "I've met so many doing good for this community and, you know, America is so friendly . . . if your car breaks down on the road, everyone stops to say, 'Can I help you?'" This is a golden moment of joy for us, one we will always remember fondly. This new American's love for America is pure and unaffected. She has been treated with goodwill and now radiates it.

Asked who she'd most like to meet, Zineta smiles broadly and says, "That's a good one! I never thought about that. This is really good, what you are doing! If I could include my family, I would like to meet my grand-parents. All four of them lived and died in Bosnia; I never met them."

Zineta tells us the best decision she made was to come to the United States. "Just because now I'm able to help my family still in Bosnia," she says. "At home, none of us would have enough to live on. I'm the only one to get out. The rest of my family is in Bosnia . . . two sisters and three brothers. There are no jobs there. Now I'm able to help them." *That's goodwill.*

Zineta glances out the door and sees far away. "Still, I hope to go back home to Bosnia and have a nice life there. At least to do this when I am old. I miss my home, especially at the holidays—I'm homesick."

Then, Zineta tells us, "I always wanted to be a doctor. When I was done with high school back home, war had started. So, I lost that opportunity. Someday, I'd still like to do that!"

Zineta Imamovic

When Pat asks about the best thing that has happened in her life, Zineta gives us a brilliant smile and says, "Marrying my husband in 1998 and having two beautiful boys with him and having them all here with me! One son is five, the other is two—my husband is Bosnian, too."

Her exuberant spirit encourages us to be more exuberant ourselves. This wonderful new friend sends the following advice: "I would say, follow your heart, be honest, and help others in need," she says.

After taking her photo, we give Zineta a spread-some-good-will ten-dollar bill and ask her to do something good with it. She tells us she is delighted by the idea.

One of our Florida interviews, Jim Seay, had used our ten-dollar bill to buy envelopes and postage for sending ten-dollar bills to thirteen other people with instructions to do something good. We loved his idea of multiplying our effort, and we enjoyed a happy surprise when we discovered that he had turned the tables on us by also sending ten dollars to Pat and ten dollars to Scott! Pat donated his to the Spina Bifida

Association of America, and Scott carried his ten dollars along on the rest of the trip, looking for just the right time and place to put it to good use.

Fargo was the place. Scott retrieved the money and presented it to Zineta with an explanation of where it came from and a request that she forward it to one of her sisters or brothers who remain in Bosnia. Contemplate the journey of a small gift from Florida, to Tennessee, to North Dakota, to Bosnia . . . and we hope, beyond. The radiant expression of joy on Zineta's face still brightens our days.

May 11, 2004, Tuesday
Angela Miller
Medora, North Dakota

Based upon Zineta's enthusiastic recommendation, we aimed for Medora, which lies all the way across North Dakota from Fargo—about 325 miles. We didn't calculate the distance beforehand; we just settled on the direction.

It was almost mid-May and cold! The wind had risen sharply, and there was a thin, mysterious fog for miles.

At Sterling, we stopped for fuel and it was thirty-four degrees! After purchasing a soft drink, Scott started to walk out to the car. The clerk told Scott he received a free bag of barbeque potato chips with his drink. Goodwill came to us! You may call it coincidence if you choose, but it struck us as being marvelous to have stopped at just the right place in the

Dear Scott,

I am writing to let you know that I have used the $10 bill that you gave me. . . A few years ago [a] Bosnian gentlemen came to USA to find a new home and after finding [it], he went to [the] doctor and found out that he has inoperable tumor on his brain. He is still being strong and is applying for green card, but since he is not feeling good he can't work so he is struggling financially.

He was able to get Social Security income and he was able to get money for green card application, but [he] needed $10 for medical information from [the] local clinic . . . He came in to let our immigration specialist know that he [couldn't] complete this application because he [didn't] have enough money.

I remembered [the] $10 bill that you left with me. When I hand[ed] him that $10 bill, he was speechless and could not say a word, [he] just looked [at] me and left.

Later he called and said that he is so happy that people still care and that he is so thankful that he can't even describe it.

Thank you so much for your help,

Zineta Imamovic

Minnesota, North Dakota & South Dakota

middle of a vast rural state and bought just the right drink and had just the right honest clerk who didn't let Scott leave without the complimentary bag of chips. As an added blessing, the back of the bag carried an inspiring story of the company's founder, along with some encouraging verses of Scripture. It was just another manifestation of goodwill as we continued our search.

Spirits buoyed, we drove onward. The capitol building in Bismarck jutted upward out of the plains, and we found the Dakota countryside quite scenic. This was another drive to make when wearied of hectic urban life. Out here, we marveled at the major league farms and amazing little towns.

Through the fog, we saw "New Salem Sue," the world's largest Holstein cow statue. She was huge and irresistible. We pulled off to inspect her close-up, and got a photo. She would stand out in New York City; here she was a landmark!

We looked at Dickinson State University, but found no prospects. By the time we reached the small cluster of motels and shops which comprise Medora, it was evening and the streets were deserted.

Uncle Ray's potato chip bags spread goodwill

The first place we tried for dinner turned out to be a saloon, no meals. Just down the street, we saw a school group leaving The Chuck Wagon. All right! We knew we could eat. The buffet was our only choice, and we weren't choosy at this point. There were about 20 other guests in a large open dining room which would probably accommodate 125. We seated ourselves at a round table set for eight and enjoyed our meal as we conversed about our adventures.

A steady crowd of college-age young people began to stream in. We figured they must work in the Theodore Roosevelt National Park. Even with this influx, the room was not even half-full. So, we were a little surprised when a young woman approached and asked if she could sit with us. Of course, we were delighted!

We introduced ourselves to Angela Miller, a college senior at the University of Mary in Bismarck. She grew up on a farm with cows and pigs in Carrington, North Dakota. She has two brothers: one, thirty; one, twenty-six. Since her dad passed away, their farm is rented out, and her mom likes to stay busy. She teaches and also works at a convenience store.

Angela loves to sing. At school, she is in a jazz singing group and the choir as well. She works in Medora during the summer; by day she handles hotel reservations, and by night she sings on stage in a local musical production.

When Angela asks, "What brings you out here?" we tell her, then seize the opportunity to interview her.

Pat asks, "What is your favorite place in North Dakota?"

Angela wears a big smile as she responds, "That would have to be back home in Carrington. Our farmstead is just two miles from the James River in an area that's kind of hilly. It's sorta homey . . . I just like being on a ranch!" She speaks energetically and to our southern ears her midwestern accent sounds somehow foreign. "Carrington's small, about twenty-five hundred people, and very community-oriented. Everybody supports all of our sporting events or musical events or our school activities."

Angela Miller

Angela pauses as she considers the best person she knows. "I'd have to say the person I think the most of right now is Sister Welder, the president of my school, the University of Mary. She doesn't just stay in her office, she's involved in lots of activities. She's always greeting students and their families. She's always willing to give her time and energy to students, to the school, and to the community. I like that she is not just a business person sitting in her office. She tries to be in the lives of the people around her!"

Angela says she would most like to meet Garth Brooks. "He has performed in Fargo, but I've never gotten to see him. I have lots of memorabilia and posters of him, but I haven't gotten to actually see him."

Pat asks, "What is the best decision you have made?"

Angela says, "Besides going to college, I'd say working for the Roosevelt Medora Foundation. The foundation works to preserve the Badlands area and boost the local economy. The people here treat you like family. Plus, I'm a nature person . . . I love being down here."

Questioned about her goals, this sweet college girl tells us of her hopes to become an elementary educator and to work with children in special education. There is a pause. She trusts us enough to speak from her heart. "I'd love to be a professional recording artist!" Angela exclaims. "I don't know if that could ever really be possible, but I'd love to try! I love being in front of people. I sing at school. I sing at church. I sing for old ladies back home; they enjoy hearing a young person sing old gospel songs." We encourage her to dream big dreams and come to Music City, U.S.A. when she's ready to give it a try.

Asked about the best thing that has happened in her life, Angela answers right away—with a bright smile and a pretty twinkle in her eyes. "That would be that I was adopted by Jean and Howard Miller when I was little, from a family that couldn't afford to have another child. I have no idea where I'd be or what I'd be doing if that had not happened to me!" What joy we feel at hearing the mature expression of gratitude in Angela's happy voice. We are so glad she chose to sit with us!

Dear Pat & Scott,

Hello from North Dakota! After all of the summer concerts I have worked on, I am finally sitting down to tell you both what I did with your $10 gift.

As you may remember, I told you about my love for singing [and that] I also had a medium-sized summer concert lineup. I know that crowd involvement can help the reaction. So, I purchased pencils with messages of love for children who were watching.

When I was three, I sang a version of "Jesus Loves Me/Oh How He Loves You and Me" for the county fair. Now the kids come on stage to help me sing this song. As [a] reward each child receives a pencil. It is so fun to experience their excitement.

Thanks again for the great experience you have given me. Someday, I'll make sure to look you up in Nashville!

With heartfelt joy,
Angela Miller

"No matter what other people may tell you, you can do anything you set your mind to. Don't give up! When I was little I was having seizures pretty often. I had a tumor about the size of a shelled walnut between the lobes of my brain. Doctors told my mother I probably wouldn't survive the surgery to remove it, and if I did there'd be no chance of me being able to do anything good. Well, I was in the hospital four days post-op, then I went home and went back to school! Here I am." Goodwill has found us!

What if Zineta had not urged us to see Medora? What if the first place we looked had been serving dinner? What if Angela had chosen to sit at one of the dozen or so empty tables instead of ours?

Now, we know her great story and you do, too. The joy of being adopted by good people, the thrill of surviving when it did not seem likely, the dream of connecting with others through song. Fabulous!

We stayed in Medora for the night; the weatherman said it was thirty degrees with a wind chill of nineteen degrees. We were grateful that we weren't camping out!

Each new friend made us all the more eager to meet the next. Who would we meet around the next bend in the road?

South Dakota

May 12, 2004, Wednesday
Jim Wilson
Deadwood, South Dakota

It was a most memorable May morning—our car wore a light coating of snow as we visited the stark, wild beauty of Theodore Roosevelt National Park. We saw what Roosevelt must have seen; even in the midst of a strange and difficult environment, life perseveres.

Leaving the park, our map showed an unpaved road leading south from Medora. We stopped at a convenience market to ask if the road had been rendered impassible by the weather. The lady there said, "No problem. It's gravel all the way, but it's good gravel." Thus reassured, we headed south through about forty miles of amazing wilderness.

For the first time in forty-eight states, we noticed we were extremely low on gas. And of course, we were in dramatically remote country. Amidon was on the map, but when we got there, it had only about six buildings and no sign of a gas station. We stopped at a tiny post office to ask where we might find gas. The sweet lady working alone there said brightly, "There's a pump behind the bar next door. Just go in and get 'em to turn it on for you." We felt rescued—and grateful.

We pressed southward on U.S. 85. In little Bowman we found Big J's was the place in town for lunch. Everyone there seemed to be enjoying being together. The place was packed and full of good cheer. Scott watched as a distinguished older gent came in with two other men and made his way through the room. Pat's back was toward the front door, and he couldn't see the gentleman. We didn't know if the gentleman saw Pat's wheelchair parked behind our booth, but for whatever reason, as he passed our table he gave Pat an encouraging pat on the back and nodded in that open, friendly manner so characteristic of rural America. We don't know his name or anything else about him, but we wanted you to know about his spontaneous gesture of goodwill.

We crossed into South Dakota and passed through Buffalo. Drifting south on U.S. 85, we passed the geographic center of the entire United States.

When we arrived in Deadwood, we looked around carefully. The name appealed to us, as did the well-preserved old buildings. Ample free parking and easy access drew us to a municipal building where we met Jim Wilson. Given our love of history, we could not have found a better person to interview in Deadwood. Jim is the chief historic preservation official for the city, and he had a great sense of humor, too.

Jim tells us he was born in Illinois, and has lived in West Virginia, Minnesota, Arizona, California, New Mexico, and Kansas; he made his first visit to Deadwood in 1979. This old

Gold Rush town was founded in 1876, and is frequently mentioned in the same breath with other Wild West towns like Dodge City and Tombstone. Jim tells us, "Wild Bill Hickok was killed here after a six-week stay." According to Jim, "The historic preservation of this old town is attributable to South Dakota voters amending the state constitution to allow casinos only in Deadwood, with the net proceeds restricted to historic preservation projects here in Deadwood."

Jim Wilson

Pat asks, "What is your favorite place in the entire state of South Dakota?"

Jim answers right away, "The Black Hills. I like to bike, and I used to run, on the Mickelson Trail there. It was once a mainline railroad bed, and it's now a 108-mile trail. On June 6, there'll be the third marathon up there; it had to be cut off at eleven hundred racers this year. It has grown steadily. The area is special—lots of community spirit and great involvement. Plus, the weather is better there . . . warm is better! I like Deadwood because it's a small town—you know pretty much everybody. You can walk to work, and it's a very comfortable place to live."

Jim says the best person he knows is his wife, Anne, laughing as he says the good thing she does is put up with him. "We've had thirty-nine and a half good years."

Jim furrows his brow as he decides who he'd most like to meet. He says, "That's a tough question. It seems cliché to pick Albert Schweitzer, or Jesus, or President Bush . . . Kevin Costner?" He punctuates the list with a question mark. After a pause, he says, "It would probably be more interesting to meet an average guy from two hundred years ago and see what it was really like!" What a fascinating reply! We love it. Jim continues, "From here to Pierre you are in the middle of nowhere. Imagine a hundred and fifty years ago, no map, some goofball took off

Minnesota, North Dakota & South Dakota

from St. Louis and walked or rode west. How and why did he do that?" We love the historian's desire to really know how it was. We say we'd like to interview the goofball, too.

When Pat asks, "What is the best decision you have made?"

Jim laughs and says, "Oh, I hate this . . . having my wife ask me to marry her!" Later he adds that the best thing in his life is "pretty much the same as my best decision—meeting my wife Anne and ending up with almost forty great years with her."

Jim's goal is, "To stay alive! So I can ride my bike. We have three lovely daughters who are grown up. I have written a book. We have lived interesting places; things are looking good!"

Jim considers the opportunity to begin a new career and laughs softly as he says, "Gee! I don't know. I'm way too old to begin a whole new career. I've been an architect, a political science professor, and a historic preservationist. I might just go up to the Mickelson Trail to sell passes and ride my bike!"

Here is parting advice from this contented man of goodwill: "A good friend told me when I turned fifty, 'If you won't do it for free, don't do it for money!' Do something you love!"

We drifted south into the Black Hills National Forest, and it was lightly snowing when we reached the Mount Rushmore National Monument. This was an awesome all-American site, inspiring under any conditions. On that strange, snowy day in May of 2004, fewer than a dozen other visitors were taking in the magnificent scene with us. Our small numbers magnify the mountain and the monument; we shiver at the thought that in some far-off May one thousand years from now, another father and son will gaze up at George Washington, Thomas Jefferson, Theodore Roosevelt, and Abraham Lincoln, and be inspired by the kind of people who have led our nation.

Onward we drove, up Route 16 to Rapid City, and after dinner, eastward on I-90. We encountered a cold wind, stunning sunset, and beautiful farmland.

The night sky was crisp and crystal clear when we stopped in Kadoka.

We traveled 398 miles that day. Rather than being road-weary, we were elated by the goodwill we encountered down every road.

May 13, 2004, Thursday
Jennifer Wagaman (WAH-gah-mon) Toupal (TOW-pull)
Chamberlain, South Dakota

The vastness of the South Dakota plains and farmland was unspeakably beautiful. For eyes weary of chasing fine print, we highly recommend a day cruising across South Dakota.

At Chamberlain, we saw a sign for St. Joseph's Indian School and the Atka Lakota museum. We went in and found the museum to be both attractive and informative.

We introduced ourselves to an attractive young woman working in the museum shop, and explained to her that we were making random visits in all fifty states to find goodwill. She was a tad wary, but definitely intrigued.

When introducing herself, Jennifer Wagaman Toupal tells us that her middle name is a German one because she was adopted. She proudly adds, "I am a Sioux Indian." We tell Jennifer that she is a rarity in our travels because she was actually born in the locality where the interview is being conducted.

Pat asks Jennifer to talk about her favorite place in South Dakota. This question has consistently put people at ease, and Jennifer is no exception.

She smiles and says, "I enjoy trout fishing in Custer, South Dakota. The open range, the hills, it's all beautiful out there. It's peaceful and quiet; you can hear the coyote in the morning when you are camping." Jennifer's enthusiasm for the outdoors shines in her eyes, and her words paint an appealing portrait of South Dakota's natural beauty. "I like Chamberlain for the beautiful Missouri River, the fishing and hunting, and its slow pace of life."

When Pat asks, "Of all the people you know, is there one who stands out for consistently doing good things?" without hesitation, Jennifer responds, "My adoptive parents. Hank and Betty Wagaman."

It's no surprise, then, that the best thing that has happened in her life, Jennifer says, was, "Being adopted by Hank and Betty."

Jennifer says she would choose to meet Sitting Bull, the Sioux chief. "I would like to see how things really ran back then, in the days he led the Sioux," she says. We agree that that would be a fascinating meeting.

Minnesota, North Dakota & South Dakota

"The best decision I made was moving back to Chamberlain in April 2004, after living in Sioux Falls for two years."

Jennifer smiles as she shares her goal. "I want to have my own buffalo herd. That's what I'm working on now."

Pat asks why, and Jennifer tells us, "To tan and sell the hides. My mom did that."

Pat asks, "Mrs. Wagaman?" Jennifer says, "No, my birth mother, Marian Middle Tent." We would enjoy learning the origin of that name, and meeting both of Jennifer's mothers.

Her goal of raising her own buffalo herd is enmeshed in Jennifer's ideas for a new career; she emphasizes her desire to be in business for herself. The entrepreneurial spirit is at work all across our land.

Jennifer offers this message of encouragement: "Whatever your dreams are, go out there and seek them!" She also notes a display nearby with a statement attributed to Spotted Tail: "There is a time appointed for all things . . . look upon the snow that appears today—tomorrow it is water . . . we are part of that life."

Jennifer Wagaman Toupal

We said good-bye and continued across South Dakota and crossed back into Minnesota to catch our flight home. A tremendous sense of joy filled us. America's heartland covers a lot of states, and we were fortunate to have seen so much of it, and to have found so much goodwill out there in it.

Pat read off the names and locations of all of our interviews so far, and we laughed over and over at the memories of so many wonderful people. We agreed that we have done a fine thing together! Now, on to Alaska!

Trip Nineteen

TRIP TWENTY
ALASKA

June 6, 2004, Sunday
Travel Day

Mindful of, and grateful for, the valor and selflessness of our countrymen who, sixty years ago today, went ashore at Normandy to free Europe, we flew to Chicago. After a brief delay, we boarded our flight to Anchorage and enjoyed dinner, a movie, and a little sleep. The approach to Anchorage by air could not be any more magnificent. At eleven thirty in the evening, the sunset was spectacular as it splashed red and golden light across snow-covered mountains and the sea.

June 7, 2004, Monday
Travel Day

We rose at six o'clock, having decided to catch the Alaska railroad train bound for Denali. A festive mood prevailed among the waiting crowd at the depot, and a fleet of tour buses arrived with passengers from various cruise lines. Each cruise ship had one or more cruise-line-branded railroad cars attached to the regular train for the exclusive use of its passengers.

Everyone loaded quickly and easily, and we departed on time. We were rapidly away from town, out into open, spacious, spruce-covered, lush, green, incredibly wet Alaska. And the rivers! Every river rushed and roared and swiftly dashed by. The snow melt brought gray silt and turned the rivers the color of slate. We rolled merrily along through wide-open spaces, often in a cold drizzle, but it was thrilling to stand in the open area between the rail cars and just breathe in the luscious fresh air.

Pat and Scott on the train to Denali

Back inside, everyone was most congenial and there was a warm spirit of common adventure amongst us. It was mid-afternoon, sunny and warm, when the train arrived at Denali Park. We were to spend the night near the main gate so we could catch the once-a-day bus that would take us into the center of the park. We had watched all day for interview prospects; we kept looking.

Our simple cabins were clustered close together in a glade and our evening meal was served family-style in a central dining room. We sat with a friendly couple from Wisconsin who had traveled on seven continents to pursue bird watching! A handsome Indian couple joined us, Mr. and Mrs. Idnani, and we learned during dinner that they not only owned these cabins, but they were the owners of the Back Country Lodge to which we would travel the next day. We enjoyed hearing their description of travels to Bali, Singapore, and Hong Kong. It was a lively, cheerful group, and we felt especially happy to have had such a pleasant day in beautiful Alaska.

June 8, 2004, Tuesday
Saroj ("Just call me Sarah, it's easier") Idnani
Denali Cabins, Alaska

Outside our cabin window, a small arctic jackrabbit hopped among the grove of slender, sturdy spruce trees. The mountains that surrounded us looked black and red and green in the morning sunlight, capped with a lovely covering of snow along their top ridges.

We talked about how pleasant our dinner companions had been the previous night, and decided to call Mrs. Idnani in her cabin and ask for an interview. We all met in the now-empty dining room.

The train traveling through breathtaking views

Sarah softly tells us her favorite place in Alaska is the Denali Backcountry Lodge, inside the Denali National Park near Kantishna. "It is the end of the road into the park. It is very secluded, quiet, and peaceful. The beautiful mountains there remind me of where I grew up in India. There were mountains behind my house in India, and this place reminds me of that."

When Pat asks, "Who is the best person you know?" Sarah doesn't delay as she answers. "We have a very good friend, Mr. Kapadia, who was our first partner in a small ten-room hotel in New Jersey. He is like a brother to us . . . so very kind."

Pat asks, "Which person, living or dead, would you most like to meet?"

Sarah says, "Probably my grandmother and grandfather . . . and my parents!" She has a poised demeanor and a soft-spoken manner of conversing. We enjoy listening to her speak.

In describing her best decision, Sarah speaks evenly. "Coming to this country and making our future. My husband had four brothers and three sisters; he is the oldest son. In India, the oldest supports the whole family. He was all the time thinking, 'How am I going to take care of my family?' We lived in that part of India which became Pakistan in the partition. It

Alaska

is Muslim, we are Hindu. We had to leave everything. In 1970, we married; in 1971, we came to America. We bought that ten-room hotel in New Jersey, fixed it up and ran it. We sold it to buy a larger one in Georgia, which we fixed up and ran and sold to buy one in Tennessee. The same then in Ohio, and Missouri, and then Phoenix, Arizona—a 300-unit hotel. By this time, our daughter was a teenager and she came up to Kantishna to work one summer. She called us and told us how beautiful it was and urged us to come for a visit. We did and we loved it! We liked it so much, my husband spent a year making the deal to acquire the Back Country Lodge, the cabins here and a Best Western Hotel in Wasilla, which is our actual residence. We sold the hotel in Phoenix last year. And, we have been able to help all of my husband's brothers and sisters move to America." We are dumbstruck by Sarah's serene account of this fabulous three-decade-long American immigrant success story. What a triumph of their determined spirit!

Saroj "Sarah" Idnani

With a sweet smile, Sarah says, "Now, my goal is to have a peaceful life and enjoy my grandchildren."

Asked about the best thing in her life, Sarah says, "We joined the Temple in Delhi, the International Society of Krishna Consciousness. We have a temple here in the U.S., too—though not much in Alaska. There's one Hindu temple in Anchorage."

If beginning a new career, Sarah says, "I would like to just do service in the Krishna Temple—be able to go and do more religious activity."

Sarah's advice is profound: "Hard work pays." It is simple, but not easy. As she explains, "We have worked very hard from the beginning and it has paid off."

This gentle lady has a backbone which seems to be made of steel. We are so glad we have found her.

After our farewells, twenty-seven of us—plus a driver—piled into a roomy, army-style bus and headed into the heart of Denali on the primitive park road. This ninety-five-mile journey provided an unforgettable display of natural beauty, mountain splendor, and amazing wildlife. Our driver was also an excellent field guide, and he stopped whenever he or anyone else spotted a wild animal. We were scarcely underway when we came upon a mother moose and her calf blocking the roadway. Everyone was given ample opportunity to look or make photographs while our driver provided informative commentary. This was repeated when we spotted a few dozen Dall sheep, three caribou, multitudes of beaver and duck, a falcon, an eagle, and a magnificent mother grizzly bear with her spring cub.

The trek took around five hours, with a couple of rest stops, but it was not tiring travel. The scenery was vast, ever-changing, and awe-inspiring. Rushing rivers abounded. Mist, showers, fog, and clouds obscured the park's dominating centerpiece, 20,230-foot Mt. McKinley, our continent's highest peak.

We were a merry troupe of friendly travelers from all over; we met folks from Oklahoma, Pennsylvania, Florida, California, Louisiana, Alaska, and India. There was lots of pleasant conversation as we enjoyed observing the fabulous panorama of wild Denali. A very fine and good thing was accomplished by setting aside this vast natural wilderness so that present and future generations may enjoy contemplating the wild earth.

When we reached the lodge, it seemed certain that we were further away from any other place than we had ever been. Everyone savored a bountiful and delicious family-style dinner, followed by an excellent presentation highlighting the park's abundant wildlife.

Natural beauty is everywhere in Alaska

Alaska

Our day was full and good. Before falling asleep, we talked of the Idnanis' remarkable journey from India to Alaska. We're glad they made it. We're glad to be here.

June 9, 2004, Wednesday
Elizabeth Potts Meier
Backcountry Lodge
Denali, Alaska

We awakened to total silence, save for the gentle tip-tap patter of raindrops on our cabin's roof. Although it was overcast and foggy outside, the crowd at breakfast inside the lodge was cheerful and energetic. Young staffers had hikes and explorations planned, and we signed up for a "flight-seeing" small airplane tour of Mt. McKinley (weather would postpone this adventure until the next day).

For two days, we carefully watched our fellow sojourners. It felt a bit like being all together aboard a cruise ship. We first noticed one particular couple upon our arrival at the Denali railroad depot after the long trip from Anchorage. With more people than our van could hold, this couple cheerfully volunteered to wait (almost forty minutes) for the van to return. Yesterday, on the trip into the park, we had the pleasure of sitting across the aisle from them. Hans (called Bill by his wife) was tall, affable, and erudite. Elizabeth was petite, radiant, and irrepressibly enthusiastic. Her unabashed love for her husband was immediately obvious, and she was remarkably cheerful and kind toward everyone with whom she interacted. She was the kind of person who truly lights up a room (or a bus). Denali's natural beauty and magnificent wildlife were amplified for us by Elizabeth's joyful exclamations throughout the long drive.

This day, we watched them at breakfast and lunch. The Meiers were a vibrant couple; smiling, joyous, always positive, and always encouraging—not just to us, but to everyone they met. Elizabeth was exactly the sort of person we looked for:

loving, open, cheerful, kindhearted, optimistic, and oh so enthusiastic and vital! She radiated goodwill.

When we told them about our nationwide search for goodwill, their response could not have been more positive or encouraging, even if we had been members of their own family! They made our spirits soar—they reinforced our sense that we were doing something worthy, something that was inherently good. We felt as though they had been our friends for decades.

We sat together in front of a warm fireplace in the library upstairs at the lodge.

Obviously not a native-born American, Elizabeth possesses an unmistakable and beautiful British accent which accentuates her lovely spirit. With eyes that are always sparkling, Elizabeth says, "I was born at Westcliff-on-Sea, near Essex, England, on the Thames River. And I have a twin sister! Our dad was a sea captain, but he didn't like being away so much. So, he started his own business in Karachi, India—which is now Pakistan—when I was four. We lived in India before World War II began. After Burma fell—I was seven—my dad put my sister, my mother, and me on a ship bound for South Africa, where we lived until the war ended. I came to America on a boat; we came to Ellis Island as immigrants. I lived with a sponsor for three months in Albany, New York, then moved to California, which is where we live—Studio City, Los Angeles." We are entranced by this remarkable woman and her unique personal history.

"My favorite place is home! Thirty years ago, I found a half-finished house with a view that was gorgeous, looking out over the San Fernando Valley. I fell in love with it! I took my husband to see it, and we bought it that evening. We have deer, raccoon, skunks . . . and rattlesnakes! I killed twenty-six rattlesnakes during the construction work to finish that house!" She seems as indomitable as Winston Churchill.

She cracks us up when she asks, "Who is the comedian on television with the long chin?" When we answer, "Jay Leno," she says, "Yes! He lives up the hill from us; we see him drive by in his various vehicles."

When Pat asks, "What do you like most about Studio City?" Elizabeth responds with her characteristic enthusiasm, "It's

Alaska

small, and conveniently located in greater Los Angeles. We have the best of living in the center of a lovely city, but it's like camping out! Marlon Brando and Jack Nicholson have donated property which helps protect the Santa Monica Mountains there—it'll always be wild."

"My husband, Bill, is the best person I know. I love him so much, ever since I first laid eyes on him. I was rooming with two other 'stews' [stewardesses]—we were all working for BOAC [British Overseas Airways Corp.] He moved in next door, and I thought he was so handsome! Apparently, he felt the same about me—we were married in 1958!"

Elizabeth Meier

Elizabeth says, "I would like very much to meet my great-great grandmother, Jane Mack. Stories I've heard about her always fascinated me. Either her father—or was it her brother?—was a pirate! Jackie Mack married an Indian princess and never came back!" Wonderful laughter. Elizabeth possesses such an original personality—we think she should have her own television show.

Asked about the best decision she has made, Elizabeth responds, "Marrying my husband and having our children. We have one daughter, who is very wild—been married three times—and one son. He's kind of the opposite. He's been married for ten years. He had spinal meningitis at eighteen and lost his hearing. He has had a cochlear implant, which is experimental, and it works! With it on, he hears about as well as we do."

Pat inquires about goals, and Elizabeth says, "I hope to keep on traveling—it's healthy activity, and I want to keep Bill with me as long as I can. So I dangle these [travel] carrots in front of him."

"So many, many good things have happened to me!" Elizabeth says. "I feel that I have sort of had an enchanted life." She has obviously shared those good things with others all along the way. She continues, "On the morning I saw the island of Santorini, I remember seeing so many beautiful sights . . . it filled me with joy." And, on further reflection, she adds, "It was the joy when John, my son, was able to hear again due to his cochlear implant—that has to be one of the greatest times in my life."

Pat asks what she would choose for a new career; Elizabeth laughs at the thought and says, "Oh gosh! I'm a little old . . . I'd be an astronomer!" She places her hand on Pat's hand, and says, "When I was in school, ladies were taught to be good wives and well-mannered. I sang in Ted Heath's band; I worked in the movie industry; I married and had babies. My mother said, 'Learn shorthand and typing'—which I did—so I've been able to help in business with my husband. He does specification consulting for the hospital industry."

Pat concludes our 106th interview by asking Elizabeth, "Do you have a message of encouragement or words of advice for our readers?" After a moment of reflection, Elizabeth replies, "The only thing I could say is be as kind as you can be to other people; always try to enjoy other people; and be happy for them."

We stepped out onto the porch to include mighty Alaska in our photo of the dynamic Elizabeth Meier. When we gave her the ten-dollar bill, she beamed and told us right away that she would add to it and use it to do something good for the children in a little school on Fanning Island in the South Pacific Ocean, which she and her husband would visit on New Year's Day 2005. (Not surprisingly, Elizabeth sent us photos of the event.)

Our farewells came later that evening as the Meiers were to depart on the next day's morning bus. We could not have asked for anything more in a goodwill interview, and we have made two wonderful new friends. It was a very good day.

Thursday morning dawned bright and clear; sunshine brightened all the world as well as everyone's spirits. At

---

Dear Scott and Pat:

Well, we did make it all the way to the Republic of Kiribati which is in the middle of the Pacific Ocean, just north of the equator. . . . We arrived there on New Year's Day 2005, and tendered from the ship over to this tiny little place where the people greeted us with songs and much goodwill. We took our school supplies consisting of boxes of colored pencils, lots of large lined paper pads, pens, erasers, rulers, etc., for the children to use. We also took a sack full of Beanie Babies for the children to play with and perhaps wonder at the wolves, otters, bears, polar bears, etc., so very different from anything they would have ever seen where they live.

The $10 you gave me certainly spread goodwill to these sweet island children. I said I would do this and by golly it did come about! . . .

Our love to you both,
Elizabeth and Hans

Alaska

mid-morning, we rode to a small airstrip and took off for Mt. McKinley. Neither words nor photographs could capture the power and majesty of this place. You must go see it in person. Massive peaks, ice, glaciers, brilliant white snow—an awesome expanse of cruel beauty.

Back at the lodge, we found an excellent passage in the library from "Spell of the Yukon" by Robert Service:

> *There are hardships that nobody reckons*
> *There are valleys unpeopled and still;*
> *There's a land oh it beckons and beckons,*
> *And I want to go back*
> *And I will.*

That's how we feel about Alaska. Hope you'll go see it.

June 11, 2004, Friday
Travel Day

We woke up at four thirty to a light rain, and turned toward home for the last time on this great adventure. The bus trip out of Denali was quicker than the trip inbound— everyone has to catch the noon train. Still, we saw rock ptarmigan, ducks, beaver, Dall sheep, grizzly bear, caribou, trees, mountains, rivers, clouds, and expansive, wild, beautiful open spaces.

At the train station in Denali, we ran into the Meiers, and enjoyed their company for much of the return trip to Anchorage in a lovely observation car.

After unloading at the depot in Anchorage, Elizabeth shook hands with Scott, then with Pat. Suddenly she hugged Pat, then gave him a kiss. Holding his face in her hands, she said, "Oh, you dear boy! You have made my trip!" It was a fitting, climactic demonstration of spontaneous genuine affection—and goodwill—which we will never forget.

EPILOGUE

During the eleven months we traveled the country, we were overwhelmed by the unfailing goodness of people we met, and the hearts full of goodwill that we found everywhere. We now have an answer to the question posed in that *Barron's* cartoon—and it is, yes, there is good news every day—if you are looking for it. Because of the people we met, we know that there will be good news tomorrow, and the next day, and for years to come.

How do we know? We know because our unscientific and random search yielded such an abundance of goodwill, we feel highly confident that there exists a vast—even overflowing—reservoir of goodwill all across the land. But remember, it must be sought, and sought diligently.

Along our way, we also learned another important lesson from the people we met. They responded with great enthusiasm and seriousness when given an opportunity to spread some goodwill. As you read, we gave each interviewee ten dollars and asked them to use it for something good. We also asked them to send us a note telling us how they used the money. We heard from some people right away. Others responded much later. Even today, we are still receiving letters from our goodwill ambassadors. (Because of space limitations, the portions of letters that appear in this book represent only some of the responses we received.) It has been a thrill to see how often the initial small gift has been multiplied, and how broadly the goodwill has rippled out.

One result that neither of us foresaw was that our quest for goodwill would change other lives. But people have told us that it did.

We heard from a young man, who wrote:

> I want you both to know that being interviewed by you and listening to some of your stories of travel was very neat and

inspirational. . . . After meeting you both, I really sat back and looked at my life, mainly to see if I display goodwill each day. I found myself shocked. I felt like I was not doing enough for those around me. . . . The honest truth is that I am a former drug and alcohol addict, and though I have successfully cleaned up my life with the help (and goodwill) of friends, family, and specialists, I felt like I needed to do more, as others have done for me. My entire life I have kept a fake smile because I was told to. I never knew why, though. Today I understand. A smile is a pure, simple form of goodwill, which everyone should be exposed to. I've learned that goodwill is everywhere, really. It doesn't necessarily take lots of effort, time, or even money. It only takes a good spirit from within and passing it on to others in any form possible. . . . I kind of think of it as another step in my recovery. I have since gotten in touch with my recovery therapist and I (when work allows) try to sit in on group meetings as a peer mediator, sharing my story with others. . . . I think I've helped some folks.

But because of you two inspiring my thoughts and my life, I have helped myself. I have moved into a cheaper apartment in order to save money for my future, something I never thought mattered before. I have enhanced my relationship with my girlfriend. And probably most important, I have improved my family's faith and trust in me. I have started to see the glass half full, instead of half empty. . . . I have been promoted to [supervisor] after I expressed to my boss that I want to take the next step in a career path. . . . I like to call it the goodwill industry, because I get to spread so much of it to all kinds of people. . . . I am happier now than I have been in a long while. It may sound a little "cheesy" but I do credit you two a lot. Taking the time to share your story with me was an encouragement. I guess that is why I'm trying to do the same for others when possible. . . . Thank you very much for spreading goodwill. . . . God bless you both.

Another goodwill correspondent who requested anonymity was inspired to reach out to tornado victims in his area. He and his wife headed south in their pickup packed with a camera, shovel, rope, an emergency kit, two coolers filled with water and soda, and a couple of boxes of doughnuts.

We came to the first demolished home . . . where we walked up and introduced ourselves and asked how we could help. . . . We worked at moving walls off of their belongings, and helped them salvage books, toys, pictures, silverware, and anything else of value to them. Many volunteers came to help, and the doughnuts and beverages were greatly appreciated by all. Several times, the homeowners got teary-eyed from the outpouring of help they were receiving from complete strangers. When things slowed down there, we moved on to another demolished house, where we asked the man if we could help . . . he needed to bury the family's husky before his wife and kids arrived. We buried the dog, then moved on to another home. . . .

My wife and I worked a long and hard, yet meaningful day, and were exhausted by the time we headed home. We were passively reflecting over the day when my wife said, "Hey, is this a good enough cause to count that ten dollars toward?"

I hope this shows there is still good in the heartland, in America, and the world.

We believe it does.

The spread of goodwill extended well beyond those we interviewed. Remember that Jim Seay in Florida took the $10 we gave him and multiplied it by sending $10 to thirteen friends, $10 to Pat, and $10 to Scott, along with instructions to use it for good (p. 215). Here's what happened to one of the thirteen.

Your letter created a great deal of wheel-turning in my head. I wanted to do something extraordinary with the $10, so I thought and thought and then I over-thought and got nowhere. Finally, when KPMG decided to send me to India on a job assignment, what I was going to do with the $10 was simple. I was going to use it to buy gifts for some children at an orphanage. I would add to the $10 myself. Seemed like a no-brainer. I shared this entire story with various colleagues at KPMG and they, too, wished to contribute to the "India Fund." Soon the $10 grew to $130 and I found myself removing various articles from my luggage to accommodate all the gifts I was taking for the children. If the story ended here, I would have felt adequate, but what happened next has forever changed my husband and me. I took the gifts to the children at an orphanage in Kengeri (outskirts of Bangalore), India. . . . My goal was to take the gifts to them and share some of my time with them. Seemed simple enough. I was definitely wrong about that.

The children were thrilled to get these fancy gifts from the U.S. and they treated me like I was royalty. I shook hands with 250 children and many of them gave me big hugs. I felt like the most fortunate person to be allowed to be part of their Saturday. The children made me promise that I would come back and visit them again. I kept my promise to them and visited with them a total of six times over the remaining two months I was there. At the end of my assignment, when my husband, John, came to India, we both went to the orphanage together. . . . During all my visits, I spoke to the director and gathered information to see how we [John and I] could continue to help. . . .

It has taken us six months and dealing with two different banks to establish an account in India. . . . At a minimum, John and I have promised to fund the third meal in the day. You see, when funds are low, the children get only two meals a day. We want to make sure the children get the third meal. Additionally, we have promised to fund the salary of a teacher. . . .

It has taken us a long time to use the $10 to its maximum, but it's been worth every moment. I kept the original ten-dollar bill that you sent to me to be my source of motivation when things didn't go as planned.

I want to thank you for sending me the $10. It's been a great experience for us.

We have been encouraged and inspired by these letters, and know that others will be, too.

Epilogue

We would love to know about the good things in your community and in your life. Just imagine that Pat is asking you each of his questions. Please take some time to think about your answers—they are worthy of your serious reflection.

1. Is there a place in your state which you especially enjoy? What is your favorite place, and why?

2. What is the best thing about your town or state?

3. Of all the people you know, is there one who "stands out" for consistently doing good things? Who is the best person you know?

4. Which person, living or dead, would you most like to meet, or meet again?

5. What is the best decision you have made?

6. Do you have a goal you still hope to achieve?

7. What is the best thing that has happened in your life?

8. If you had an opportunity to begin a new career, what would you choose to do?

9. Do you have a message of encouragement or words of advice for our readers all across the land?

Contact us at:

Pat and Scott Price
1032 Tyne Boulevard
Nashville, TN 37220

Be sure to include a photograph. If we receive enough responses, we will try to compile another book!

Epilogue

In the same vein, we urge you to personally experience the joy of spreading some goodwill, right where you are. Use a ten-dollar bill to do something good. Then write to us and let us know how it turned out. If you are so inclined, include your name and address. Perhaps we may be able to interview you in person one day.

This was a very good year (eleven months, actually, but who's counting?). Writing this allowed us to re-visit these wonderful people, and compounded and magnified the joy and goodwill which we found in them—and which they shared so readily in our initial meetings.

We fondly hope that you will be inspired by these good people, as we have been, to seek the good that is all around you—and to spread some goodwill all along your way.

Epilogue